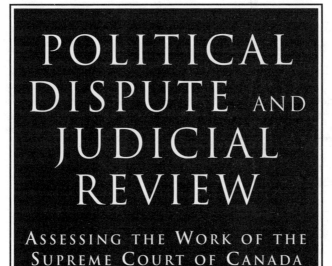

POLITICAL DISPUTE AND JUDICIAL REVIEW

ASSESSING THE WORK OF THE SUPREME COURT OF CANADA

EDITED BY

HUGH MELLON
KING'S COLLEGE, UNIVERSITY OF WESTERN ONTARIO

MARTIN WESTMACOTT
UNIVERSITY OF WESTERN ONTARIO

Australia • Canada • Denmark • Japan • Mexico • New Zealand • Philippines
Puerto Rico • Singapore • South Africa • Spain • United Kingdom • United States

1120 Birchmount Road
Scarborough, Ontario M1K 5G4
www.nelson.com
www.thomson.com

Canadian Cataloguing in Publication Data

Main entry under title:

Political dispute and judicial review: assessing the work of the Supreme Court of
    Canada
Includes bibliographical references.
ISBN 0-17-616744-7

1. Canada. Supreme Court.   2. Political questions and judicial power – Canada.
3. Judicial review – Canada.   I. Westmacott, M.W. (Martin William), 1943– .
II. Mellon, Hugh.

KE8244.P64 1999   347.71'0352   C99-932540-X   KF9058.ZA2P64 1999

Acquisitions Editor	Nicole Gnutzman
Project Editor	Jenny Anttila
Production Editor	Natalia Denesiuk
Production Coordinator	Hedy Later
Marketing Manager	Kevin Smulan
Art Direction	Angela Cluer
Cover Design	Julie Greener
Senior Composition Analyst	Alicja Jamorski
Copy Editor	Erika Krolman
Proofreader	Jim Zimmerman
Cover Image	CP Picture Archive (Tom Hanson)/ Supreme Court of Canada
Printer	Webcom

Printed and bound in Canada
1 2 3 4 03 02 01 00

CONTENTS

ACKNOWLEDGMENTS

The editors gratefully acknowledge the kindness and cooperation of the University of Western Ontario and of those special individuals who aided our project with their expertise. Jane Borecky served as our trusted editorial guide, while Janice Brown offered helpful support. Translation support was provided by Diane Roussel.

LIST OF CONTRIBUTORS

Herman Bakvis is professor of political science and public administration at Dalhousie University. His current research interests include the role of think tanks and management consultants in the policy process, party finance and electoral reform, and more generally, cabinet government and government organization. His publications include *Regional Ministers: Power and Influence in the Canadian Cabinet* (University of Toronto Press, 1991) and *The Centralization–Decentralization Conundrum* (IRPP, 1988) (with Peter Aucoin). From 1990 to 1992 he was research coordinator with the Royal Commission on Electoral Reform and Party Financing.

Paul Barker teaches politics at Brescia College, at the University of Western Ontario. He has published articles on health policy, decision making, and fed-eral–provincial fiscal relations in Canada. He is also the coeditor of a book of readings on Canadian politics.

Ian Brodie joined the Department of Political Science at the University of Western Ontario in 1997, after completing his graduate work at the University of Calgary. His research focuses on courts, interest group litigation, and legal issues. He has published articles on political culture and the Charter of Rights, patterns of evidence presented to the Supreme Court of Canada, interest group litigation, the Court Challenges Program, and competition for constitutional status in Canada.

Peter Clancy is professor of political science at St. Francis Xavier University. His research interests include politics in the Canadian North, business–government relations in Canada, and the political economy of forestry. He is the coauthor of *Against the Grain: Foresters and Politics in Nova Scotia*, which is forthcoming from UBC Press. Recent publications include "Concerted Action on the Periphery? Voluntary Economic Planning in 'The New Nova Scotia,'" *Acadiensis*, XXVI, 2 (Spring 1997).

Pierre Coulombe is a political theorist who specializes in language policy. He has taught at McGill University, the University of Ottawa, the University of New Brunswick, and the University of Western Ontario. He has written on language rights in Canada, constitutional reform, and Quebec politics.

Susan Delacourt has a B.A. in political science from the University of Western Ontario (1982) and served for more than ten years as a parliamentary correspondent for *The Globe and Mail*. In her sixteen years at *The Globe*, she also worked as an editorial writer, an editor, and a general assignment reporter. She is currently writing freelance for a variety of publications and interests, and working on a book about the late Shaughnessy Cohen, the Liberal MP who died in the Commons in December 1998.

Roy Flemming is professor of political science at Texas A&M University, which is in College Station, ninety miles north of Houston. With the financial support of the National Science Foundation in the United States, he is currently writing a book on the leave to appeal process in Canada's Supreme Court. He is the author or coauthor of numerous journal articles and four books, including most recently *The Craft of Justice: Politics and Work in Courthouse Communities* (University of Pennsylvania Press).

Samuel LaSelva is a member of the Department of Political Science at the University of British Columbia, where he teaches in the areas of political theory and Canadian constitutional studies. His publications include *The Moral Foundations of Canadian Federalism*, which was awarded the 1998 Smiley Prize by the Canadian Political Science Association.

Hugh Mellon has worked with Martin Westmacott on two previous collections, one on Canadian federalism and the other on public administration. He is an associate professor at King's College at the University of Western Ontario. His research interests lie in the field of Canadian public policy and intergovernmental relations.

Andrew Robinson is a lecturer in the Department of Political Science at the University of Western Ontario. His teaching interests include introductory political science, political theory, and Canadian politics. He is currently working on problems of identity and community in liberal democracy.

Laura Shanner is an associate professor at the John Dossetor Health Ethics Centre and at the Department of Public Health Sciences at the University of Alberta, where she teaches a graduate course called "Public Health: Ethics, Law, and Policy." She is also currently a co-coordinator of the International Network for Feminist Approaches to Bioethics. A philosopher by training (with a Ph.D. in this discipline from Georgetown University, awarded in 1994), she has previously taught bioethics and philosophy at Georgetown University, Johns Hopkins

University, and the University of Toronto. Her publications have appeared in books and journals in law, medicine, philosophy, and women's studies. Her current primary research project is an exploration of models of maternal–fetal relationships.

Jennifer Smith is an associate professor in the Department of Political Science at Dalhousie University. She writes on issues of electoral politics, as well as on Canadian government and politics and comparative government. She has also served on federal and provincial electoral boundaries commissions for the province of Nova Scotia. Recently, she and Ronald Landes coauthored "Entitlement Versus Variance Models in the Determination of Canadian Electoral Boundaries," *International Journal of Canadian Studies* 17 (Spring 1998).

Richard Vernon is professor of political science at the University of Western Ontario, where he teaches political theory. From 1993 to 1996, he served as English-language coeditor of the *Canadian Journal of Political Science*. His most recent book, *The Career of Toleration* (McGill-Queen's, 1997), won the Canadian Political Science Association's C.B. Macpherson prize. His current research is on the theory of liberal democracy.

Martin Westmacott teaches political science at the University of Western Ontario, including the first-year course in politics, and courses in intergovernmental relations and Canadian federalism. He has coedited books on Canadian federalism and public administration.

José Woehrling was born in Alsace (France) and studied law in Strasbourg and Montreal. He teaches Canadian and comparative constitutional law in the Faculty of Law at the University of Montreal.

FOREWORD

The following collection offers an introduction to the role and importance of the Supreme Court of Canada by looking at different aspects of the Court's operations and the judicial resolution of various kinds of important legal cases. The contributing authors have worked at providing an accessible account of the issue(s) or case(s) before them, thus providing material suitable for instructional use. In reading through the volume, students should reflect on the variety and significance of the cases before the Court and the responsibilities that fall to the judiciary. The justices of the Supreme Court are entrusted with challenging, multifaceted cases that often provoke heated debate in household discussions and editorial-page commentaries, and on open-line radio and television programs. Cases sufficiently important to reach the Supreme Court often involve profound questions of values, political and social structures, cultural expression, rights and liberties, and/or major patterns of economic and commercial activity. Hearing and adjudicating such matters is a demanding task that needs to be understood by students and observers of Canadian politics.

This collection is intended for an undergraduate or generalist audience. The various chapters examine the issues facing the Court, the contending parties and principles, and the political ramifications of the legal outcomes. It is hoped that this collection will spark interest in the judiciary, particularly in the Supreme Court, and encourage further inquiry into the topics raised here.

The book is made up of five parts, the first of which is an introductory section. The purpose of the three chapters in the first section is to acquaint readers with the fundamental importance of the Court and its workload. This should allow readers to position the Court within the political landscape and to appreciate its relevance. In Chapter 1, Hugh Mellon provides an overview of the Court's responsibilities and an institutional history of its evolution. In addition, concepts such as judicial review and an independent judiciary are explained, and reference is made to the history of the Judicial Committee of the British Privy Council and to the growth in the Supreme Court's prominence in the post–World War II era. There is also reference to the Supreme Court's composition and appointment, topics about which there is ongoing discussion across Canada. In Chapter 2, Susan Delacourt looks at the communications challenges associated with the Court. The legitimacy of the Court as an institution depends on a variety of things, including public and professional respect, efficiency in operation, adherence to sound legal principles, and accessibility. One of the ingredients in maintaining trust and breaching the walls of geographic isolation is to make the Court more open and people more aware of its proceedings. Effective communication planning can help address concerns over openness and public awareness. Ongoing attention has been paid to this element of Court operations in recent decades, and Delacourt, a veteran journalist, offers her assessment of the resulting developments. The Supreme Court has considerable discretion over its caseload, and the criteria and procedures by which cases reach the Court are important considerations. Roy

Flemming explores the complex question of how cases reach the Court in Chapter 3, as well as providing a helpful introduction to the broader debates over judicial agenda-setting and an interesting comparison of agenda-setting practices in the high courts of Canada and the United States.

Part 2 of the book deals with the Supreme Court's handling of complex cases involving issues of democracy, legitimacy, and consent. The three chapters in this section examine critically important cases whose adjudication has had widespread political and social impacts. In Chapter 4, Jennifer Smith and Herman Bakvis look at the relationship between judicial review and electoral law, with particular emphasis on judicial assessment of fairness and appropriateness in governmental regulation of elections and party competition. Their commentary goes right to the heart of the national contentiousness over the relationship between interest groups and elections and the rules that may (or should) guide elections or referendums. In Chapter 5, José Woehrling works through the Supreme Court's landmark ruling on the legality of Quebec secession, a case watched attentively by Canadians from coast to coast. His discussion of the judicial reasoning serves as a helpful guide to the complicated issues and to the implications of the Court's ruling. In Chapter 6, Peter Clancy provides an account of an important case relating to relations between Aboriginal peoples, land, and governments. The case concerned territory and practices in British Columbia, but the lessons go far beyond the boundaries of one province. Aboriginal groups and peoples are turning to the courts to address contemporary problems and historic grievances. It thus falls to the judiciary to adjudicate Native claims and to assess the associated grievances. Through their rulings, the Supreme Court justices are recasting Aboriginal–government relations and offering an opportunity for judicial declaration of what constitutes just outcomes.

In Part 3, attention turns to matters of autonomy and expression. In Chapter 7, Samuel LaSelva and Richard Vernon deal with the philosophical and policy debates over regulation of pornography. Where should the boundary between what is and what is not acceptable be drawn? Is it consistent or inconsistent with liberal values to accept a measure of public regulation and restriction on certain forms of activity or expression? These and other equally difficult questions are studied by the authors. In Chapter 8, Laura Shanner reviews the Court's major decisions relating to matters dealing with reproduction. There has been much litigation in this field and many new developments since the Charter of Rights and Freedoms came into effect. Given the breadth of change and the importance of the judicial rulings, her survey offers a useful overview.

Part 4 includes essays on two cases that featured the intersection of parliamentary traditions and prerogatives with the realm of judicial activity. Pierre Coulombe, in Chapter 9, focuses on a dispute arising from regulation of language usage and the competing claims of rights and freedoms. This dispute reflects yet again the tension in Quebec over language matters and fears of assimilation. The Court had to weigh these public policy considerations against individual and corporate rights of expression and self-presentation. Ultimately, the notwithstanding clause was called upon by the Quebec government, and governmental and parliamentary priorities became pitted against claims of rights and freedoms. The ensuing events had an impact not only on language legislation and perceptions of the notwithstanding clause, but also on the Meech Lake discussions and the possible constitutional inclusion of a distinct society clause. Paul Barker follows in Chapter 10 with his discussion of a case concerning another element of our parliamentary heritage, namely, the principle of parliamentary sovereignty and its status in regard to federal–provincial shared-cost programs. When the federal government unilaterally changed the rules and its share of contributions, aggrieved provinces asked the courts to set matters right. Ottawa responded by claiming the British tradition of parliamentary sovereignty. Ultimately, it was up to the Supreme Court to resolve the intensifying conflict. Barker sets out the issues and then offers his legal and political evaluations.

The fifth and final part of the book tackles the intricate connections between notions of rights and court protection with the activities of groups within society. In Chapter 11, Andrew Robinson points to the tough choices facing the courts when they hear cases in which group rules or sanctions are challenged by members who are upset. Should the judges recognize groups as having discretion over rule-setting and internal discipline, or should individual members be protected in their assertions of individual beliefs and practices? Robinson selects three cases in which these questions come into play, one involving a religion, and two involving Aboriginal organizations. His commentary on the prevailing direction of Supreme Court conclusions in such matters illuminates an interesting field of legal, philosophical, and political debate. Ian Brodie, in Chapter 12, addresses the use of legal action by groups. It is widely believed that groups of various sorts are more willing than ever to pursue claims through the courts. Brodie notes the history of group use of legal action, and observes the issues raised by such interest-group tactics. He also comments on the topic of whether governments should encourage or even fund the legal efforts of various types of groups deemed to be disadvantaged.

In going through the book, students should bear in mind certain key questions. What is the basis of the disputes or debates at hand? How and why do issues like this get reviewed through the judiciary? How does judicial action differ from those of the legislature or the executive? How does the judicial resolution of complex issues frequently involve not only legal, but also philosophical and social considerations? Why might groups or individuals turn to the courts for resolution of their complaints or grievances? How are the Supreme Court justices selected? Why do Supreme Court rulings often have important political ramifications? To explore these and other critical questions, review the articles, follow up the sources in the endnotes, contemplate media discussions of legal topics, and be bold enough to move on to reading the Court decisions in their original form. We wish you well in these endeavours, and urge you to consider the enduring salience of the Supreme Court.

Hugh Mellon
Martin Westmacott
July 1999

INTRODUCTION
TO THE COURT

PART | 1

INTRODUCTION:

APPRECIATING THE
SUPREME COURT'S
NATIONAL SIGNIFICANCE

Hugh Mellon

The Globe and Mail's front page of January 18, 1999, carried this headline: "Cory to Leave Supreme Court—Speculation Favours Arbour as Successor."[1] The Cory referred to is Justice Peter Cory of the Supreme Court of Canada, while Arbour is Justice Louise Arbour of the Ontario Court of Appeal, then serving a three-year term as chief prosecutor for the United Nations' International War Crimes Tribunal. Rumours of Cory's impending resignation sent shock waves through the country's political and legal communities, leading *The Globe* to report that this would lead to "unleashing what is likely to be another onslaught of lobbying at the highest levels over his replacement."[2] *The Toronto Star* sounded a similar note: "The seat on Canada's top court is not yet officially vacant, but already the federal government is bracing for keen interest in Justice Peter Cory's job, and trying to forestall the lobbying."[3] Chief Justice Antonio Lamer was so troubled by the lobbying that had accompanied a recent past appointment that he publicly cautioned prospective candidates. He also worried about the impact of past competition among members of the Ontario Court of Appeal (the seat at stake had become vacant with the death of Justice John Sopinka from Ontario): "I think it was unfortunate ... I wasn't privy to it except when I was alerted to the fact there was campaigning. I think it is divisive. And if it's going on in a collegial court, it is even more divisive."[4]

While a certain portion of the lobbying referred to has been, and will continue to be, a product of ambition, competition, and interpersonal rivalry, there is more at stake. Jousting among the partisans of legal and judicial notables interested in a Supreme Court appointment is only one element of a much broader set of public issues related to the Court. Operating as the court of last resort for

Canadian legal disputes, the Canadian Supreme Court has found itself embroiled in national controversies. It has been called on to adjudicate many of the most contentious problems facing the country, including the effort of Prime Minister Trudeau to seek patriation and amendment of the Canadian constitution without significant provincial consent, the legality of potential Quebec separation, federal legislation regarding abortion, the legitimacy of the federal government's imposition of price and wage controls, the nature and extent of Aboriginal treaty rights, and the relation of Canadian law to assisted suicide. Cases with national repercussions make their way to the Supreme Court for adjudication. Students of Canadian political life, therefore, need to appreciate its responsibilities and significance.

INSTITUTIONAL INDEPENDENCE AND JUDICIAL REVIEW

Deciding complex cases and giving effect to Canada's constitutional documents and provisions involves the judiciary in tough choices. As the ultimate interpreter of the law and constitutional legitimacy, the Supreme Court has an important role in Canadian public life. Given this significance, there are institutional safeguards built into place to establish the importance of an independent judiciary. In its evaluation of disputes, the Canadian judiciary must be free from partisan influence and governmental interference. This institutionalized insulation is meant to help foster respect for the fairness and impartiality of the legal system.

An independent judiciary is a vital element of a democratic political system, for it promotes the open and fair resolution of conflicts. Andrew Heard has asserted that "[a]n independent judiciary is a fundamental element of liberal democracy."[5] A key feature of Canada's legal heritage is the belief that laws and their associated penalties should be made and enforced openly, publicly, and consistently. Open government, featuring the voicing of alternative ideas and policies, is indeed a hallmark of liberal democracy. Why should someone be held responsible for violating a law if it can be changed by the arbitrary decisions of a partisan adjudicator? The operation of an open legal system, in which rules and procedures are consistently and fairly applied according to established guidelines, is characteristic of the rule of law. Chief Justice Antonio Lamer has asserted that "[t]he rule of law, interpreted and applied by impartial judges, is the guarantee of everyone's rights and freedoms. We cannot expect judges to be superhuman; we can expect them to be as impartial as it is humanly possible to be, and to allow them, indeed require them, to work in institutions where the conditions promote and protect that impartiality."[6] Impartiality in the administration of law promotes public respect for its outcomes and encourages people to utilize the courts rather than other, potentially violent or physical, dispute resolution mechanisms. This impartiality is built into the institutional fabric of the judiciary through such means as protection of judicial tenure, limitations on the public political involvement of judges, and the reference in the Charter of Rights to "an independent and impartial tribunal": "11. Any person charged with an offence has the right ...

(d) to be presumed innocent until proven guilty according to law in a fair and public hearing by an independent and impartial tribunal."

In their workload of appeals and governmental reference cases (in which they have been assigned a question(s) by the federal government) the Supreme Court judges have laboured over many kinds of disputes. Federal–provincial struggles have often ended in adjudication of which powers are federal and which are provincial. In the early 1980s the workload of the judiciary expanded with the Constitution Act, 1982 and the arrival of the Canadian Charter of Rights and Freedoms. Canadian courts were now responsible for giving effect to the Charter. Section 24(1)[7] of the Constitution Act declares that "[a]nyone whose rights and freedoms, as guaranteed by this Charter, have been infringed or denied may apply to a court of competent jurisdiction to obtain such remedy as the court considers appropriate and just under the circumstances." The remedy designed by the country's top political leaders for infringement of these rights and freedoms was recourse to the judicial system. Section 52(1) of the 1982 Constitution Act establishes that Canada will be governed by the Constitution: "The Constitution of Canada is the supreme law of Canada, and any law that is inconsistent with the provisions of the Constitution is, to the extent of the inconsistency, of no force or effect." This further established the key responsibilities of the courts, especially the Supreme Court. In addition to their traditional role of adjudication, "the courts are now responsible for determining the constitutionality of laws in relation to the absolute standard of the Constitution of Canada."[8] Hence, Canadian courts exercise full judicial review of the actions of governments. This entails more than determining the appropriate bounds of federal and provincial authorities, or the hearing of appeals or questions referred by the federal government—it encompasses the review of governmental actions (or inactions) to ascertain that they are in keeping with what is deemed to be Canada's formal Constitution. The term "the Constitution of Canada" is dealt with in greater detail in the 1982 document, but for our purposes at present, the main point is that Canada moved decisively to a form of constitutional government in which the judiciary is assigned great authority over assessing governmental actions and giving meaning and effect to fundamental freedoms and rights. This accorded great authority to the judiciary, for they were to oversee the constitutionality of government decisions and practices.

All of this has repercussions not only for rights protection, but also for public policy. In the words of Roger Gibbins, "With the Charter in place, legislation can now be struck down on grounds other than a violation of the federal division of powers. The court [Supreme Court] therefore has the constitutional authority and the public legitimacy to play a more central role in the evolution of public policy."[9] Given the controversial nature of the public policy issues that do wind up in the Supreme Court (such as reproductive freedoms, rights of accused persons, obscenity laws, provision for possible provincial separation), it should not be surprising that Court rulings provoke occasional consternation and laments from various segments of society. Note in the subsequent chapters the associated constellation of players involved with the particular legal disputes discussed and their reactions to the legal outcomes.

THE WORKLOAD OF THE SUPREME COURT

The Supreme Court's diet is composed largely of cases being appealed from decisions in other courts. As already noted, this is occasionally supplemented by special questions referred to it by the federal government. As the final appeal court, the Supreme Court must deal with those seeking to have their cases re-examined. It is the Court's role to select cases raising significant matters of law, including matters relating to its application to particular fact situations, but not to rehear basic findings of fact.

What the members of the Supreme Court do in hearing an appeal is delineate the key questions they will consider in their assessment of the case. Granting leave to be heard by the Supreme Court does not generally include a lengthy re-presentation of the evidence submitted at previous trials. Established provisions regulate the length and nature of the presentations the Court will hear. After the appeal has been heard, the members of the Supreme Court work on coming to a decision, which usually follows the hearing of the case by several weeks or months.

Supreme Court judgments serve to clarify points of law or to settle uncertainties. This may, for example, involve elaboration of the legal definition of particular terms or constitutional requirements, or the re-evaluation of legislative enactments in light of Charter requirements and the application of the law to particular situations or settings. The Supreme Court can order new trials if it finds significant problems or weaknesses either with how a case has proceeded through police and court channels or with the understandings that guided police actions or lower court reasoning. Its findings will then serve as guides for others throughout the political community and the attendant judicial system. Russell, Knopff, and Morton point to this critical element of the Court's workload when they note that "[t]he Supreme Court's function is to select those cases which raise difficult and contentious questions in all areas of law—not just constitutional law—and to write opinions on these which will serve as principled guides to the lower courts and to the lawyers who advise citizens and governments on their legal rights and duties."[10] As already noted, the federal and provincial governments of Canada may occasionally assign questions to the courts that they believe are so important and pressing that recourse through ordinary channels is inappropriate. Rather than wait for a concrete dispute between differing parties to arise and to pass through the legal system, provincial and federal governments may refer questions to the courts (federal government to the Supreme Court; provincial governments to their provincial court of appeal) for an answer. While not necessarily binding, the resulting advisory opinions carry great weight. Governments have referred different types of matters to the courts over the years.

Questions may, as noted, be referred by the federal government directly to the Supreme Court, or by provincial governments to their provincial courts of appeal. One of the most striking examples of a provincial government taking this kind of initiative occurred in response to the constitutional tactics of Prime Minister Pierre Trudeau. On October 2, 1980, Trudeau informed Canadians that the federal government was prepared to work toward constitutional amendment without provincial consent. A set of federal government–inspired constitutional reforms was drafted. Unilateral action of this sort troubled provincial premiers, who argued that consultation with provincial governments was necessary and that provincial support was required for actual amendment. The governments of Manitoba, Quebec, and Newfoundland submitted questions to their provincial courts of appeal. Differing conclusions were arrived at by the various provincial courts amid much national discussion. The entire issue ultimately was the subject of an appeal to the Supreme Court of Canada where it was ruled that substantial provincial consent for the kind of amendments in question was in keeping with Canada's constitutional conventions, that is, our traditions and past practices.[11] More recently, the federal government submitted a list of questions to the Supreme Court dealing with legal issues related to the legality of a possible provincial separation from Canada. Known as the *Quebec Secession Reference* (1998), it is dealt with in a subsequent chapter in this volume.

Canadian legal traditions are rooted in adversarial proceedings wherein participants argue their respective cases. Defendants are recognized as needing good legal counsel and are believed to be innocent until proven guilty. Procedural safeguards, such as the already noted independence of the judiciary, are employed to promote fairness. Given these elements of Canada's legal heritage, there are those who are troubled by the availability of the reference procedure. One criticism of the reference mechanism is that reference proceedings allow a governing executive to shape a set of questions in self-serving ways. Rather than allow others to define the issue in a real-world setting, they force an immediate answer on question(s) that in other circumstances might have been framed differently. Another concern is the potential blurring of lines between the political executive, which oversees the execution of laws and directs the flow of legislative business in a parliamentary system, and the judiciary, which hears disputes arising from the application of laws and which interprets what is legally and constitutionally appropriate. References, it is argued, provide a way for the executive to be advised directly by the courts without facing a real-world dispute.[12] In Australia and the United States such referrals are regarded as unconstitutional.[13] The advantage of reference cases is that they facilitate expedited treatment of an issue before deeper and more complex problems emerge. In the unilateral patriation debate of the early 1980s, for example, reference proceedings were seen as a way of clarifying what was constitutional before the Trudeau project became too far advanced. Whichever side of the debate one prefers, provision for reference proceedings seems likely to remain a feature of the Canadian legal system.

CANADA'S COMMON LAW TRADITION AND EMPHASIS ON THE APPLICATION OF PRECEDENT

Public trust in the courts is enhanced not only by preservation of their independence, but also by the clarity and wisdom of judicial findings. A key element of such findings is reasoned recourse to the principles and guidelines established by past legal judgments. Consistency of application promotes advance public knowledge about laws and the sanctions associated with their transgression. Such information is readily available to lawyers and trained legal professionals through recourse to past statutes and their interpretation in past judicial decisions. Public access to legal counsel is in fact protected by the Charter which, among other protections, includes the following: "10. Everyone has the right on arrest or detention (a) to be informed promptly of the reasons therefore; (b) to retain and instruct counsel without delay and to be informed of that right."

Canada operates with a common law tradition inherited from Great Britain, wherein reference to past judicial decisions or precedents is a fundamental component of legal reasoning and decision making. The application of precedent, which is so central to the common law tradition, is implemented by the principle of *stare decisis*. As explained by Greene, "*Stare decisis* is a particularly rigid version of the doctrine of precedent that holds that the decisions of higher courts in the same jurisdiction are always binding on lower courts concerning the interpretation given to the law. As well, the decisions of courts of equal or higher status in other common-law jurisdictions are persuasive. How a particular law will be interpreted by the courts, therefore, is contingent on the whole history of interpretation of other relevant laws."[14] In this way, the determination of what is illegal rests upon legislation and constitutional documents and conventions, judicial interpretation, and application of the relevant precedents.

Quebec's legal system is distinguished by the maintenance of the civil law tradition inherited from France. Put simply, civil law "regulates relationships between two private parties such as individuals or corporations."[15] Civil law in Quebec operates via a formal code—the implementation of a comprehensive legal code, as opposed to the accumulation and application of precedents. Their civil code heritage involves "important differences ... in the concepts and forms of action in relation to personal and property law, particularly regarding the status of minors, the succession to estates and the transmission of property."[16] Quebec's unique legal tradition leads to debates over issues such as Quebec's number of positions on the Supreme Court and Quebec's desires for constitutional recognition of its provincial distinctiveness.

Working on difficult cases that involve tough and complex choices produces the earlier-mentioned "principled guides" that Russell and his coauthors speak of. Supreme Court judgments and opinions help clarify contentious matters and shine light where previously vagueness or uncertainty prevailed. This carries with it power, for as Rand Dyck points out: "While the Supreme Court hears fewer cases per year than any lower court, it is interested almost exclusively in questions of law.

Thus, of all courts it is the most heavily engaged in a 'law-making' role, and its decisions are binding on all lower courts."[17] By "law-making" Dyck means, of course, the explication of law and judgments through Supreme Court decisions and Court determination of what is constitutionally required from a legal–judicial vantage point. Judicial rulings help give practical meaning to words and concepts: i.e., in these kinds of circumstances this is how these statutes, for example, come into play.

JUDICIAL REVIEW

Settling noteworthy legal conflicts and helping to regulate the interactions between citizens, as well as between citizens and their governments, entails more than the explication of ordinary statutes and/or regulations. As was already pointed out, Canadian courts, especially the Supreme Court, are also occupied with the function of judicial review—the determination by members of the judiciary of what is constitutionally acceptable. As Peter Russell has observed, "One kind of jurisdiction traditionally exercised by Canadian courts that may well be entrenched is judicial review of the constitutionality of government activity. The power of the courts to veto legislation or executive activities which in the judiciary's view violate the law of the Constitution is the most dramatic political role played by Canadian courts."[18] Checking against violations of the Constitution can pit the courts against governments (federal and/or provincial) or political parties intent on projects of their own design. It may also lead the courts into positions in which the judiciary takes a stand contrary to public opinion.

The landmark case of *Marbury v. Madison* (1803) established the authority of the United States judiciary to review governmental actions in terms of their constitutionality. It came at a time of political turbulence and upset over the character of the judiciary generally and the particular reforms to the judiciary proposed by the incoming Republican administration.[19] At issue in the case was a dispute over commissions to the position of justice of the peace and the decision of the incoming president, Thomas Jefferson, not to reappoint William Marbury despite the fact that a commission identifying Marbury for this post had been prepared, but not delivered, by the outgoing administration of President Adams. Marbury felt aggrieved, and action was begun to request Secretary of State Madison to indicate why the Supreme Court should not direct him to deliver the commissions not acted on by Jefferson, among which was Marbury's. Subsequently, a request was made by certain opponents of the new presidential administration for the Supreme Court to direct that Marbury's commission be delivered to him. In the end, the Supreme Court dismissed the case due to complex constitutional factors revolving around the ability of the Court to issue such directives, but Chief Justice John Marshall took the opportunity to declare the Court's responsibility to enforce the law, including the Constitution. "The Constitution is either a superior, paramount law, unchangeable by ordinary means, or it is on a level with ordinary legislative acts, and like other acts, is alterable when the legislature shall please to alter it."[20] Hence, it was up to the courts to review legislation and rule on what was constitutionally acceptable. Constitutions were to be seen as fundamental "law," protected from shifting legislative majorities and public feelings and hence not easily changed.

Judicial review of constitutionality carries with it some element of ongoing tension between the judiciary and its institutional counterparts—the legislature and the executive. For, as Manfredi alerts us, "Judicial review occupies an ambiguous position in liberal democratic theory. On the one hand, it performs a positive function by safeguarding individual rights and liberties by enforcing constitutional limits on legislative and executive power. On the other hand, judicial review can become an antidemocratic force to alter the fundamental nature of a regime's constitution without popular participation."[21]

CANADA'S HERITAGE OF JUDICIAL REVIEW

In Canada, the early practice of judicial review was shaped by colonial relationships and the evolutionary character of the country's progress toward full political independence. With colonial status came the application of Britain's Colonial Laws Validity Act, which was meant to prevent discrepancies between Canadian and British statutes. Lack of complete political autonomy brought with it final recourse to British rather than Canadian courts, and oversight of legislation, even when it was passed within the new Dominion of Canada. Dominion legislation was reviewed in light of imperial direction, adherence to the federal–provincial division of powers, and legal principles and practices. Great Britain's Judicial Committee of the Privy Council (the JCPC) served as the ultimate appeal court for Canada for over sixty years after Confederation. Access to the JCPC was rooted in the ability of colonials to appeal "to the foot of the throne."[22] The means for handling these appeals involved creation of "a committee to advise the Crown on how to respond to such appeals. In 1834 the practice was given a statutory basis by the Imperial Parliament, and the Judicial Committee that was to play such a large role in Canadian history came into existence."[23]

From the first, judicial review in Canada was tied to the imperial connection, but the most controversial dimension of this review by far was its application to federalism and the division of powers. Adoption of a federal set of governing arrangements for the new Dominion meant that legislative authority would have to be allocated. This was carried out via the Constitution Act, 1867 (known before 1982 as the British North America Act or BNA Act), in which lists of federal and provincial powers are presented. The list of federal powers was extensive, as the subjects of power were important and the rhetoric expansive. Among the powers of the national government were the following: authority under the preamble to section 91 to legislate for "the Peace, Order, and good Government of Canada, in relation to all Matters not coming within the Classes of Subjects by this Act assigned exclusively to the Legislatures of the Provinces";

enumerated authority over such weighty matters as trade and commerce, all forms of taxation, military affairs, navigation and shipping, currency, savings banks, bankruptcy and insolvency, Aboriginal peoples and lands reserved for them, and criminal law; concurrent powers with the provinces, but with federal paramountcy over agriculture and immigration; federal power to pass remedial legislation to safeguard certain endangered denominational school systems; and the powers of reservation and disallowance, which could be exercised over provincial governments. Provincial powers, meanwhile, were narrower. They included such matters as direct taxation, provincial public lands, municipal institutions, licences for such things as shops and saloons, marriage solemnization, property and civil rights within the province, incorporation of companies with provincial objects, local works and undertakings, save for interprovincial ship, railway, canal, telegraph, or other works connecting provinces, interprovincial and international steamships, and works declared by the federal Parliament to be for the general advantage of Canada.

Even a cursory glance at the division of powers shows the possibilities for disagreement. By way of examples, one might easily imagine the difficulty of sorting out rival claims when federal authority over "The Regulation of Trade and Commerce" (91.2) encountered provincial authority over "The Incorporation of Companies with Provincial Objects" (92.11) and "Property and Civil Rights in the Province" (92.13); or when federal authority over "The raising of Money by any Mode or System of Taxation" (91.3) met "Direct Taxation within the Province in order to the raising of a Revenue for Provincial Purposes" (92.2). Beyond the possible semantic ambiguities lay an even deeper dilemma, one that, in fact, took shape over the ensuing decades. How could such a distribution of powers, with an expansively presented list of federal powers, work within an emerging country marked by strong regionalism/provincialism and strong federal and provincial leaders? Federal–provincial rivalry was not slow in coming after Confederation. Provinces felt confined and sought to carve out a greater role. Federal politicians often found themselves confronted by determined opposition from some or, on occasion, most or all of the provinces. Legal challenges ensued, and review of jurisdictional boundaries became a hot topic.

By their very nature, federal governing arrangements presuppose some method of resolving jurisdictional quarrels. In contemporary society, this role is often assumed to be the natural responsibility of the courts. In the 1860s this had not yet been established in Canada. Jennifer Smith reminds us that at the time of the Quebec Resolutions and Confederation there was questioning of whether judicial review was necessary, given the extent of federal government powers: "Under the Resolutions, the central government possessed the power to disallow local laws just as the British government retained the power to disallow Parliament's enactments, a parallel feature not unnoticed by critics of the scheme like Christopher Dunkin. Disallowance not only undermined the need for judicial arbitration, whether by the Judicial Committee or a national court, it also suited partisans of parliamentary supremacy...."[24] This federal predominance suggested by the power of disallowance was soon challenged in the courts and elsewhere.

Over time, the courts became central in the resolution of federal–provincial conflicts, but the long decades of rule by the law lords of Britain delayed independent Canadian jurisprudential thinking and interpretation of the division of powers. Such fundamental questions as the approach to be taken in understanding the words and implications of constitutional documents and conventions, or in determining how high court judges should be selected, were not fully reflected on by Canadians. The same was true for the criteria for Supreme Court appointment. The possibility of direct provincial input in the selection process remains an unresolved constitutional issue to this day.

Finally freed in the post–World War II era from the JCPC's oversight, the Supreme Court slowly came into its own. By the 1980s it had achieved a higher profile than ever before. With the already discussed patriation reference and the development of a Charter of Rights and Freedoms, the Court was regarded with respect, if not always passive public agreement. Among those who participated in this maturation was Chief Justice Bora Laskin (chief justice from 1973 to 1984), of whom Peter McCormick has asserted: "I take it as axiomatic that the Chief Justiceship of Bora Laskin was the pivotal period for the emergence of the modern Supreme Court of Canada."[25] Laskin had been appointed chief justice by Pierre Trudeau over a number of more senior colleagues. His influence was widely felt.[26] Snell and Vaughan describe Laskin as having acted in contrast to the traditional conservatism of the judiciary: "only the rare justice—such as Chief Justice Bora Laskin—falls easily into the category of judicial innovator."[27] Since Laskin, the Court has been led, successively, by Brian Dickson and Antonio Lamer. As this book went to press, Lamer retired and was replaced as chief justice by Beverley McLachlin, and Louise Arbour was appointed to replace Cory.

The Constitution Act, 1982, ushered in the Canadian Charter of Rights and Freedoms, which brought judicial review to a new frontier—the review of government legislation and action (or, on occasion, inaction) in the interest of enforcing and protecting entrenched rights and freedoms. Included among the Charter's provisions are the limitations of section 1 ("The Canadian Charter of Rights and Freedoms guarantees the rights and freedoms set out in it subject only to such reasonable limits prescribed by law as can be demonstrably justified in a free and democratic society."); the fundamental freedoms (section 2, which refers to freedoms of conscience and religion; thought, belief, expression; peaceful assembly; and association); democratic rights (section 3); mobility rights (section 6); legal rights (sections 7–14); equality rights (section 15); Canada's official languages (sections 16–22); minority language education provisions (section 23); enforcement (section 24); relation of the Charter to Aboriginal treaty or other rights and freedoms (section 25); Canada's multicultural heritage (section 27); equality of the sexes (section 28); the application of the Charter (section 32); and provision for the notwithstanding clause (section 33). The famous, or possibly notorious, notwithstanding clause allows for the passage of legislation notwithstanding the Charter protections of sections 2 and/or 7 to 15; a declaration made pursuant to this provision can have effect for up to five years and may be re-enacted.

As prime minister, Trudeau saw the Charter as a fundamental element in the building of nationwide political loyalties and citizenship within a bilingual and multicultural country. Many have adopted it as a key element of their conception of Canada.[28] Its implementation is frequently cited as an important national achievement. Groups came to call on the Charter as an aid to particular causes. Various business interests used it to question restrictions on things such as Sunday shopping and tobacco advertising. Aggrieved minorities sought protection under provisions such as the section 15 equality rights. All of this and more led Cairns to observe that "[t]he Charter is imperialistic. Its various clientele seek to extend its jurisdiction."[29]

The task of interpreting the general language of constitutional documents such as the Charter and giving it meaning fell to the courts. Many of the clauses reflect aspirations and political principles. Giving them day-to-day practical content requires painstaking legal analysis and argumentation over tough choices. For example, do guarantees of freedom of expression preclude restriction of pornography or hate speech? Do guarantees of free expression prevent governments from imposing financial limits on spending related to referendum or election campaigns? How will the Charter affect reproductive matters? What is a reasonable limit on a right or freedom, and what values come into play when reasonableness gets weighed? These and many other questions ensure the ongoing salience of the Supreme Court to Canadians.

ORGANIZATION AND OPERATIONS

The Supreme Court is the product not only of political history, but also of modern legislation. The Supreme Court Act[30] sets out the Court's structure and operation. Membership consists of a chief justice and eight puisne judges, all of whom are appointed by the federal government via the Governor-in-Council. Justices can be selected from the ranks of either superior court justices or barristers with at least ten years of experience at the Bar of a province or territory.[31] Unlike the appointment process for the U.S. Supreme Court, no public hearings are held to approve or reject an appointment to the Canadian Court. In the United States, proposed appointments go to the Senate where vigorous hearings can, and frequently do, occur. Appointees to the Canadian Court may serve until their mandatory retirement age of seventy-five. Because of Quebec's civil law system, three judges must be appointed by law from Quebec. Conventional practice has been that the remaining justices are divided as follows: three from Ontario, two from Western Canada, and one from Atlantic Canada. Within the regional groupings (Western or Atlantic Canada), there is often pressure to spread out the appointments among the constituent provinces, but this is not a necessity. Administration of the Court is a responsibility of the chief justice. A small organizational staff complement attends to the Court's functioning, but the chief justice is the Court's public face.

Judgments may go through a number of draft versions before being released to the public. In their private discussions after hearing the legal arguments, the judges meet and voice their initial feelings about the case in reverse order of seniority. Former justice Bertha Wilson describes the ensuing events this way: "The first tentative expression of views at our conference will usually disclose whether there is any prospect of unanimity or whether there is clearly going to be more than one judgement. We decide at this conference who is going to prepare the first draft. This will be a member of the group which appears likely to form the majority."[32] From here on, an exchange of ideas develops as the written opinion(s), and dissent(s), if any, take shape. Such differences reflect the independence of mind and diversity of opinion within the Court. When Justice Cory was interviewed by *The Globe and Mail* on his impending retirement, his comments on intra-Court deliberations were illuminating: "When you see a decision reserved for a particularly long time, there have been extra meetings and a flood of memos back and forth," he said. "Memos are circulated to everybody. You will get one back saying: 'I agree to A and to B, but not to C—and over my dead body to D.'"[33]

Over time, the written judgments and public statements of justices help mould the broader legal environment. This can involve speaking out on occasion to raise the profile of emerging and important issues. For example, at the Canadian Bar Association's 1998 annual meeting in St. John's, Newfoundland, Chief Justice Lamer raised questions about whether the judiciary should be more willing to speak out publicly in defence of their judgments.[34] Another example would be the reflections on the place of women in the judiciary offered in learned papers by Justices Wilson[35] and L'Heureux-Dubé.[36]

The Supreme Court's influence over the entire legal and judicial community is profound. According to Laskin,

> the Supreme Court's main function is to oversee the development of the law in the courts of Canada, to give guidance in articulate reasons and, indeed, direction to the provincial courts and to the Federal Court of Canada on issues of national concern or of common concern to several provinces, issues that may obtrude even though arising under different legislative regimes in different provinces. This is surely the paramount obligation of an ultimate appellate court with national authority.[37]

HISTORICAL EVOLUTION OF THE COURT'S CONSTITUTIONAL STATUS

Looking at the lengthy process through which the Supreme Court evolved may offer some indication of the difficulties associated with the development of independent Canadian thinking about issues of jurisprudence and the constitutional status of the Supreme Court. Provision was made in the Constitution Act, 1867, for the potential creation by the Parliament of Canada of a general court of appeal: "101. The Parliament of Canada may, notwithstanding anything in this

Act, from Time to Time provide for the Constitution, Maintenance, and Organization of a General Court of Appeal for Canada, and for the Establishment of any additional Courts for the better Administration of the Laws of Canada." This general court of appeal was not created until 1875 under the Liberal government of Alexander Mackenzie, and even then there existed ambiguity about its role. Divergent understandings of the new Court's relationship to Canada's federal–provincial battlefield co-existed. Smith's evaluation of the parliamentary debates of the time suggests that some saw the new Court as an institutionalized restraint on provincial ambitions, while others foresaw a transition to judicial umpiring of federal–provincial disputes.[38] The former conception envisioned the Court as a tool for rejecting provincial advances, while the latter understood the Court as arbitrating federal–provincial disputes as a learned and impartial adjudicator. These contrary conceptions lived on in political discussion even after the ultimate ascendancy of the latter model.[39]

Canada's colonial ties and the provisions of section 101 set in place certain important institutional features of the newly created Supreme Court. Note that the section provided for a Court created by the federal parliament. Provincial input into the creation or appointment of the Court was not provided for. Observe further that the provisions allowing for the Court's creation did not stipulate a further process of constitutional ratification or amendment before the Court would become operational.

Since Supreme Court judgments could still be appealed to the JCPC, the rulings of the JCPC shaped the terrain for legal argument. Their rulings became the basis for precedent. For legal minds of great promise and ambition, the Supreme Court presented limited inducements. Snell and Vaughan have concluded that "[f]or many decades the Canadian public and political leaders neither expected nor allowed the Supreme Court of Canada to become a conspicuous and influential institution. Viewed in our political and legal culture as a body subsidiary to the legislature and the political executive, the Court occupied an ambiguous place in the judicial hierarchy and was used as a minor political instrument at the disposal of the federal government."[40]

Making sense of the JCPC's legacy for the Constitution Act, 1867, and for Canadian jurisprudence generally, has been labelled by Alan Cairns as "one of the most contentious aspects of the constitutional evolution of Canada."[41] Given the stakes, it should not come as a shock that the JCPC handiwork lingers as a source of dissension.[42] The cumulative impact of the JCPC rulings on the public policy environment was to focus attention on the headings of provincial powers in section 92 of the Constitution Act, 1867; to weaken the national government's capacity to act on its own in many fields of endeavour; and to strengthen the interests of provincial governments. Grand allocations of power such as "trade and commerce," assigned to the federal government under section 91.2, were cut down by the JCPC.[43] It was judged that such phrases understood expansively would confine provincial authority to the margins, and that, therefore, it might be better to respect some sphere for provincial action and to adopt a narrower understanding of the federal power. The handiwork of the British law lords bedevilled various federal legislative initiatives: for example, federal regulation of labour relations ran into the roadblock of *Toronto Electric Commissioners v. Snider*, 1925; the "Bennett New Deal" of the 1930s encountered decisions such as *Attorney General of Canada v. Attorney General of Ontario* (Employment and Social Insurance Act Reference), 1937.[44] Advocates of a strong central government response to challenges such as the Great Depression or the development of Canada's social safety net lamented the JCPC's reluctance to recognize what they regarded as national problems needing a nationwide attack. Typical of those wishing for an enhanced national presence was the eminent lawyer, professor, and poet F. R. Scott, who was bitterly disappointed in the JCPC's response to the reference cases submitted by Prime Minister Mackenzie King on the Bennett initiatives. He declared that the "Privy Council is and always will be a thoroughly unsatisfactory court of appeal for Canada in constitutional matters; its members are too remote, too little trained in our law, too casually selected, and have too short a tenure."[45] Scott was far from alone, particularly during the 1930s. On the other hand, Cairns has suggested that "the policy output of British judges was far more harmonious with the underlying pluralism of Canada than were the confused prescriptive statements of" those who criticized the JCPC's views on the distribution of powers.[46] Even Pierre Trudeau observed that "[i]t has long been a custom in English Canada to denounce the Privy Council for its provincial bias; but it should perhaps be considered that if the law lords had not leaned in that direction, Quebec separatism might not be a threat today: it might be an accomplished fact."[47]

Over time, the constitutional landscape evolved, and the calls for Canadian judicial autonomy grew in volume. With the Balfour Declaration of 1926 and the Statute of Westminster in 1931, "the formal legal subordination of the self-governing dominions to the imperial Parliament" was ending.[48] Judicial autonomy was finally ushered in after the completion of World War II. In *Attorney General of Ontario v. Attorney General of Canada* (Reference re: Abolition of Privy Council Appeals), 1947,[49] the JCPC ruled that, with the Statute of Westminster, the way was clear for the Canadian government to bring appeals to Great Britain's law lords to a close. The requisite legislation was finally passed after the 1949 election.

On September 20, 1949, federal Minister of Justice Stuart Garson rose in the House of Commons to begin second reading debate of the bill to abolish the practice whereby cases from Canada could be appealed to the Judicial Committee of the British Privy Council, making the Canadian Supreme Court the final appeal court for Canadian legal disputes. This would formally end the authority of British legal minds to chart the course of Canadian destiny directly, although, naturally, their rulings would live on. Abolition was depicted as further progress on the road to Canada's ultimate nationhood. It would remove one of Canada's "badges of colonialism," the other being the need for British approval to amend Canada's constitution.[50] Removal of appeals to the JCPC would encourage the Supreme Court to be a more capable court of final appeal.[51] Garson's colleague, Prime Minister Louis St. Laurent, reminded parliamentarians that the Liberals had pledged to end appeals in the preceding election campaign. Having won a huge victory, they had a "mandate" to act.[52] St. Laurent and Garson prevailed, and the Canadian legal and political landscape was fundamentally changed. The Canadian Supreme Court would now, in fact, be supreme within Canada for cases beginning after the passage of the 1949 amendments to the federal Supreme Court Act.

Notwithstanding the 1949 legislation, Peter Russell regards the Supreme Court as "one of the country's most important items of unfinished constitutional business."[53] Aside from the earlier noted clause within the Constitution Act, 1867, allowing for the Court's establishment, there are only limited references to its organizational and institutional characteristics in formal constitution documents. The composition of the Supreme Court is covered by the unanimous consent features of the amendment process in section 41(d) in the Constitution Act, 1982. There is reference to the Court in the general amendment provisions of section 42(d), but the importance of this is limited, for the Supreme Court Act is a piece of federal legislation, not the product of a federal–provincial constitutional accord. There may be said to be additional ambiguity about all the implications of these references to the Court in the amending provisions of the Constitution Act, 1982, given the absence of the Supreme Court Act in section 52 of the same document in which the country's formal Constitution is set out.[54]

APPOINTMENTS

The whole issue of appointments might at first seem straightforward; federal governments seek out willing and talented legal and judicial practitioners. However, potential appointments send out shock waves that generate debate about such matters as the division of powers and federal–provincial relations, gender representation, the political outlook of minority groups individually and/or generally, Aboriginal perspectives and grievances, and lobbying among the loyalists of possible contenders. Various groups in society suggest to governments that selection of one of their number would be a welcome gesture of recognition. Journalists, academics, and prospective appellants monitor the past decisions of possible appointees. Unfortunately, the politics of judicial appointments has traditionally not received sufficient academic attention. As Russell and Ziegel have declared: "For far too long political scientists and lawyers have focused on what courts do but not nearly enough on *how* they do it and *who* does it."[55]

Political tensions and sensitivities surround the issue of appointments. First, there are the tensions surrounding the relationship of this arrangement to Canada's federal system. Construction of the Court with such overt provincial/regional representation is a manifestation of intrastate federalism—the use of central government institutions to represent Canada's provincial and regional identities within elements of the national government. Like appointments to the Canadian Senate, appointments to the Supreme Court follow a provincial or regional allocation. This may have some value in knitting together the fabric of Canada, but the jury may be said to be out on its long-term effectiveness. A critical point is that while judges may be drawn from a province and may have lived and/or worked there, they may not (and maybe should not) see themselves as representative of that province's political outlook. Judges operate amid institutionally protected and loudly proclaimed professional norms of impartiality and independence.

For much of Canada's history, judicial review was largely about adjudicating the federal–provincial division of powers. Provincial governments feeling constrained by federal leadership sought to move beyond a narrow reading of their jurisdictional sphere in hopes of reflecting the aspirations of provincial political communities. Federal governments sought to act and spend with broad jurisdictional aspirations in the interest of things like unity, common national standards, or responses to serious national emergencies (for example, actions to combat severe economic difficulties). At issue were, and are, governing powers and the shaping of the policy agenda.

A feature of both the Meech Lake and Charlottetown Accords was provision for entrenching a standardized process for direct provincial input into the appointment of Supreme Court justices. Some variant of provincial lists with federal concurrence seemed to be the consensus choice as a mechanism, although this would carry with it complications in the event of discord over the selections.[56] The failure of these accords to become approved amendments to the Constitution leaves the issue on hold, pending further talks.

Aside from the inclusion of provincial input, there are other representational worries. Women's groups have pointed out the numerical underrepresentation of women throughout the ranks of Canada's judiciary.[57] The first female member of Canada's Supreme Court was Bertha Wilson, who was not appointed until the early 1980s. Since then several other women have been named, but there have never been more than three at any one time. This situation existed for almost two years after Justice Beverley McLachlin joined Justices Wilson and L'Heureux-Dubé on the Court in March 1989. Wilson retired in January 1991. While these numbers are marginally superior to those of the U.S. Supreme Court (where there never have been three at once, and for a long period—after the appointment of the first, Justice O'Connor, by President Ronald Reagan—there was only one), much room for improvement remains. In a widely cited paper, "Will Women Judges Really Make a Difference?" Justice Wilson tackled the issue of women and the work of judging. Her conclusions suggest that appointing women and integrating the different life experiences of the two genders may offer a richer understanding of issues.[58]

Aboriginal peoples also suffer from numerical underrepresentation in the ranks of Canada's judiciary. Given the range of important Aboriginal issues working their way through the courts, this is a serious concern. That justice should not only be done, but also be seen to be done, is an often repeated adage which may have relevance here. The respect people have for the political system can depend in part on whether they feel a part of that system. Underrepresentation over long periods of time might lead to underlying credibility problems.

Representation in Canada's judiciary that reflects its socioeconomic diversity is another area of concern. In alerting Canadians to "the inevitable class bias of the legal profession," Michael Mandel has pointed out that "[j]udges still have to be lawyers with some prominence in the profession, and the profession is still almost entirely the domain of the white and the upper class."[59] Such elite backgrounds and the limited representation of society's marginalized members may affect attitudes and predispositions.

There is also the underlying issue of appointment and party connections. Russell and Ziegel's work cited above shines a welcome light on the significance of past political involvement in the discussion of appointments. Many former politicians and political activists have, over the years, received appointments to positions at different levels within the court system. Patronage appointments are not often a source of hot contention in regard to Supreme Court appointees since they rarely occur. This may be a reaction to the hostile outcries when the St. Laurent government appointed cabinet minister Douglas Abbott to a slot on the Court in 1954.[60]

A FEW WORDS ON THE TASK OF JUDGING

Judging can involve tough choices. Statutes are often complex. Constitutions are meant to recognize long-lasting fundamental practices and understandings; given this, constitutional documents are often written in general language. While such language conveys basic beliefs and aspirations, conflicting understandings can arise over interpretation of phrases or differing means of implementing constitutional principles. Circumstances change once a law is passed. Rulings on specific questions arising in the complex circumstances of daily life lead to debates over the intent and application of statutes, government actions, political conventions, or constitutional accords such as the Charter. It is in the complexities of daily life that diverse and possibly competitive understandings of legal principles and past decisions come to the fore.

While precedent is vitally important, it is not the only tool employed in judicial reasoning. Reliance on precedent is complicated by several factors. One is, of course, the emergence of new laws or constitutional agreements necessitating a rethinking of how past decisions and practices will relate to new provisions. Another, trickier factor is the creation in life of new twists or variations on past situations. This may render past decisions less pertinent or raise questions about which of several possible precedents to apply. These and other difficulties associated with reasoning via the use of precedents have to be considered. Boyd, for example, asserts that among such difficulties are "the danger that, in trying to mesh current situations with pre-existing case law, the courts and counsel may make illogical distinctions," and the realization that "the Supreme Court must occasionally depart from its past decisions, weighing the value of new evidence or responding to new conceptions of a problem."[61]

There are also debates about the attitude to be adopted when approaching statutory or constitutional interpretation. For example, one commonly cited school of thought is that judges should seek out and adhere where possible to the original intent of those who drafted the provisions at issue. This original intent strategy is most often referred to in matters arising from constitutional agreements, for they might be argued to reflect momentous occasions when people and their elected representatives consciously opted for certain major choices; hence, these decisions and the sentiments behind them should be recognized and applied. These original intentions should receive prominence until the formal Constitution or key statutes are amended. Adoption of such an approach to interpretation would assign primacy over legislative and constitutional reform to the legislative and executive institutions where statutes and accords are debated and implemented. Meanwhile, the judiciary would be charged with recognizing past decisions and the motivations and intentions that accompanied them. While this interpretive strategy has many adherents, it has also gained critics. Among its merits are its respect for parliamentary debate as representative of the people's views and of legislative objectives, and the restraints it puts on the possibility of an unrepresentative and headstrong judiciary. Among its limits are difficulty in dealing with situations unimagined by the creators of the laws or accords, and the complexities associated with conclusively determining legislative intentions. For example, whose views on what is intended by certain sections of the Charter take precedence: those of Prime Minister Trudeau, the various premiers, the lawyers and experts who did the legal drafting, political and/or legal commentators, or others? The consistent use of the past as a reference point rather than taking into account contemporary values may also pose difficulties.

Another commonly referred-to orientation toward legal and constitutional analysis sees the Constitution as akin to a "living tree" that adapts and is refined over the years. Lord Sankey of the JCPC came up with this phrase in the celebrated *Persons* case.[62] The analogy of the living tree suggests growth and vitality wherein the courts and other elements of the political system carry on with the process of adaptation to new and changing circumstances. Evidence of this approach can be found in the words of Lamer in Reference re *B.C. Motor Vehicle Act,* 1985, in which he cautioned against heavy reliance upon past debates and understandings even if they could be found expressed in a source such as the records of a past special committee studying the Constitution. Lamer stated, "If the newly planted 'living tree' which is the Charter is to have the possibility of growth and adjustment over time, care must be taken to ensure that historical materials, such as the Minutes of Proceedings and Evidence of the Special Joint Committee, do not stunt its growth."[63] As with other interpretive strategies, strengths and weaknesses accompany this one. Among its strengths are an awareness of new and evolving circumstances and openness to new ideas. The rigidity involved in seeking out original intent is removed. However, as an interpretive approach, it seems open to as many interpretations as there are gardeners aspiring to direct the tree's growth. Who is best suited to prescribe the needs of the growing tree? How much flexibility should be accorded the judiciary and their recommendations?

In short, there are various understandings of the work of judging and the means of dealing with statutory and constitutional interpretation. Presented here are only some examples of prominent schools of thought. Those considering the general task of judging and the associated responsibilities may find it helpful to supplement their reading with biographies of celebrated judges and to contemplate the values they brought to their work.[64] Also consider the challenge of judging amid technological and cultural changes. These changes bring forth new disputes, different types of information and evidence, and evolving attitudes on the part of the public and legislators. In late April 1999, for example, a collection of judges from the Massachusetts Superior Court spent two days at the Whitehead Institute for Biomedical Research "to trade their gavels for pipettes and learn firsthand what DNA is all about."[65]

The justices of the Supreme Court may on occasion use a decision or a set of decisions to alert Canadians to the need for social and legal reform. Such is the case in their 1999 unanimous decision in the case of Jamie Tanis Gladue, a decision that raised questions about the high rates of incarceration for Aboriginals and appropriate sentencing practices. Fears over the future impact of these high rates drove the justices to express their concerns. The situation, in the Court's words, is "so stark and appalling that the magnitude of the problem can be neither understood nor explained away."[66]

JUDICIAL DECISION MAKING AND THE UPROAR OVER JUDICIAL ACTIVISM

Contemporary discussion of the work of Canada's courts often revolves around the extent of judicial review and the vigorousness of judicial intervention. This dialogue has been constrained to a degree by the heritage of JCPC dominance and the slow development of an independent Supreme Court, limiting the development of jurisprudential thinking. Cairns has argued that critics of the JCPC were more effective at criticism than they were at developing guiding beliefs for judicial review in the Canadian context. "In sum, Canadian jurisprudence was deeply divided on the question of the relevant criteria for the guidance of judges in the difficult process of constitutional interpretation. Neither critics nor supporters of the Judicial Committee were able to develop consistent and defensible criteria for judicial review."[67] This lack of consensus about the role and extent of judicial review is pointed to by Katherine Swinton when she observes that "[e]ven though the justification for judicial review has rarely been addressed openly, the traditional form of the Canadian debate nevertheless implicitly raised fundamental questions about the role of the judiciary in resolving jurisdictional disputes between the federal and provincial governments."[68] For years, the overriding concern of scholars was debate over the degree of faithfulness displayed in JCPC rulings to the vision of the architects of Confederation. In modern times, the focus of distress over judicial review has shifted. The Charter's enactment moved the debate to a new stage and gave the courts new responsibilities. The judiciary's interpretation of Charter requirements and consequent treatment of government or legislative intentions has led to active scrutiny of judging and the degree of activism or restraint displayed by the judiciary, particularly those on the Supreme Court.

Activism and restraint refer to the level of willingness shown by a judge or collection of judges to assert judicial perspectives over legislative intentions and the relative breadth of definition accorded to constitutionally protected rights. Knopff and Morton offer this helpful explanation: "Judicial activism refers to the disposition to interpret rights broadly and to enforce them vigorously.... An activist court uses the power of judicial review to intervene and to influence the making and enforcement of laws. A self-restrained court tends to avoid such intervention."[69] Activism and restraint imply the degree of respect or acceptance judges show toward the intentions of legislators and/or those drafting constitutional or legal texts. Activist judges are assumed to be those most willing to substitute their outlook or values for those of legislators and constitutional drafters, while restraint implies a willingness to apply the wishes of these people and to hold in check one's own beliefs and values. Critics of the judiciary often denounce what they perceive as expansive interpretations of individual rights offered by an insulated and appointed, not elected, judiciary. Charter advocates, meanwhile, point to the merits of assertive judges seeing beyond the political passions of the moment, offering a reasoned protection of fundamental liberties—one which does not equate the bureaucratic decisions of government administrators with democracy. There is a large and growing literature on the Charter and its enforcement by the courts[70] where the judicial activism issue often enters the discussion. What follows is a brief attempt to introduce the topic of activism and to suggest some factors relevant to understanding its dimensions.

Those worried over the possibility of ongoing judicial activism often stress the following themes. One is the limited accountability of judges, given their place as part of the nation's social and political elite. Judges are not unaccountable, but the lines of accountability through the Canadian Judicial Council remain largely within the ranks of the profession and may be relatively closed to an outsider. This is clearly suggested in the wording of a *Globe and Mail* headline for an article dealing with a dispute involving two prominent judges: "Close Ties Cloud Process of Judges Judging Judges—Settling Fate of McClung, L'Heureux-Dubé Hard for Judicial Council That Knows Them Very Well."[71] This issue of accountability becomes more complex when judges face disputes over public policy debates whose full dimensions exceed issues of jurisprudence and legal expertise. Lawyers are trained to reason along lines that emphasize precedent, jurisdiction, and legal formulations of matters such as intent and culpability, and they do so using a specialized vocabulary. Their approach to problems may on occasion reflect neither the surface meaning of words or statutes nor the outcomes expected by observing nonlawyers. Resultant tensions can produce outcries against presumed judicial arrogance or shortsightedness. When, for example, the Supreme Court became absorbed with the issue of criminal intent and ruled in 1994 that extreme intoxication could be used as a defence against a sexual assault charge,[72] the public outcry was deafening. The resulting disquiet extended even to the Justice Department.[73]

Accompanying concerns over judicial accountability are criticisms of the salaries and benefits received by judges. Judicial independence helps promote fair and impartial justice, but some question the protective cover it offers the judiciary in pursuit of good salaries and working conditions. Evidence of such sentiment may be found in the following headline for an article in *Alberta Report* on the introduction of amendments in 1998 to the Judges Act by Justice Minister Anne McLellan: "The Judicial Lobby Strikes Again—Another Bill Before Parliament Sweetens Pension Provisions for Judges."[74] Those interested in such issues can observe the Supreme Court's perspectives on judicial independence and compensation in their ruling in *Reference re Remuneration of Judges of the Provincial Court of Prince Edward Island; Reference re Independence and Impartiality of Judges of the Provincial Court of Prince Edward Island.*[75] While setting or describing an appropriate range for judicial compensation is beyond the scope of this essay, it should be noted that the justices of the Supreme Court are talented legal minds who could likely otherwise command very good salaries in the legal marketplace.

There is a more profound set of concerns regarding the extent of judicial review and the activism of various members of the judiciary.[76] These concerns arise from the assignment of complex, highly political questions to a small group of individuals, such as the Supreme Court, for resolution, no matter how highly trained they may be. Interpreting vital political matters like rights and freedoms requires the justices to engage in what might be seen as political judgments. For example, determining when limits on a right are reasonable in a free and democratic society (section 1 of the Charter) is ultimately a political challenge beyond the confines of traditional statutory interpretation. Judicial assessments of the reasonableness and inclusiveness of legislative attempts to deal with an issue, and the Court's weighing of these attempts in light of guaranteed rights and freedoms, involves the justices in contemplation of political values and choices.

The general language of the Charter is a mixed legacy for Canada's judiciary. At one level, the argument could be made that it gives judges room to act and give operational meaning to valued provisions such as equality or mobility rights. Yet, simultaneously, there is the dilemma of value conflicts when judicial understandings are presumed to be inadequate. A useful contribution to discussion of this issue is made by Thomas Bateman in a recent article in the *Canadian Journal of Political Science.*[77] Bateman points to divergent understandings within the ranks of the Supreme Court over such basic questions as the extent of the Charter's coverage and the essential purpose of charters of rights. It is generally understood that the Charter applies to governmental actions, yet the boundary of what is governmental remains contested. What is more, an ongoing tension between liberal and what Bateman calls "postliberal" constitutional thinking frequently divides the Court. Liberal constitutionalism stresses the threat to individual liberty posed by government authority and actions at the same time as it "exalts liberty, affirming the formal equality of persons before the law."[78] The Charter is seen as protecting the freedom of individuals from an overbearing government. Adopting this viewpoint, one seeks a judiciary able to restrain unjustified governmental intrusion and protective of private, social, and economic choices. Postliberal thinking views the public–private distinction (that is, the Charter's application to government, not private, conduct) as a limitation on the ability to see broader social patterns of inequality and exploitation. Charters encapsulate political bargains that reflect underlying distributions of social and economic power. "The state, argue the postliberals, is part of a hegemonic ideological order of privilege for some and oppression for the many."[79] Those adopting this perspective emphasize the limits of formal liberal equality and imagine a broader set of challenges to the prevailing social and economic status quo. This would entail unravelling the neat public–private divide and investigating below the surface of power arrangements and the accommodative government policies that facilitate them. Equality of condition, rather than formal equality of opportunity, is a key aspiration for postliberals.

Examples of philosophical division lie in regard to the equality provisions of section 15 and in the Supreme Court's treatment of labour relations issues. As might be expected, disagreement persists over the proper way to apply and understand the Charter's guarantee of equality (section 15). Is the issue formal equality of individuals? after-the-fact equality of outcome? or equality tempered by respect for legislative intentions and discriminations specified in statutes (those people in a particular area, of a particular age, with particular medical or social conditions)? Note Chief Justice Lamer's acknowledgment of difficulty for the Court in arriving at a common approach to equality rights: "If you read the judgments coming out of this court, I think it is apparent that we are struggling ... And the courts below are struggling. There is so much social impact.... How far do we go in terms of seeing that everyone is equal? How far can we afford to go?"[80] While the Court continues to work at reaching a generally agreed-on approach to equality, another aspect of its jurisprudence has generated much hostile commentary. Court decisions on disputes involving organized labour and the Charter have not been kind to the expectations of Canada's unions. The public–private divide and the focus on protecting legally equal individuals from government action have not served the interests of unions and their allies in working through organized means to challenge the current economic order. The Supreme Court has ruled fairly consistently against the hopes and practices of organized labour. Those worried about the underlying equality of social and economic forces have been left deeply troubled. Writing in the *Osgoode Hall Law Journal,* H. J. Glasbeek asserted that Canada's Supreme Court has, in its judgments, displayed contempt toward workers, and he condemned various judicial decisions as illustrating the "untrammelled expressions of the courts' sense of self-importance, inflated by their new role under the *Charter,* and as evidence of their continued anti-working class biases."[81] David Beatty argues along similar lines: "A close reading of the Charter decisions which the Supreme Court has authored shows precisely the same bias against the interests of workers and their unions that plagued the common law rules of tort and crime employed by the judges to control the behaviour of the working class throughout most of the nineteenth and first half of the twentieth centuries."[82] The more inclusive the judicial-political debate becomes, the better able Canadians will be to understand the significance of judicial review and the authority of lawyers and the judiciary.

For the moment, however, let us return to the discussion of judicial activism and restraint. As concepts they are suggestive of tendencies, but one must be careful in their usage. Judicial reasoning that may appear activist in one aspect may appear restrained in regard to another. For example, one of the first highly publicized Charter cases to reach the Supreme Court entailed complaints from an organization called Operation Dismantle that held that government participation in certain weapons testing efforts jeopardized rights under section 7 ("Everyone has the right to life, liberty and security of the person and the right not to be deprived thereof except in accordance with the principles of fundamental justice.").[83] The complainants lost, but their case provoked serious debate. A key question was whether the whole case was justiciable, that is, whether the issue was suitable for resolution by a court of law. Were there specific facts and a legal question to be dealt with, or was the issue one involving political judgments and value differences? If the latter, then the government should be allowed to exercise the prerogatives that come with its authority. The federal government declared that Crown prerogative should insulate the issue from legal review, and that the matter was essentially a political question and therefore not suitable for legal resolution. Political questions were argued by the government to raise problems of evidence, for there would be virtually insurmountable problems in determining what could be recognized as explicit facts as opposed to judgment or perceptions. The political executive felt it had to use judgment and guile rather than be bound by strict legal facts and rulings. The Court ruling on this case manifested the two kinds of obvious complications referred to above. Powers of foresight sufficient to predict this sort of legal challenge were not widespread at the Charter's inception, but now the justices had to grapple with the resulting court challenge. The second kind of complication was the coexistence of activist and restraint views within the judicial reasoning. Take the case of Justice Wilson, who bluntly rejected federal views on justiciability, but rejected the protesters' position because, in her view, the rights contained in section 7 were designed for individual citizens, not for general decisions that might affect the broad populace. Putting together these elements of her decision is interesting. As Russell, Knopff, and Morton observe, her position on justiciability "initiated her reputation as the most activist judge on the Court," while her "narrowing of the scope of section 7 suggests an element of judicial self-restraint."[84] In the end, a majority of the Supreme Court ruled that the issue of heightened risk of war was a subjective matter not suited to fact-based adjudication.

Another prominent complication with the activist/restraint conception is that its use may lead to an oversimplification of the problem of intent. Much of the popular original intent criticism of activist judges assumes that there is a clear and reasonable legislative intent that may be identified. This is often not the case, and furthermore, it underestimates how difficult it is to discern intent unquestionably in a court of law. For example, section 3 of the Charter states: "Every citizen of Canada has the right to vote in an election of members of the House of

Commons or of a legislative assembly and to be qualified for membership therein." The general language offers few detailed qualifications. No explicit reference is made to minors or other groups who have often faced restrictions on their voting (for example, judges, psychiatric patients, incarcerated individuals). Recourse might be made to the reasonable limits clause in section 1 cited above, but there is serious ongoing debate over the impact of this clause and phrases in it such as "reasonable limits prescribed by law as can be demonstrably justified in a free and democratic society."[85] While expressing reservations about facile reliance on the activist/restraint formulation, the purpose here is not to reject it outright. It is suggestive of a general orientation to the task of judging and is an easily explained formulation.

A broad-brush way of describing the attitudes of certain judges on particular types of questions is often a helpful guide. Furthermore, various judges do have distinctive outlooks and these warrant examination and comparative analysis. An example of such helpful comparative work done from a different perspective is that conducted by Peter McCormick in which he seeks to assess numerically the levels and patterns of agreement and disagreement among the Supreme Court's membership over a broad range of its cases.[86] Using sophisticated quantitative methodology, he examines the various groupings of judges that each case has created based on agreement with the prevailing judgment or participation in dissent. He cautions his readers against using his findings to support simplistic conclusions (these judges win when they stick together or some similar inference), arguing that the aim is "rather to use them to find the values and principles and areas of law around which the agreement clusters—as well as the values and principles about which frequently agreeing justices no longer agree."[87] Another notable project with a quantitative element is the effort to chart the interaction of courts and legislators. For example, Hogg and Thornton speak of a "Charter dialogue" between them and monitor specific outcomes. They assert that legislators often employ statutory responses to judicial outcomes they find unacceptable: "our research has indicated that most of the decisions of the Supreme Court of Canada in which laws have been struck down for breach of a Charter right have in fact been followed by the enactment of a new law."[88] This research is not, however, without critics who argue that this work underestimates the important issue of the resultant law's content, that is, whether the outcome favours a judicial tendency toward absolute outcomes rather than legislative or parliamentary compromises.[89]

CONCLUSION: TRANSITION TO THE SUBSEQUENT CHAPTERS

Looking at cases in isolation permits elaborate analysis of arguments, careful assessment of a specific legal dilemma, and extensive reflection on the particularities of a situation. Case-by-case analysis is challenging, but keep in mind that the law in any given field is shaped by a multitude of different decisions on related, yet dissimilar, situations. This might be most visible in matters of criminal law in which different dimensions of violence, forethought, plotting, networks of allies and accomplices, age, and many other variables have to be evaluated in any dispute. However, the point may be more effectively made if we consider a less obvious example. Toward that end, let us make note of the general field of education and the diverse kinds of education-related disputes dealt with by the Supreme Court in just the last few years. There is the *Adler* case,[90] in which competing claims of denominational educational rights and rights to religious freedom and equality of treatment had to be resolved. *Ross v. School District No. 15* involved the discriminatory comments and writings made by a teacher against adherents of a particular religion and the regulatory and judicial assessment of appropriate sanctions.[91] Another case, this one having to do with unacceptable behaviour by a teacher and the associated sanctions, involved the Board of Education for the City of Toronto.[92] Inappropriate intimacy between a teacher and a fourteen-year-old former student, and the issue of how one understands the idea of teachers as people in authority, was adjudicated in *R. v. Audet*.[93] The issue of teachers' authority status and their responsibility toward students came up in a very different context in *R. v. M. (M.R.)*.[94] By a wide majority the Court concluded that teachers not only were able to undertake searches of students without elaborate procedural restrictions, but may also have a responsibility to do so. Yet another aspect of the responsibilities of teachers and educational institutions was dealt with in *University of British Columbia v. Berg*.[95] Here discussion swirled about discrimination in the treatment of students and issues of human rights regulation and judicial review. The treatment of extraordinary students and the selection of a suitable classroom or learning environment arose in *Eaton v. Brant Board of Education*.[96] A very different kind of case related to education matters was *Ontario Home Builders' Association v. York Region Board of Education*.[97] This emanated from the application of a means for regulating land development designed to raise money for educational facilities. Educational financing also figured, albeit indirectly, in *Union of N.B. Indians v. N.B. (Minister of Finance)*, in which a dispute arose in New Brunswick over the provincial Social Services and Education Tax, the federal Indian Act, and the treatment of goods purchased by Aboriginals off reserves.[98] These and other disputes in the education field made their way into the legal system. Realizing the breadth and multiplicity of cases helps us to appreciate the role of the courts, especially the Supreme Court; the frequency with which public disputes end up before the legal system; the interrelationship of different cases involving related themes or subject matter; and the potential for contentiousness over which past precedent best suits present circumstances.

ENDNOTES

I wish to thank Martin Westmacott and Richard Vernon for their insights and commentary.

1. Kirk Makin, "Cory to Leave Supreme Court—Speculation Favours Arbour as Successor," *The Globe and Mail*, 18 January 1999, A1 and A4.

2. Makin, "Cory to Leave Supreme Court."

3. Tonda MacCharles, "Top Court Speculation Begins All Over Again—Louise Arbour May Be Top Contender for June Vacancy," *The Toronto Star*, 19 January 1999, A7.

4. Kirk Makin, "Lamer Blasts Unseemly Lobbying for Positions on Supreme Court—Campaigning Divisive, Chief Justice Warns as Vacancy on Bench Looms," *The Globe and Mail*, 5 February 1999, A2.

5. Andrew Heard, *Canadian Constitutional Conventions: The Marriage of Law and Politics* (Toronto: Oxford University Press, 1991), 118.

6. Quoted in Martin L. Friedland, *A Place Apart: Judicial Independence and Accountability in Canada, a Report Prepared for the Canadian Judicial Council* (May 1995), 1.

7. For elaboration on the meaning of section 24, see Chapter 17, particularly p. 231, in Robert J. Sharpe and Katherine E. Swinton, *Essentials of Canadian Law—The Charter of Rights and Freedoms* (Toronto: Irwin Law, 1998).

8. Bayard Reesor, *The Canadian Constitution in Historical Perspective: With a Clause-by-Clause Analysis of the Constitution Acts and the Canada Act* (Scarborough: Prentice Hall, 1982), 404.

9. Roger Gibbins, *Conflict and Unity: An Introduction to Canadian Political Life* (Scarborough: Nelson, 1994), 75.

10. Peter H. Russell, Rainer Knopff, and Ted Morton, " Introduction," in *Federalism and the Charter: Leading Constitutional Decisions, A New Edition* (Ottawa: Carleton University) Press, 1989), 26–27.

11. For a very good overview of the genesis of this case and its treatment by the Supreme Court, see Russell, Knopff, and Morton, 706–59.

12. For elaboration on this point, see Peter H. Russell, *The Judiciary in Canada: The Third Branch of Government* (Toronto: McGraw-Hill Ryerson, 1987), 91–92.

13. Sharpe and Swinton, 71.

14. Ian Greene, "The Courts and Public Policy," in *Governing Canada: Institutions and Public Policy*, ed. Michael M. Atkinson (Toronto: Harcourt Brace Jovanovich Canada, 1993), 192–93.

15. Rand Dyck, *Canadian Politics: Critical Approaches* (Scarborough: Nelson Canada, 1993), 521.

16. J.R. Mallory, *The Structure of Canadian Government*, rev. ed. (Toronto: Gage, 1984), 311.

17. Dyck, 528.

18. Russell, *The Judiciary in Canada*, 93.

19. Among the many sources one might call on for a fuller explanation of the period and *Marbury v. Madison*, there is an interesting account in Jean Edward Smith, *John Marshall: Definer of a Nation* (New York: Henry Holt and Co., Owl Books, 1996), 296–326.

20. Quoted in Jean Edward Smith, 322.

21. Christopher P. Manfredi, "Judicial Review and Criminal Disenfranchisement in the United States and Canada," *The Review of Politics* 60, no. 2 (1998): 305.

22. Quoted in Garth Stevenson, *Unfulfilled Union: Canadian Federalism and National Unity*, 3d ed. (Toronto: Gage, 1989), 46.

23. Stevenson, 46.

24. Jennifer Smith, "The Origins of Judicial Review in Canada," *Canadian Journal of Political Science*, 16, no. 1 (1983): 124.

25. Peter McCormick, "Follow the Leader: Judicial Power and Judicial Leadership on the Laskin Court, 1973–1984," *Queen's Law Journal* 24, no. 1 (1998): 238.

26. See, for example, the account in McCormick, "Follow the Leader," 239, or the assorted commentaries in R.C.B. Risk and J.R.S. Pritchard, eds., "Chief Justice Bora Laskin: A Tribute," *University of Toronto Law Journal* 35, no. 4 (1985).

27. James G. Snell and Frederick Vaughan, *The Supreme Court of Canada: History of the Institution* (Toronto: Osgoode Society and University of Toronto, 1985), 253.

28. Dale Gibson, for example, cites a 1981 survey that found over 70 percent of Canadians supportive of the Charter's enactment. See Dale Gibson, "The Deferential Trojan Horse: A Decade of Charter Decisions," *The Canadian Bar Review* 72, no. 4 (1993): 418.

29. Alan C. Cairns, "The Charter: A Political Science Perspective," *Osgoode Hall Law Journal* 30, no. 3 (1992): 616.

30. R.S.C. 1985 Chapter S-26. The Act has been, and remains, subject to periodic amendment by the federal Parliament.

31. www.scc-csc.gc.ca/generalinfo/history.htm; p. 1 of 2.

32. Madam Justice Bertha Wilson, "Decision-Making in the Supreme Court," *University of Toronto Law Journal* 36, no. 3 (1986): 236.

33. Kirk Makin, "Top-Court Judge Defends Bench: Retiring Justice Peter Cory Speaks out Against Grilling of Potential Jurists," *The Globe and Mail*, 3 March 1999, A5.

34. Remarks of the Right Honourable Antonio Lamer, P.C., to the Canadian Bar Association, August 23, 1998, St. John's, Newfoundland; copy provided by the Supreme Court offices in Ottawa.

35. Madam Justice Bertha Wilson, "*Will* Women Judges Really Make a Difference?" *Osgoode Hall Law Journal* 28, no. 3 (1990): 507–22.

36. Madam Justice Claire L'Heureux-Dubé, "Making a Difference: The Pursuit of a Compassionate Judge," *University of British Columbia Law Review* 31, no. 1 (1997): 1–15.

37. Bora Laskin, "The Supreme Court of Canada: The First One Hundred Years, A Capsule Institutional History," *The Canadian Bar Review* 53, no. 3 (1975): 475.

38. Jennifer Smith, 124–33.

39. Ibid., 132.

40. Snell and Vaughan, 258.

41. Alan C. Cairns, "The Judicial Committee and Its Critics," in Douglas E. Williams, ed., *Constitution, Government, and Society in Canada: Selected Essays by Alan C. Cairns* (Toronto: McClelland and Stewart, 1988), 43.

42. For a recent example of this ongoing intellectual dispute, see the review of Patrick Monahan's *Constitutional Law* by Ronald I. Cheffins in *Canadian Public Policy* 24, no. 3 (1998): 403–6, particularly 404.

43. See, for example, their ruling in *Citizens Insurance Co. v. Parsons*, 1881, which is discussed in Russell, Knopff, and Morton, 37–42.

44. For excellent introductions to these cases and overviews of the judicial reasoning that prevailed, see Russell, Knopff, and Morton, 73–77 for Toronto Electric Commissioners, and 97–100 for the Employment and Social Insurance Act Reference.

45. Quoted in Sandra Djwa, *The Politics of the Imagination: A Life of F.R. Scott* (Vancouver: Douglas and McIntyre, 1987), 151.

46. Cairns, 83.

47. Pierre Elliott Trudeau, "Federalism, Nationalism, and Reason," in *Federalism and the French Canadians* (Toronto: Macmillan, 1968), 198.

48. Peter H. Russell, *Constitutional Odyssey: Can Canadians Become a Sovereign People?* 2d ed. (Toronto: University of Toronto, 1993), 53.

49. See Russell, Knopff, and Morton, 122–29.

50. *House of Commons Debates* (henceforth cited as *Debates*), 20 September 1949; 69.

51. *Debates,* 20 September 1949; 73.

52. *Debates,* 23 September 1949; 198.

53. Russell, *The Judiciary in Canada,* 363.

54. This is explained more fully in Reesor, 405.

55. Peter H. Russell and Jacob S. Ziegel, "Federal Judicial Appointments: An Appraisal of the First Mulroney Government's Appointments and the New Judicial Advisory Committees," *University of Toronto Law Journal* 41, no. 1 (1991): 35.

56. For an account of the proposals for the Supreme Court in the Charlottetown Accord, see Ronald L. Watts, "The Reform of Federal Institutions," in Kenneth McRoberts and Patrick Monahan, eds., *The Charlottetown Accord, the Referendum, and the Future of Canada* (Toronto: University of Toronto, 1993): 30–31.

57. The representation of women and the legal profession, and the broader issue of social elitism and the profession, is dealt with in many books and articles. See, for example, Joel Bakan, "Constitutional Interpretation and Social Change: You Can't Always Get What You Want (Nor What You Need)," *Canadian Bar Review* 70, no. 2 (1991): 318–24.

58. Madam Justice Bertha Wilson, "*Will* Women Judges Really Make a Difference?" 522.

59. Michael Mandel, *The Charter of Rights and the Legalization of Politics in Canada,* rev. ed. (Toronto: Thompson Educational Publishing, 1994), 48.

60. Snell and Vaughan, 199–200.

61. Neil Boyd, *Canadian Law: An Introduction,* 2d ed. (Toronto: Harcourt Brace and Company, 1998), 51.

62. *Henrietta Muir Edwards v. A. A. Canada* (1930) A.C.

63. Quoted in Russell, Knopff, and Morton, 446.

64. A recent example of such a work is Jean Edward Smith's biography of John Marshall, which the *New York Times* cited as one of the notable books of 1996.

65. Carey Goldberg, "Judges' Unanimous Verdict on DNA Lessons: 'Wow!'," *The New York Times,* 24 April 1999, A10.

66. Quoted in Kirk Makin, "Top Court Appalled as Natives Fill Canada's Jails—Judges Must Stop Sending So Many Aboriginals to Prison, Court Declares," *The Globe and Mail,* 24 April 1999, A4.

67. Cairns, "The Judicial Committee and Its Critics," 82.

68. Katherine E. Swinton, *The Supreme Court and Canadian Federalism: The Laskin–Dickson Years* (Toronto: Carswell, 1990), 21.

69. Rainer Knopff and F.L. Morton, *Charter Politics* (Scarborough: Nelson, 1992), 19.

70. See, for example, F.L. Morton, Peter H. Russell, and Michael J. Withey, "The Supreme Court's First One Hundred Decisions: A Statistical Analysis," *Osgoode Hall Law Journal* 30, no. 1 (1992): 1–56.

71. Kirk Makin, "Close Ties Cloud Process of Judges Judging Judges—Settling Fate of McClung, L'Heureux-Dubé Hard for Judicial Council That Knows Them Very Well," *The Globe and Mail,* 8 March 1999, A4.

72. *R. v. Daviault* [1994] 3 S.C.R.

73. Gay Abbate and Tu Tranh Ha, "Drunkenness Defence For Rape Worries Justice Department—Ways to Lessen Impact of Supreme Court Ruling Being Considered," *The Globe and Mail,* 4 October 1994, A7.

74. Celeste McGovern, "The Judicial Lobby Strikes Again—Another Bill Before Parliament Sweetens Pension Provisions for Judges," *Alberta Report,* 19 October 1998, 38.

75. [1997] 3 S.C.R.

76.   The arguments in this and the immediately ensuing paragraphs were clarified by comments offered by Richard Vernon in a helpful commentary on an early draft of this chapter.

77.   Thomas M. J. Bateman, "Rights Application Doctrine and the Clash of Constitutionalisms in Canada," *Canadian Journal of Political Science* 30, no. 1 (1998): 3–29.

78.   Ibid.

79.   Ibid.

80.   Quoted in Kirk Makin, "Lamer Worries About Public Backlash—Angry Reaction Could Affect Judges' Decisions, Chief Justice Says," *The Globe and Mail*, 6 February 1999, A1.

81.   H. J. Glasbeek, "Contempt for Workers," *Osgoode Hall Law Journal* 28, no. 1 (1990): 18. In this section of the article his commentary was directed particularly at decisions in *Newfoundland Association of Public Employees v. Attorney-General for Newfoundland and Chafe (1988)*, [1988] 2 S.C.R., and *British Columbia Government Employees' Union v. Attorney General of British Columbia, Attorney General of Canada, Intervenor (1988)*, [1988] 2 S.C.R.

82.   David M. Beatty, "Labouring Outside the Charter," *Osgoode Hall Law Journal* 29, no. 4 (1991): 842.

83.   *Operation Dismantle, Inc. v. The Queen* [1985] 1 S.C.R.

84.   Russell, Knopff, and Morton, 415–16.

85.   For an illustration of this debate, see Troy Q. Riddell and F.L. Morton, "Reasonable Limitations, Distinct Society and the Canada Clause: Interpretive Clauses and the Competition for Constitutional Advantage," *Canadian Journal of Political Science* 31, no. 3 (1998): 467–94.

86.   See his earlier cited "Follow the Leader," as well as "Birds of a Feather: Alliances and Influences on the Lamer Court 1990–1997," *Osgoode Hall Law Journal* 36, no. 2 (1998): 339–68.

87.   McCormick, "Birds of a Feather," 367.

88.   Peter W. Hogg and Allison A. Thornton, "The Charter Dialogue Between Courts and Legislators," *Policy Options* 20, no. 3 (1999): 22.

89.   For example, F.L. Morton, "Dialogue or Monologue," *Policy Options* 20, no. 3 (1999): 23–26.

90.   *Adler v. Ontario* [1996] 3 S.C.R.

91.   *Ross v. School District No. 15* [1996] 1 S.C.R.

92.   *Toronto (City) Board of Education v. O.S.S.T.F., District 15* [1997] 1 S.C.R.

93.   *R. v. Audet* [1996] 2 S.C.R.

94.   *R. v. M. (M.R.)* [1998] S.C.R.

95.   *University of British Columbia v. Berg* [1993] 2 S.C.R.

96.   *Eaton v. Brant Board of Education* [1997] 1 S.C.R.

97.   *Ontario Home Builders' Association v. York Region Board of Education* [1996] 2 S.C.R.

98.   *Union of New Brunswick Indians v. New Brunswick (Minister of Finance)* [1998] 1 S.C.R.

THE MEDIA AND THE SUPREME COURT OF CANADA

Susan Delacourt

Journalism is not an exact science. It writes history on the run and makes up its own rules as it hurries along. And there is no such thing as just one media filter. Styles and methods of reporting are as varied as the people who practise it. Men write differently from women. French-language reporting is not the same as English-language reporting. Moreover, print, radio, and TV journalists all do their jobs in markedly different ways.

But in Ottawa, the seat of power for the country's national government and its laws, the most important media filter revolves around reporters' attitudes to institutions. Generally, it can be said that there are two types of reporters: those who see themselves as part of the institutions they cover, and those who believe that it's the media's job to crusade against the institutions where they work. The second category of reporting has increased exponentially since Watergate in the 1970s and the dramatic, president-felling exploits of *Washington Post* reporters Bob Woodward and Carl Bernstein. Now, it is fair to say that for every one institutionally minded reporter in Ottawa, there is at least one reporter with an anti-institutional bent.

The Supreme Court of Canada is an institution, of course, and it has seen its share of institutional and anti-institutional reporting over the past couple of decades. Ironically, perhaps, the trends in those two types of reporting may well be rooted most deeply in two separate provisions of the Charter of Rights and Freedoms. The institutional reporters have picked up the freedom-of-the-press ball and run with it, while the anti-institutional reporters have been emboldened by the equality provisions in the Charter, which seem to indicate to them that no one in Canadian society, not even a Supreme Court judge, is better than any other person.

But up until recently, the Supreme Court of Canada has been spared much of the intense, knock-down-the-place kind of reporting that has become common in coverage of the House of Commons and the Senate since the days of Woodward and Bernstein. This chapter will examine how and why the Supreme Court of Canada has enjoyed such a high degree of institutional reporting since the advent of the Charter of Rights and how it is just now, in the last moments of the twentieth century, starting to feel the heat of anti-institutional journalism.

INSTITUTIONAL REPORTING

Canadians might be surprised to learn that the Supreme Court of Canada is an international trailblazer in terms of media relations. It has gone a lot further than the U.S. Supreme Court, in fact, in making itself accessible to the media. Like any other cooperative phenomenon, good institutional reporting is based on mutual agreement; in this case, on the idea that the media truly should act as the middle step between the production and distribution of information. The Supreme Court of Canada and the reporters who have covered it have built a model of successful institutional reporting—one that other institutions might do well to emulate.

The best description of the Supreme Court of Canada's handling of the media is contained in a paper written by the Court's executive legal officer, James O'Reilly, which will be published in a forthcoming issue of the *St. Louis University Law Journal*. The paper was written after O'Reilly had what he calls an "illuminating" conversation with an American legal academic at a conference in Panama City in 1998, resulting in the two men learning that there are vast differences between the way the Canadian and the U.S. Supreme Courts deal with journalists. In O'Reilly's words:

> I am of the view that the Supreme Court of Canada goes to quite extraordinary lengths to accommodate the media. Whether the U.S. Supreme Court or the Supreme Court of Canada is in fact doing enough in this respect is for others to judge. What is clear, however, is that the two Courts do things differently.[1]

The very position that O'Reilly holds is a vivid illustration of the Canadian Court's attention to media relations. The sixth person since 1984 to hold the job of executive legal officer of the Supreme Court of Canada, O'Reilly's function is to serve as the principal liaison between the Court and the media. This isn't just a matter of answering the telephone when a reporter calls. The executive legal officer holds briefings before and after judgments, helps reporters identify key legal issues in complicated rulings, and is crucial to setting the tone with which the Court is covered in the national media. It would be wrong to call the executive legal officer a "spokesman" for the Court, since his dealings with the press are strictly off the record. Reporters work on the understanding that the Court "speaks" only through its rulings and official speeches.

The executive legal officer's position owes its origins to the pioneering work that former chief justice Brian Dickson did to spruce up the court's image in the early days after the Charter of Rights and Freedoms was introduced. As reporter and author Peter Calamai writes:

*In Brian Dickson's seven years as Chief Justice, the Supreme Court of Canada
shifted from an institution that regarded the media as a necessary nuisance,
often barely tolerated, to one that actively encouraged media attention and was
not above advancing its own agenda through the press and broadcasting. This
transition was undoubtedly inevitable, given the profound transformation of
the Court brought about by the Canadian Charter of Rights and Freedoms, but
Chief Justice Dickson helped it to happen faster and more smoothly than
anyone could have predicted.*[2]

David Vienneau, a Global-TV news reporter who worked for almost twenty
years as the *Toronto Star's* chief legal reporter and Ottawa bureau chief, also
believes that Chief Justice Dickson took a visionary approach to establishing the
Supreme Court's image with the public. He recalled that before Dickson's tenure,
lawyers could be publicly lambasted before the Court if they had spoken to the
media before the hearing. Back then, said Vienneau, the Supreme Court didn't see
much of a distinction between a lawyer explaining his case and defending his
case—all of that was to take place within the hallowed chamber of the Court and
not in the pages of the newspapers.[3]

But during Dickson's time a rigorous system of cooperation was set up
between the media and the Supreme Court. This saw the advent of the executive
legal officer; the first meeting of the chief justice with newspaper editorial boards;
the first advance release of speech texts; the first of a series of interviews with the
chief justice by journalists; and the arrival of TV cameras for documentary film-
making in the Court's private dining room, conference chambers, and individual
judge's offices.[4]

This is not just a matter of the court coming to grips with the times. In
many ways, the Supreme Court is ahead of other institutions in Ottawa in facili-
tating media access. O'Reilly's article lists in some detail all the ways in which the
Court anticipates media needs. For example, he says that there are no fewer than
four special types of briefings for media: presession briefings, judgment-day briefings, prehearing briefings, and briefings before judgment days. The court is also
on the doorstep of introducing a "lock-up" style of briefings on big judgments.
The lock-up, used routinely on budget day in Ottawa, is a system by which
reporters get to spend a few hours reviewing complicated information several
hours in advance of its official release. On budget day, reporters are actually
locked up—once they enter the room where the briefing is held, they are not
allowed to leave or communicate with the outside world until the time of the official release of the information.[5]

Much of the increased journalistic access during the 1980s and 1990s
revolved around the Media Relations Committee that has a rotating membership
of three Supreme Court justices and three or four representatives of the
Parliamentary Press Gallery.[6] David Vienneau and *Ottawa Citizen* reporter
Stephen Bindman spent many years on this committee. (Bindman is now a special adviser to the federal Department of Justice.) In the mid-1980s, when the
issue of TV coverage began to be a hot issue in relations between the Court and

the media, the Media Relations Committee also invited CBC-TV's Don Newman to serve. In just over a decade, Newman has witnessed the move by the Court from stony resistance to open welcome for television cameras,[7] and he was one of the three news anchors who actually set up their desks in the lobby of the Supreme Court building in October 1998, when the Quebec secession reference judgment was released. No one who had seen the Court conduct itself twenty years ago and watched it on that day, with the hubbub of reporters, TV commentators, and spectators milling around, along with the heavy cables and technical equipment littering the marble floor, could have failed to notice how far the Court had come to opening its doors to the media.[8]

The Media Relations Committee meetings are reportedly rather informal affairs, held over dinner, once or twice a year. They have a set list of topics to discuss, and about which they are generally expected to agree. On the agenda for the May 1999 meeting, for example, was the topic of allowing audio recorders in the courtroom. (Up to this point, the only taping that could be done in the Supreme Court building was through a "feed" in the media room of the Supreme Court.)

All these steps take the Court far away from the pre-Charter days, when almost any media scrutiny was seen as a potential violation of the Court's dignity or a dangerous invitation for unseemly "performances" in the court. The CBC's Don Newman says that the steady progress has come for two reasons: first, the conservative, media-wary judges have largely retired and been replaced by more progressive, media-savvy judges; and second, each step that brought positive results—as did TV coverage, which the judges saw as healthy and positive—emboldened the Court to go further.[9]

The introduction of TV, though, was a wary, multi-staged process for the Court. It began tentatively in 1990, with a remarkable "dress rehearsal" one evening in the chamber, as a few judges and journalists discreetly staged a mock hearing to test how the Court would handle the presence of television. Don Newman was there. He recalls most vividly what the high-wattage TV lights did to the courtroom itself. Squinting in the glare, Justice Charles Gonthier joked that at least he could read his papers more clearly. (One of the chief findings of this experiment was that the lights were too bright.[10] Watchers of Supreme Court broadcasts will notice that the courtroom does appear darker than the average meeting room or TV studio.) As well, for the first years of TV broadcasts from the Supreme Court, the media were allowed to broadcast entire cases only, and not just show "clips." But in 1997, two years after the Cable Public Affairs Channel (CPAC) began regular, gavel-to-gavel broadcasts, the Supreme Court relaxed the rule, on the basis that the full context was available to TV viewers somewhere, so the clips from then on could be seen.[11]

Stephen Bindman is one of the longest serving practitioners of institutional journalism at the Supreme Court. Indeed, his current position as a special adviser to the Justice Department could well be seen as a natural evolution of his role within the institution of the law. He and David Vienneau believe that a close, working relationship between judges and reporters is healthy, and that it need not just be formal.[12] Legal reporters saw the late justice John Sopinka as a champion of this informal style of rapprochement.[13] When Sopinka died unexpectedly in November 1998, the loss of his trademark openness was publicly lamented.

In a 1996 speech to the University of New Brunswick, Bindman urged judges to cultivate good ties with reporters—not to help the reporters, but to help the public get better information.

... I think judges should go one step further, and here I point again to Mr. Justice Sopinka's practice. After a ruling is handed down in which he wrote or participated, he is often available informally to select reporters to explain, clarify or discuss certain points. We are not talking here about an interview or quotes, we are talking about helping reporters, and through them the public, to understand what are very complex issues for lawyers. More judges should make themselves available and break their silence to assist the public in understanding the process.[14]

ANTI-INSTITUTIONAL REPORTING

In 1998, a new phrase began to find common use in the Canadian media: "judicial activism." Suddenly, it seemed, someone had declared open season on judges' power and the media were beginning to give prominence to people who questioned whether the Supreme Court had seized too much authority over lawmaking in Canada.

The declaration of war on judges in fact came from several, but related, quarters. The Western-based Reform Party and Alberta Premier Ralph Klein openly acknowledged their desire to put judicial activism on the public agenda. The Reform Party used one of its allotted "opposition days" in the Commons in June 1998 to debate whether judges had too much unfettered power. In August of the same year, Klein arrived at the annual premiers' conference, saying that judicial activism was for him one of the leading items on the agenda for the meeting with his counterparts. News organizations whose editorial slant leaned the way of Reform and Klein—notably the magazine *Alberta Report*[15] and the brand-new national newspaper, the *National Post*—began in 1998 to give ample coverage to criticism of the Supreme Court's power.

Two extraordinary media stories in the first months of 1999 illustrated how the anti-institutional bent was starting to affect the Supreme Court. The first was the unusual and quite sensational exchange in the media between Alberta Court of Appeal Justice John McClung and Supreme Court Justice Claire L'Heureux-Dubé. It began when Justice L'Heureux-Dubé publicly rebuked Justice McClung for his 1994 ruling in a sexual-assault case. In overturning his judgment, the Supreme Court had harsh words for comments that Justice McClung had made during that trial. In turn, the Alberta judge launched an unprecedented personal attack on Justice L'Heureux-Dubé, implying that attitudes such as hers were provoking a high rate of male suicide in Quebec. In the midst of this public battle, the very personal information emerged that Justice L'Heureux-Dubé's husband had in fact committed suicide. Hence, Judge McClung's attack was seen as all the more vicious. The question underlying this whole story, though, was: Would such a personal story about a judge have become so public in a previous era? Undoubtedly not.

The second story was less of a headline-grabber, but equally telling of the new attitude insinuating itself into court coverage. In May 1999, the Supreme Court justices held a retreat in Winnipeg—the first time they'd ever held one outside of Ottawa. The *National Post* treated the story as it would a politicians' junket, reporting on the "imperial procession" of judges and their expensive receptions with elite folks in Western Canada.[16] The *Post*, in fact, has made no secret of its willingness to declare a public-relations war on the Court, devoting pages of commentary to judicial activism and spending many editorial inches slamming the Court's power. A succinct description of that editorial position, in fact, was provided by one of the *National Post*'s own columnists. Andrew Coyne noted: "For the *National Post* and for the ultraconservative legal theorists it has adopted and promoted, the day the Charter of Rights and Freedoms became law, in the words of one, Canada 'surrendered any claim to democratic self-government....' The *Post* is against any attempt on the part of unelected judges to impose their will on a democratically elected legislature."[17] For instance, an editorial on April 20, 1999, written after a Toronto conference called "Are Judges Too Powerful?" took place, strongly chided the conference for "smugly" defending the Supreme Court's role. Noting one study that showed the Court had overturned only 80 laws in its 250 rulings since the Charter, the *Post* editorial said: "What restraint! What circumspection! What heroic self-control! Were they taking long vacations? Or advised by their doctors to have a siesta over lunch?"[18] That editorial, clearly sarcastic and verging on personal attack, is an indication that the Supreme Court should be braced for more anti-institutional reporting. In tone, it is remarkably similar to the one that the anti-institutional media have used on MPs and senators since the mid-1980s.

The *Globe and Mail*'s justice reporter, Kirk Makin, says the *National Post* has indeed had a profound effect on Court coverage. The *Post*, he says, is leading the charge on more harsh criticism of the Supreme Court. But it isn't just the *Post*, Makin notes. He believes it's part of something broader.[19] "With few exceptions, a hands-off attitude toward judges in the press was the tradition up until quite recently," Makin says, adding,

> *Either that or utter neglect, that is. This was a direction engendered in part by the judicial habit of never speaking to reporters. As their reluctance to speak out has faded, our interest in them has simultaneously grown. The news media is now in the midst of a 180-degree turn. Having demystified and demythologized every other institution in society, I see the media now turning a great deal of attention to judges, judicial behaviour, and actual judgments.*[20]

This development can't be seen in isolation from other trends in the media. A big trend in journalism in the 1990s is to "personalize" stories, in an attempt to make the stories more relevant or entertaining to information-overloaded audiences. The anecdote has become a popular "lead," or opening, for serious news stories; budget coverage inevitably focuses in on a typical family or person to show how the numbers affect ordinary people. The Supreme Court judges are under some media pressure to show a more personal side, too—a demand that does not sit comfortably with the traditional notion of the court as a faceless, distant, objective arbiter in society. In other words, as the judges become more human in the eyes of the public, and more of society than above it, by what authority will they claim to sit in judgment of people and events? The "judge bashers" argue that it's the media's job to crusade against any person or institution that sets itself above the rest of society.

Seasoned legal reporters, such as Stephen Bindman or Kirk Makin, warn that the Court should not overreact to the trend of judge bashing. In his 1996 speech at the University of New Brunswick, Bindman said:

> I should make it clear at the outset that judges, like all public officials, should
> expect a certain amount of criticism and scrutiny of their work and their lives.
> After all, judges are called upon to decide some of the most difficult issues
> facing us. They are unelected and have tenure, and it is virtually impossible to
> get rid of them once they are appointed. Moreover, there are always going to be
> winners and losers in every case and that makes judges an easy target.[21]

Makin, for his part, believes that judge bashing is a temporary development.

> I think one sees this phenomenon with regard to any institution that has
> remained relatively unexamined, unscathed and protected from press scrutiny.
> Once that scrutiny finally starts, it can be quite unrestrained for a time. The
> media attacks we see on the judiciary these days remind me of a pack of exuberant puppies discovering a turtle waddling across a field. The pawing and
> barking are sure to reach a fever pitch for a while, but eventually the little darlings will spot a nearby kitten and head off to make its life miserable.[22]

WHAT'S NEXT?

In terms of institutional reporting, the Supreme Court of Canada is expected to continue its bold march toward improved access for journalists. The willingness to allow tape recorders into the courtroom itself and the openness to the idea of lock-up style briefings for reporters are just two signals of the Court's continuing campaign to make itself more open to media scrutiny.

The Court's enthusiastic participation in the Internet revolution also bodes well for improved access on the institutional-reporting front. Since the mid-1990s, the Supreme Court has made its judgments immediately accessible on its Web site, which means that reporters like Vienneau and Makin are no longer the prime filter for the Court's decisions. In other words, the public can read for itself what the judges say, as soon as they've said it. This makes for a more educated, legally literate audience. The consequences of the Supreme Court's openness via the Internet will be interesting to monitor in the next century.

But the fear exists that all these accessibility advances will be offset by developments on the anti-institutional front—developments that could make judges more skittish and fearful of the media. Even more worrying is the fear that judges might start to shy away from making unpopular decisions.

Chief Justice Antonio Lamer, in an interview on February 6, 1999, with *The Globe and Mail*'s Kirk Makin, publicly aired his apprehensions on this score. "It is in these cases I am concerned that as a result of virulent or harsh comments by the press or public, the most popular thing to do might become the outcome," the Chief Justice said, adding, "Judges are human beings. I would be remiss if I were to say that we are superhuman or that we are not influenced sometimes."[23]

The Chief Justice took some of that heat himself several months earlier after his address to the Canadian Bar Association's annual meeting in the late summer of 1998, when he openly mused about whether the Supreme Court justices should speak out more after their rulings, to explain them in person to the public.[24] Editorial and media reaction was swift—many commentators accused the Chief Justice of flirting with an idea that would make the justices into TV celebrities and diminish the value of the considered, carefully written ruling.[25]

The fact that the Chief Justice is speaking out on judge bashing, however, is a strong indication of the Court's overall trepidation about the anti-institutional reporting it is beginning to feel. Will the Supreme Court react as other institutions have, that is, defensively or in a pandering, apologetic fashion? For those who continue to see the Court as an important and vital institution in the nation, this is the big question about media coverage of the Supreme Court in the next century.

ENDNOTES

1.   James W. O'Reilly, "The Supreme Court of Canada and the Media," *St. Louis Law Journal*, (forthcoming), 1999.

2.   Peter Calamai, "The Media and the Court's Public Accountability," in *Brian Dickson at the Supreme Court of Canada 1973–90*, ed. DeLloyd J. Guth (Winnipeg: University of Manitoba, Faculty of Law, Canadian Legal History Project, 1998), 290.

3.   David Vienneau, interview with author, 25 March 1999.

4.   Calamai, 293.

5.   O'Reilly, forthcoming.

6.   Ibid.

7.   Don Newman, interview with author, 21 May 1999.

8.   Ibid.

9.   Ibid.

10.   Ibid.

11.   O'Reilly, forthcoming.

12.   Stephen Bindman, interview with author, 21 May 1999.

13.   David Vienneau, interview with author, 25 March 1999.

14.   Stephen Bindman, "Judicial Independence and Accountability," *University of New Brunswick Law Journal* 45 (1996): 62.

15.   See Paul Bunner, "Editor's Notes: The Usual Suspects: Is the Charter or the Judge the Villain in the Child Porn Ruling?" *Alberta Report* 26 (8 February 1999), for elaboration on the magazine's stand on judicial activism.

16.   Marina Jiminez, "A Supremely Imperial Tour," *National Post*, 1 May 1999.

17.   Andrew Coyne, "The Charter under Attack," *National Post*, 3 May 1999.

18.   "The Defence Reclines," editorial, *National Post*, 20 April 1999.

19.   Kirk Makin, interview with author, 7 April 1999.

20.   Ibid.

21.   Bindman, "Judicial Independence and Accountability," 63.

22.   Kirk Makin, interview with author, 7 April 1999.

23.   Quoted in Kirk Makin, "Lamer Worries about Public Backlash," *The Globe and Mail*, 6 February 1999, A1.

24.   Antonio Lamer, Chief Justice of the Supreme Court of Canada, speech to the Canadian Bar Association Annual Conference, St. John's, Newfoundland, 23 August 1998.

25.   See, for example, Stephen Bindman, *Montreal Gazette*, 25 August 1998, B2.

PROCESSING APPEALS FOR JUDICIAL REVIEW:

The Institutions of Agenda Setting in the Supreme Courts of Canada and the United States[1]

Roy B. Flemming

A court's agenda is the set of cases it selects for review. The impact of this process can be far-reaching. Which cases are heard direct and mould the development of the law. Furthermore, the choice of cases and the court's emphasis on particular areas of the law can lead to major public policy changes. In assembling its agenda, a high court also necessarily creates winners and losers. At the same time, the decision to hear some cases and not others imposes the court's priorities on the politics of the country and its government.

The emergence of Canada's Supreme Court as an influential policy maker has drawn wide and often vocal attention. Little of this attention, though, focuses on the way the Court selects cases for review. While an extensive literature exists on agenda setting on the United States Supreme Court, comparable research in Canada is limited.[2] Studies of the Supreme Court's "application for leave to appeal" process were first published in 1982 by Canada's *Supreme Court Law Review,* and have continued ever since on an annual basis. These surveys, however, are "practice notes" addressed to the legal profession and are of limited analytical value.

This chapter is a survey or overview of the process in Canada with comparisons to the process followed in the United States. The account will be largely descriptive, and at some points tentative or speculative, as it is part of a larger project designed to develop an empirical understanding of how the Canadian Supreme Court selects appeals for review. The project began in May 1996 with the collection of information from over 1250 leave to appeal applications filed with the Court and from the factums or briefs filed by the applicants' attorneys between 1993 and 1995. Data collection continued through 1998 on various other aspects of the process, including a mail survey of the attorneys involved in the cases. The central purpose of this project is to determine the extent to which findings about agenda setting on the Supreme Court of the United States can be replicated in Canada. To do this, a framework for the comparison is needed. This chapter lays out this framework by contrasting the institutions and norms that shape the agenda setting processes in the two Courts. The first step toward this framework is to take a brief look at the evolution of Canada's Supreme Court.

What makes the Canadian and American Supreme Courts' selection of cases for judicial review significant political acts is the influence these choices have on their countries' policy making processes. To be more specific, the role of Canada's Supreme Court has grown over the past fifty years to the point where its position in Canadian politics is very nearly equivalent to that reached by the Supreme Court in America. Since World War II, the Supreme Court of Canada has undergone a significant transformation as a governmental institution. It is substantially more autonomous and more capable of rendering decisions with deep implications for Canadian politics and society than in the past. Three major events strengthened the Court as an authoritative institution: the abolition of appeals to the Judicial Committee of the Privy Council; entrenchment of a Charter of Rights and Freedoms; and the granting to the Supreme Court of greater discretion over its agenda.

In the mid-1970s, Parliament amended the *Supreme Court Act* to limit the right to appeal in civil cases and, with a couple of exceptions, in criminal cases as well. The 1975 amendment, analogous to the "Judges' Bill of 1925" in the United States, which gave the American Court discretionary authority over what to hear, freed the hands of the justices to select those appeals they felt were important and deserving of judicial review.[3]

An appeal means that a lower-court proceeding is reviewed by a higher court. The party appealing a decision, the "appellant," argues through written briefs and oral arguments that the errors made by the lower court are sufficiently serious that the outcome in the lower court should be invalidated or "overturned." The "appellee" is the winning party in the lower court and argues against judicial review. A court of final appeals, such as Canada's Supreme Court, is not concerned about factual errors, nor does it heed new findings of fact when it exercises its power of judicial review. Instead, it focuses on the constitutional or procedural questions raised by the appellant. Appeals are either obligatory or discretionary. When Parliament limited the right of appeal, it made discretionary appeals, or those appeals which the Court could choose to hear, the main avenue to judicial review. For the first time, Canada's Court held substantial control in its hands over the kinds of cases it wished to hear.[4]

THE INSTITUTIONS OF AGENDA SETTING: CANADIAN AND AMERICAN SIMILARITIES AND DIFFERENCES

The differences in procedures and norms relating to the components or dimensions that make up the institutions of agenda setting in the Canadian and U.S. Supreme Courts are summarized in Table 3.1. These differences are then described in more detail in this section.

In both Courts, deciding what to decide moulds the policy-making process for the Courts as well as for other governmental actors and society as a whole. In setting their agendas, the Courts elevate the public visibility of some issues while downplaying others. There is a strong likelihood that the Courts' choices will shift the attention paid by other governmental institutions and the media to issues that reflect its cases.[5] Discretionary authority is pivotal to this process. The discretion of both Courts to choose the cases they want to hear is unfettered by statutory or legislative restrictions.

Reforms in the mid-1970s gave Canada's Court wide latitude, declaring that the decision to grant leave to appeal rested on the Court's determination of the "public importance" of issues raised by an application. According to Section 40(1) of the Supreme Court Act, applications would be granted leave if

> *The Supreme Court is of the opinion that any question involved therein is, by reason of its public importance or the importance of any issue of law or any issue of mixed law and fact involved in such question, one that ought to be decided by the Supreme Court or is, for any other reason, of such a nature or significance as to warrant decision by it.*[6]

This section does not define "public importance" and is as vaguely phrased as Rule 10 governing writ of certiorari decisions in the United States. *Certiorari*, a Latin word, means "to be informed of." When the Court grants certiorari, or "cert" in the vernacular, it is an order to the lower court to forward the record of the case to the Court.[7] Rule 10, written by the Supreme Court to its own specifications, reads as follows:

> *Review on writ of certiorari is not a matter of right, but of judicial discretion. A petition for a writ of certiorari will be granted **only for compelling** reasons. The following, while neither controlling nor fully measuring the Court's discretion, indicate the character of reasons the Court considers:*
>
> *(a)   A United States court of appeals has entered a decision in conflict with the decision of another United States court of appeals on the same **important** matter; or has decided an **important** federal question in a way that conflicts with a state court of last resort; or has so far departed from the accepted and usual course of judicial proceedings, or sanctioned such a departure by a lower court, as to call for an exercise of this Court's power of supervision.*

TABLE 3.1 Institutions of Agenda Setting in Canada and in the United States

Procedural Features	Canada	United States
Discretion over agenda	Broad: some mandatory appeals and reference questions	Broader: very few mandatory appeals and no advisory opinions
Jurisdiction	Broader: both federal and provincial laws, plus constitutional and Charter questions	Narrower: federal law only; diversity, plus constitutional questions
Volume of discretionary appeal and acceptance	Much smaller volume; higher rate of acceptance	Much larger volume; very low acceptance rate
Interest group involvement	Rare before Court hears appeal	Frequent before Court hears appeal
Who sets agenda	Three panels of three justices each; followed by conference of nine justices as needed to add or delete cases	Chief Justice prepares "discuss list" followed by conference vote by all nine justices who may add cases to the list
Agenda decision rule or norm	Unanimity norm	Rule of Four and Join-3 vote
Are agenda votes public	Yes; panel only	No
Who decides on merits of appeal granted leave or certiorari	Panels of 5, 7, or 9 justices	All 9 justices sitting en banc
Reversal rate of appeals	Lower	Higher
Dissents on final opinion	Less frequent	Very frequent

(b) When a state court of last resort has decided an **important** federal question in a way that conflicts with the decision of another state court of last resort or of a United States court of appeals.

(c) When a state court or a United States court of appeals has decided an important question of federal law which has not been, but should be, settled by this Court, or has decided an **important** federal question in a way that conflicts with applicable decisions of this Court.[8]

Rule 10 underscores the Court's discretion. Rule 10 seems to stress conflicting court decisions as the chief criterion governing certiorari decisions, but this interpretation is undercut by the declaration that the criterion and indeed even Rule 10 is neither controlling nor a full measure of the Court's discretion. The Court revised Rule 10 in 1995. I have put in bold type the changes the Court made in the rule, all of which tightened the standard putatively used by the justices. For example, "compelling reason" replaced the phrase "special and important reasons" and "important" now precedes references to "federal question," which previously had gone unmodified. Like their Canadian peers, the American justices did not identify what "compelling reasons" would lead to grants of certiorari, nor did they define "compelling" or "important." As one eminent scholar of the certiorari process put it, "In short, the rule is almost a tautology: cases are important enough to be reviewed by the justices when justices think they are important."[9]

Attorneys thinking about filing applications for leave to appeal or petitions for the writ of certiorari get little help from the courts in deciphering the meanings of the terms specified in the rules. The two Courts rarely explain their decisions because they refuse to develop a jurisprudence delineating the meaning of "public importance" in Canada or the terms of Rule 10 in the United States. One exception that marks a difference between the Courts is that Canadian justices evidently do not publicly dissent when their Court denies leave. In the United States, Justices Brennan and Marshall routinely published written dissents when cert was denied in cases involving capital punishment. Scholars also find that American justices who disagree with a cert denial circulate written dissents among their colleagues with the implicit threat of publishing them as part of the negotiating process to change the Court's decision.[10] Still, the publication of dissents alone by justices of either Court would not build a jurisprudence for lawyers to follow when they file their briefs. The views of both Courts about explaining their decisions were summed up by the remarks of Chief Justice Antonio Lamer in a 1995 opinion that illustrates this "norm" for both Courts:

> The ability to grant or deny leave represents the sole means by which this Court is able to exert discretionary control over its docket. In order to ensure that this Court enjoys complete flexibility in allocating its scarce judicial resources towards cases of true public importance, as a sound rule of practice, we ... do not produce written reasons for grants and denials of leave.[11]

The justices' reticence and insistence on case-by-case assessments of the public importance of applications leaves the question in the hands of lawyers to ponder. The late Justice Sopinka coauthored a book on appellate practice in which he offered several hints to litigators about how the Court interpreted the "public importance" criterion. Leave applications heeding these suggestions, he advised, although he provided no empirical data on the matter, stood a better chance of being granted by the Court than those that did not.[12] Public importance, the justice explained, involves one or more of the following characteristics: a novel constitutional issue; the interpretation or application of a significant federal statute of general application; interpretation of a provincial statute with corresponding similar legislation in other provinces; an issue in respect of which there are conflicting decisions in the provincial courts of appeal; and an issue that requires revisitation by the Supreme Court on an important question of law.

It was left to the interpretative skills and imaginations of attorneys to figure out what Justice Sopinka and the Court might consider to be "novel," "significant," or "important" issues. Similar kinds of clues can be found in American books on Supreme Court practice, but these clues also rest in varying degrees on informed speculation. Lawyers can try to divine how the justices interpret Rule 10 by looking for patterns in the cert decisions, although a more prominent and per-haps reliable source is the justices themselves, who may reveal in their written opinions after the case has been heard why certiorari was granted.[13] These helpful gestures, however, do not reveal why petitions were *denied*, which may be as important as knowing why cases were accepted for review.

In sum, the Courts have similar discretion over the selection of cases that come to them through the leave to appeal process in Canada or by way of peti-tions for writs of certiorari in the United States. Important differences remain, of course. The Canadian Court does not have full control over its agenda. Approximately a third of the cases it hears are criminal appeals that come to it as a matter of right where the issues in dispute are limited to the matters addressed by the provincial courts of appeal. (If an attorney wishes to raise an issue not addressed in the dissent in the lower court or that was not a factor in reversing the defendant's acquittal at trial—the two major criteria establishing an appeal as of right—the lawyer must file a petition asking for leave to appeal.) Thus, in Canada, there is a significant stream of criminal cases over which the Court has little con-trol and that it must hear. Moreover, the Canadian Court issues advisory opinions for cases that it must hear.

The United States Supreme Court, shortly after the ratification of the Constitution of 1789, refused to offer advisory opinions on several questions put to it by President George Washington. This refusal quickly settled into a firm tra-dition. As a later chief justice put it, "It has become the Court's considered practice not to decide abstract, hypothetical, or contingent questions."[14] This is not the case in Canada, where reference questions that the Court is compelled to answer can be put to the Supreme Court by the government of the day or by the provinces.[15] References arise in Canada because the Constitution Act of 1867 does not separate the powers of government into legislative, executive, and judicial functions, unlike the United States. As a result, Canadian courts have nonjudicial functions. In the instance of the Supreme Court, the government can ask the Court for an advisory opinion on a legal question, since this is considered an executive function of the Court and not a judicial function.[16] The Court's inability to shun references means that, contrary to its better judgment, the Court can be drawn into politically charged controversies that threaten its standing in the country.

The jurisdiction of Canada's Supreme Court is broader than that of the U.S. Supreme Court.[17] The Canadian Court hears appeals raising questions of consti-tutional law, federal law, or provincial law. This reflects the fact that the Canadian legal system is not structured according to the "dual federalism" model that exists in the United States. Canada's system is more centralized and more unified in the sense that, with the exception of appeals from the Federal Court of Canada, which hears primarily administrative law matters, almost all appeals involving either federal or provincial laws (including Quebec's civil code) come from provincial courts of appeal, whose judges are federally appointed. The upshot is that the range of the Canadian Court's jurisdiction is potentially much broader than in the United States. Questions dealing with tort law, which includes personal injury disputes, professional negligence, medical malpractice issues, and family law questions dealing with child custody or support, may find their way onto Canada's docket. But, in the United States, unless a constitutional issue or a federal law is involved, tort cases rarely are heard by the American Court, and family law controversies are the exclusive jurisdiction of the states. The jurisdictional reach of the Supreme Court in the United States touches state laws only as far as the judicially developed (and often controversial) "incorporation doctrine" extends the protection of the federal Bill of Rights to include state legislation or court decisions.

The nine justices of Canada's Supreme Court review far fewer requests for judicial review than do the nine justices of the U.S. Supreme Court, even though the number of requests has increased in both countries. Figure 3.1 shows the trends in the number of leave applications and cert petitions for 1970 to 1995.

Applications for leave to appeal in Canada nearly trebled from 158 in 1970 to 456 in 1995. This comparison is somewhat deceptive, though, because for the most recent ten years the number of applications has remained rather steady at between 450 and 475 applications a year. Trends in the United States are more complicated.

In the United States, the total number of petitions rose from 4192 to 7554 between 1970 and 1995—an 80 percent increase—but most of this growth occurred in one part of the Court's certiorari docket. The U.S. Court divides petitions for writs of certiorari into two categories, depending on whether petitioners paid the docketing fee of $300. "Paid petitions" are almost always civil cases, while those for which the Court waives the docketing fee are "unpaid" petitions or *in forma pauperis* cases, and are predominantly criminal cases. Figure 3.1 shows that paid petitions rose from 1903 to 2456 cases—a 30 percent increase—while the unpaid petitions jumped from 2289 to 5098, more than a twofold increase in *in forma pauperis* cases. This change undoubtedly reflects the substantial increase in imprisonment rates in the United States.

In Canada, leave to appeal applications, which include criminal appeals, do not show the same trajectory, even though rates of incarceration have risen. At first blush this seems odd. While the Court's rules do not offer indigent applicants the opportunity to request leave to appeal *in forma pauperis*, the filing fee is only $50.[18] (The true expense lies in the preparation of the application and in the attorney's time.) The reason the number of leave applications is stable may reside in the fact that criminal appeals, which most often involve indigent applicants, are unlikely to go forward without the approval of the provincial legal aid committees who pay for the appeals. In a very real sense, legal aid becomes the chief gatekeeper to the Supreme Court for criminal appeals if convicted defendants cannot

FIGURE 3. 1: **Number of Appeals for Judicial Review in Canada and the United States, 1970–1995**

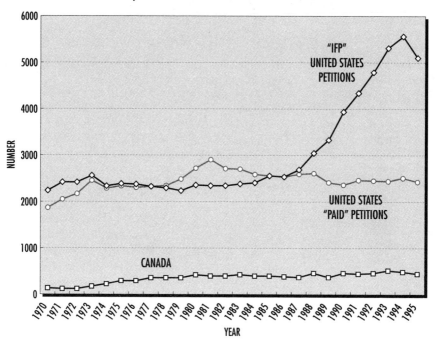

SOURCE:
(1) For Canada, *Supreme Court Law Review, 1982–1995* (Toronto: Butterworths).
Beginning in 1982, a review article has been published annually that contains statistics
on the leave to appeal process. The 1982 edition contained statistics on the period from
1970–1981. Since 1990, the publication has been referred to as the *Supreme Court Law
Review, Second Series.*
(2) For the United States, Lee Epstein et al., *Supreme Court Compendium* (Washington,
D.C.: CQ Press, 1996), 79.

afford to pay for an attorney or are unable to find an attorney willing to take the
appeal on a pro bono basis. This rationing function also applies to appeals as of
right. Applicants whose trial acquittals have been overturned on appeal at the
provincial level or when there has been dissent at the appellate level cannot expect
to receive legal aid assistance unless their conviction carries a life sentence.

While Canada's justices process fewer cases, they grant leave proportionately
more often to applicants than do the American justices. Figure 3.2 shows the dramatic difference in the acceptance rates of appeals between the two Courts, but it
also reveals a similar downward trend in the direction of these acceptance rates;
both Courts are granting proportionately fewer appeals for judicial review.

Before the 1975 reform expanding the Canadian Court's discretion over its
selection of cases for review, the proportion of applications granted leave to

FIGURE 3.2: **Percentage of Appeals for Judicial Review in Canada and the United States, 1970–1995**

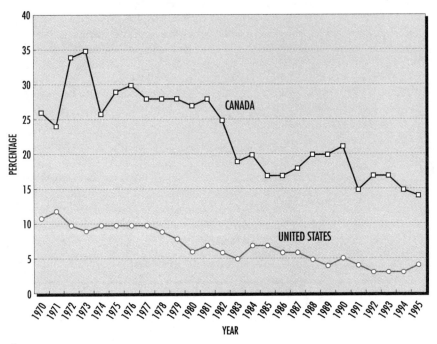

SOURCE:
(1) For Canada, *Supreme Court Law Review, 1982–1995* (Toronto: Butterworths).
(2) For the United States, Lee Epstein et al., *Supreme Court Compendium* (Washington, D.C.: CQ Press, 1996), 82.

appeal in this country ranged from 25 to 35 percent, whereas in the United States the rates hovered around 10 percent. In more recent years, Canada's Court granted leave to between 15 and 17 percent of the applicants filing for leave. In the United States, the rate has been 3 to 4 percent for paid cases. The acceptance rate for unpaid petitions, always lower than for paid cases, has been about 0.2 percent, or one out of 500 cases.

In the United States, declining acceptance rates—even with dramatic increases in the number of certiorari petitions—have shrunk the size of the docket and the number of cases the justices review on the merits. The number of cases disposed of by signed opinions dropped to 87 in 1995 compared to 161 ten years earlier.[19] In Canada, a "Special Edition" of the Court's *Bulletin of Proceedings* shows that the number of cases heard by the Court fell from 91 in 1990 to 59 in 1994.[20] The total number of appeals heard, however, remained relatively steady as the number of appeals as of right rose. For the period 1990 to 1994, the number of appeals heard by the Court ranged from 115 in 1990 to 133 in 1993; the number fell to 115 in 1994. Thus, even though the justices granted leave to fewer applicants, the number of cases heard by the Court remained relatively the same. This undoubtedly was part of the justification for a 1996 reform that placed new restraints on appeals as of right.

The impact of Court decisions on public policy has drawn the attention of organized interests in both countries. Interest group participation in litigation before the United States Supreme Court and, more specifically, the presence of organized interests in the Court's agenda setting process, are well-documented facts.[21] The *amicus curiae,* or "friend of the court," brief provides the vehicle for this participation by groups or associations. An amicus curiae brief offers an opportunity for groups or individuals that are not direct parties to the dispute to express their views about the issues in the case. In Canada, organized interests gain access by motioning the Court for intervener status. The justices rarely decline motions by groups to intervene in cases.[22]

Interest group participation in Supreme Court litigation in Canada, nevertheless, is not as widespread as it is in the United States. Not only are interveners typically few in number, but their involvement is focused exclusively on the stage *after* leave applications are granted. The Court's rules do not forbid or preclude such briefs at the leave stage, but they are rare.[23] Presumably, if the parties to a case establish its public importance to the satisfaction of the Court, there is no need to hear from interveners. The burden of proof, so to speak, is on the direct parties to convince the justices to take a case. Interveners are neither responsible nor necessary for this purpose. The United States justices clearly feel otherwise.

The Canadian Court's negative views about interveners' participation in the leave process are well known among lawyers. The absence of interveners also reflects the reluctance of some attorneys to expend time and resources in organizing interveners at this stage as part of their litigation strategy.

Given this major difference, interesting contrasts emerge when one looks only at those cases heard by the Courts. For the years 1993 to 1995, amicus curiae briefs were filed in nearly 79 percent of the cases in the United States Supreme Court compared to 30 percent in Canada in which interveners were present.[24] Provincial and federal governments appeared most often as interveners, when they were not direct parties. Of the 612 appearances made by interveners over the three-year study period, 429, or roughly 70 percent, were made by Canadian governments. In the United States the comparable proportion is approximately 15 percent.

The mix of nongovernmental groups involved in litigation before the Courts also differed. Table 3.2 presents a breakdown of the organized interests that participated in *amicus curiae* briefs or that filed intervener briefs.

Businesses and corporations, trade groups, and professional associations accounted for over half of the organized interests in the United States. In Canada, these interests made up less than one-quarter of the groups. Canadian public interest or citizen groups, in contrast, amounted to 48 percent of the group interveners, compared to 24 percent in the United States. In a sense, the compositions of organized interests in the two Courts are the opposite images of one another.

TABLE 3.2 Composition of Organized Interests Appearing as Interveners or Amici Curiae, 1993–1995

Types of Organized Interest	Canada (percentage)	United States (percentage)
Business	13	21
Trade	6	23
Professional	13	9
Unions	5	7
Public/citizen	48	24
Legal advocacy	7	7
Govt. association	2	6
Aboriginal	7	3
	101%*	100%
	(N=122)	(N=299)

*Note: Percentage does not equal 100 due to rounding.

SOURCE: Canadian data were compiled from "Agenda Setting in Canada's Supreme Court" database, developed by myself. The United States data were compiled from monthly editions for relevant years of *Preview of United States Supreme Court Cases*, Division of Public Education, American Bar Association. Reprinted by Permission.

Privately organized interests predominate in the United States, while publicly organized groups hold sway as interveners in Canada.

The two Courts differ markedly in the way they select cases for review and in their decision-making rules or norms. I will explore some of these details later in this chapter. For the moment, a sketch of these differences will place these details in a broader context. All nine American justices meet in a weekly conference to decide which cases they will hear. (When all of a court's judges meet to decide an issue, they are said to be sitting *en banc*.) The justices sit *en banc* and review the certiorari petitions on Fridays during the Court's term and on Thursdays in May and June when the Court does not hear oral arguments.[25] In contrast, the Canadian justices sit in panels of three to review applications for leave to appeal. The use of panels arose out of a 1956 amendment to the *Supreme Court Act* that required at least three justices for the review of leave to appeal applications.[26] The chief justice assigns justices to these panels in November at the start of the Court's term, and the membership generally is changed the following November—although this did not occur in 1996.

Two of three justices on a panel may decide the question of whether to grant leave, but, for reasons I will discuss shortly, there may be a "public unanimity norm" regarding the panels' deliberations. In the United States, the justices follow the "Rule of Four" and a recently developed norm of "Join-3." The Rule of Four is the only nonmajoritarian rule followed by the Court; all other decisions or actions by the Court rest firmly on majority rule. The Court adopted the Rule of Four after the passage of the Judges' Bill of 1925 to assuage congressional anxieties that access to the Court would become too restrictive under majority rule.

The Rule of Four sets a lower voting threshold for putting cases on the docket, although in practice the vast majority of petitions are disposed of by unanimous votes. During the 1980s and early 1990s, only 20 to 30 percent of the cases on the Court's docket were placed there with only four votes.[27] The seed of Join-3 sprouted in the early 1970s, and the norm soon proved to be popular among some justices. Join-3 votes occur when three justices vote to grant a writ of certiorari and a fourth justice switches his or her vote to join the triad of justices; this fourth vote is not recorded as "grant" but simply as Join-3 and thus is a form of "weak grant." The Join-3 norm lowered the threshold set by the Rule of Four, making it easier for the Court to accept cases. Concerns over the size of the Court's caseloads did not lead the justices to abandon Join-3, but rather to write new, more restrictive language into Rule 10.[28]

The American norm of *en banc* proceedings is not followed in Canada, which adopted a modified form of the English tradition on the size of merits corams, or the court that will actually hear oral arguments in cases granted leave. Until recently it was rare for the Canadian Court to sit *en banc* when deciding appeals. Between 1981 and 1990, for example, all nine justices sat to hear only 13 percent of the cases decided by the Court on the merits; the rest of the appeals were decided by panels of either five or seven justices.[29] A preliminary look at the data for this study reveals a dramatic switch in this pattern, at least for cases granted leave. From 1993 to 1995, 90 percent of the cases were more or less evenly distributed between corams of seven or nine justices; the remaining cases were decided by five justices.

Canada's Court also typically affirms lower court decisions, rather than reversing them as the U.S. Supreme Court usually does. Over the past twenty or so years Canada's justices affirmed roughly 60 percent of the cases they heard on review, in contrast to the U.S. Court, whose justices affirmed at about half this rate, 36 percent.[30] Norms about dissents on merits decisions offer a final contrast between the Courts. Dissents weaken the force of opinions, while unanimity strengthens them. Unanimity is more common in Canada than in the United States, where a tradition of dissent has taken hold in the Supreme Court over the past fifty years. From 1990 to 1994, Canada's justices unanimously decided an average of 72 percent of their cases.[31] In the United States, the comparable proportion was roughly 33 percent.[32]

When the norms regarding reversals of lower courts and dissents are taken together, then, Canadian justices can expect that, when leave is granted, the Court's traditions strongly favour an affirmation of the lower court decision, usually by a unanimous vote. American norms create the opposite set of expectations. When justices grant certiorari, they can expect that the lower court decision will be reversed and that it will not be a unanimous decision. As I suggest in the next section, the use of panels, varying sizes and composition of corams, and norms regarding affirmance of lower court decisions and dissents may play a part in determining whether Canadian justices select appeals for judicial review with strategic considerations in mind.

AN OVERVIEW OF HOW THE SUPREME COURTS OF CANADA AND THE UNITED STATES SELECT APPEALS FOR JUDICIAL REVIEW

In October 1996, interviews with thirty "repeat player" attorneys and former clerks to the Supreme Court were conducted in Toronto. The purpose of these interviews was to develop a feel for the process from the point of view of the attorneys and clerks. In this section, I describe the process based in part on these interviews and on a limited analysis of the case-level data dealing with the panel decisions. Throughout this section I will make comparisons with the United States in order to highlight the differences between the two Courts. For the sake of convenience I divide the process into four steps.

STEP ONE: CANADA'S ANALOGUE TO THE "CERT POOL"

To begin with the basic mechanics of the process, applications are filed first with the Process Clerk of the Registrar's Office, where the applications are certified as to whether they meet the requirements outlined in the Court's rules. This stage is directly analogous to the first step in the U.S., in which the Clerk of the Court reviews certiorari petitions to determine whether they meet the Court's rules.

Leave applications satisfying the basic format requirements are forwarded to the Registrar's legal services section, which has prepared "objective summaries" of the applications since 1988–89. The section normally has half a dozen full-time attorneys, including the legal services supervisor. The objective summaries were originally intended to relieve the clerks working for the justices of the burden of drafting "leave memos" for the oral hearings that previously had been part of the leave to appeal process but were later eliminated.[33] The summaries provide a history of the case, outline the facts, list the legal grounds or issues raised by the applicants, and recommend whether leave should be granted.

In some ways, the legal services section functions like the "cert pool" in the United States, where the clerks for most of the justices share the task of writing memoranda on the cert petitions. The summaries, however, are not distributed to the entire Court, nor does the chief justice winnow out cases for possible review as in the United States, where the chief justice prepares the "discuss list" that structures the Court's deliberations. Instead, the section's supervisor, who earlier assigned the applications to the panels, forwards the summaries to the appropriate panel. The supervisor generally follows an equality norm, that is, each panel receives roughly equal numbers of applications, though there are exceptions.

For example, because of Quebec's civil code, applications from that province were formerly sent to the panel with two of three Quebec justices. In 1994, the chief justice established a fourth panel, comprised entirely of the three Quebec justices, to review applications from Quebec. Another exception is the case of applications raising special issues, which are sometimes sent to panels consisting of justices with particular expertise in these areas. Finally, while the panels may process equal numbers of applications, the mix of applications, except for the Quebec applications, may not be random. Clerks volunteered, for instance, that it seemed the more challenging criminal cases found their way to the panel on which the chief justice sat, because of his keen interest in this area of the law.

STEP TWO: THE LAW CLERKS' REVIEW

Each justice in Canada has three law clerks who serve with the Court for a year; almost all of the clerks are recent law school graduates. Unlike the United States, where the justices, using their own contacts on the federal courts and with law schools, personally select their clerks (each has four, although the chief justice prefers three), the Canadian justices pick their clerks from a central pool of applicants who apply to the Court on their own, albeit with the encouragement of their law professors, many of whom are former clerks. The current clerks play a part in evaluating their future replacements, which may reinforce the existing network of referrals and recruitment.[34] The justices then choose according to rank, with the chief justice picking first, and then the others in order of seniority in three successive rounds until each justice has three clerks, at least one of whom is usually a francophone.

Canada's twenty-seven clerks work together in a separate, large room set aside for them on the same floor as the Supreme Court library. Unlike the U.S. law clerks, they do not have offices in the chambers of the justices to whom they are assigned. As a consequence of their work location in the Supreme Court building, the ecology of work for Canadian clerks is less chambers-oriented than it is for American clerks who work in the justices' chambers.

The clerks' workloads are strikingly different in the two Courts. Assuming each clerk is assigned the same number of applications or petitions, a Canadian clerk is responsible for between 20 and 25 applications during the year, or roughly one leave application every two weeks over the calendar year. American clerks, on average, handle many more cert petitions. In 1994, when the total number of petitions exceeded 8000, there were roughly 225 petitions per clerk.[35] Canadian clerks thus have ample time to review leave applications, and it shows in the length of their leave memos. Despite the fact that objective summaries were available to them, the justices continued to have their law clerks write leave memos for the applications. While American clerks typically prepare one-page memos, clerks in Canada reported that the length of their memos ranged from five to ten pages.[36] Memos obviously are longer when cases are complicated and shorter when they are simple. The law clerks said they might spend as many as three days reviewing these appeals for judicial review. The staff attorneys' recommendations were of little value to the clerks. Very often the choice between granting leave and not granting it was clear-cut.

The summaries, applications, and the attorneys' factums were sent to the appropriate panel, where the nine clerks informally distributed the leave requests amongst themselves. A rough equality rule guaranteed that each clerk got his or her fair share. Clerks, though, looked for cases that interested them or for those in which they had some expertise. Of course, clerks did not always have a choice; all clerks eventually worked on dull applications or those involving unfamiliar legal issues. Each group of clerks selected a leader to oversee the process. Because clerks found leave applications to be a chore, the group leaders occasionally rode herd on their peers to make sure that leave applications were not set aside in favour of more glamorous tasks.

The clerks did not routinely discuss leave applications among themselves. Leave applications did not involve the kinds of interesting complications that arose in the preparation of bench memos. These memos summarize a case that would be heard on the merits after being granted leave. Draft opinions for the justices are based on the justices' instructions and may involve fleshing out the outlines of their tentative opinions.

Until fairly recently, the Court offered the clerks little advice about how to review leave applications. The clerks were as much in the dark about the meanings of "public importance" as the attorneys filing applications for leave. In 1994, Justice Sopinka started informal seminars during the orientation of new clerks in which he explained to them what to look for in applications. Soon afterward, checklists were tacked on the clerks' work cubicles as reminders of the criteria. New clerks learned from older clerks as they left the Court what standards they should apply. But, as former clerks acknowledged, putting meat on the bare bones of the "public importance" criterion remained an uncertain task. There was, as in the United States, a presumption that most applications should be denied. One clerk recalled that he did not recommend leave for any of the twenty-two applications he reviewed.

The presumption that leaves should be rationed occasionally raised a dilemma for clerks. There were times when clerks felt the merits of a case deserved attention, but for one reason or another the leave application failed to clearly identify or raise an important issue. As Justice Binnie recently pointed out, "All kinds of cases that appear to have been wrongly decided [by the lower court] are denied leave."[37] Clerks recognized the possible injustice that denying leave might impose on an appellant, but they also felt that other cases would come along with similar issues. More importantly, they realized that a poorly presented case could lead to a greater injustice. A final and related point is that clerks were tempted now and then to serve as advocates on particular issues. The empirical problem in assessing the impact of the clerks' role is that, while it is possible to identify which ones worked for which justices, it is not possible without access to the memos or assignment records to determine whether the clerks influenced the justices' decisions.

STEP THREE: THE PANELS' REVIEW

Memos prepared by clerks in the "cert pool" in the United States circulate to all the justices except one, who prefers to have his own clerks review the petitions. The justices and their clerks then "mark up" those memos for the cases on the discuss list and some they think should be on the list prior to conference. In Canada, a clerk's memos are sent to the panel on which the clerk's justice sits, with single-page summaries forwarded to the other six justices. The justices, besides the memos, have the applications and factums prepared by the applicants, the respondents' responses, and the objective summaries at hand. Still, the clerks' memos represent a considerable distillation of information in the Canadian system. More to the point, a single clerk and two or three justices conceivably could determine the outcome of a leave application. Justice Sopinka, perhaps recognizing this possibility, had his clerks review all leave applications, even when they were not assigned to his panel. The other justices apparently depended on the one-page summaries to keep track of the review process on the other panels.

The panels, it appears, do not routinely meet face-to-face to make their decisions.[38] In a 1997 speech in Toronto, Justice Sopinka stated simply, "The judges vote by written memorandum."[39] While only two votes may be required to grant leave, the published votes of the leave panels are almost always shown as being unanimous; a mere thirty judgments coded by the project were not unanimous. At the risk of seeming overly skeptical, how likely is it that the justices actually agree this often?[40] The meaning of the reported votes thus becomes ambiguous. It could be that dissenting justices on the panels acquiesce when there are two votes against them as a matter of comity, not unlike the Join-3 norm in the United States. It is also possible that the votes reported in the *Bulletin of Proceedings* are often the final votes after the conference has met, and not the initial panel votes. If a justice on the panel disagrees with a decision and asks the conference to reassess the panel's choice, but fails to change the decision, the final vote reported in the *Bulletin* could reflect a change in the vote by the dissenting panel justice. Although the conference votes of justices in the United States are secret, scholars have gained insights into how the justices vote at this stage through the papers and docket books of individual justices released to the public after they leave the bench. A major consequence of not having comparable information about the actual panel and conference votes in Canada is that it is not possible to determine the extent to which justices vote strategically on leave applications, as justices in the United States do with regard to cert petitions.

Is it possible that the selection of cases for judicial review is linked to deciding the cases on their merits in Canada? Do the justices on the panels anticipate how cases will be decided on their merits, and do these anticipations influence their decisions to grant leave? The American literature strongly suggests that this happens in the U.S. Supreme Court.[41] When U.S. justices feel they have the votes to win on the merits, they vote to grant cert. If they believe they will lose on the merits, they vote to deny cert. In other words, instead of voting on the basis of whether the petitions meet the standards of Rule 10, or even according to their individual policy preferences, United States justices vote strategically, that is, they either make "aggressive grants" or cast "defensive denials" depending on their expectations of success on the merits.[42] Evidence exists that strategic considerations, and not just legal considerations or individual policy preferences, influence American justices' votes on petitions for a writ of certiorari.

The "certiorari game" in the United States grows out of the norm that all nine justices participate in *both* decisions. Because of this norm, the justices act strategically, based on their informed expectations about the other justices' voting habits or preferences. In Canada, the situation is less certain for justices who might want to take the likely outcomes of cases into account during their leave deliberations. Because merits corams vary in size as well as composition, strategically inclined justices on the leave panels do not know with assurance which justices will hear and decide a case if leave is granted. The data for this research indicate that members of the leave panels almost always are assigned by the chief justice to the merits corams. And all three Quebec justices routinely sit on the merits panels in the instance of Quebec civil code cases. The upshot is that Canadian justices, while selecting cases for judicial review, can be sure that they will also hear the appeals. This does not mean, however, that they know with great certainty who the other justices on the merits panel will be or what the size of the coram will be. Unless the justices through experience gain strong inklings of how the chief justice decides on the sizes of corams and whom he assigns to them *before* they grant leave, the institutions and norms of agenda setting in Canada create a more uncertain context for the justices than in the United States.

A final consideration regarding strategic behaviour by the justices is the direction of their leave votes. To the extent that strategic voting takes place, are the justices more likely to defensively deny or more likely to aggressively grant leaves? The answer depends in part on the Court's norms governing the final disposition of cases. The Canadian Court affirms more often than it reverses, and dissents are relatively infrequent. This means that if a "leave to appeal game" exists on Canada's high bench, the justices are more likely to aggressively grant leaves. A justice seeking to affirm a lower court decision has more favourable odds of success than his or her counterparts in America. A Canadian justice hoping to overturn a lower court decision on the merits, however, faces poorer chances of success than a justice in the United States, although the odds of reversal are higher for private law cases than for public law cases in Canada.[43]

STEP FOUR: THE CONFERENCE REVIEW

A panel notifies the other six justices of its decisions prior to conference by placing its decisions on one of three appendices.[44] If a panel chooses to defer an application because the issues are currently before the Court in another case, the application is placed on "Appendix C," pending the outcome of the case. Applications approved for leave are placed on "Appendix B" for consideration by the conference. Appendix B is analogous to the discuss list in the United States. However, the American chief justice is largely responsible for drawing up the discuss list, while Appendix B reflects the decentralized deliberations of the panels. If a panel decides to dismiss an application, the application is placed on "Appendix D," a date is set for the application's dismissal, and the other justices are notified accordingly. Appendix D is comparable to what was once called the "dead list" in the United States. If a justice not on the panel disagrees with a dismissal, the decision is deferred until it can be considered in conference. A similar procedure takes place in the U.S. Supreme Court when a justice asks that a certiorari petition not on the discuss list be reviewed by the justices when they meet in conference.

Conference discussions, according to the late Justice Sopinka, could "get quite spirited."[45] The consequences of these discussions are not known, however. There are no public records of how the justices vote in conference on cases placed on Appendix B or how often a justice asks that an application placed on Appendix D be reconsidered by the conference. The justices may simply ratify the decisions made by the panels, overturning few decisions to grant leave, and rarely adding cases to the Court's agenda that the panels have rejected. In contrast to this practice of passively accepting the panels' decisions, the conference may assume the alternative posture of actively urging panels to reconsider their decisions when the conference disagrees with their choices, but with the understanding that in the interests of collegial and professional reciprocity, panel justices are not compelled to change their votes. The common view is that panels' decisions are the final word, although no empirical evidence exists to support this view. It is not known how often the panel changes its decision as a result of being asked to reconsider its recommendation. At the conclusion of the conference, the decisions of the panels become final. There was variation among the panels. The proportion of leave applications granted ranged from 11 to 20 percent over a three-year period.

One thing this suggests is that the conference may not smooth out differences among the panels. If it did, the outcomes of the panels' deliberations presumably would be more similar. This is a significant difference between Canada and the United States, a difference reflecting the institutional arrangements adopted by Canada's Court. By devolving authority to make leave decisions to panels, the Court has created a process by which the outcomes of leave applications vary according to the panel to which they are assigned.

Before this conclusion can be accepted, explanations for these differences must be considered. For example, did the panels review dissimilar kinds of applications? Is the explanation for different grant rates due solely to differences in the substance or kinds of issues raised in the applications? If so, the assignment of leave applications to the panels cannot be seen as purely random. It is also possible that the applications are similar in substance but the panels apply different jurisprudential standards when reviewing them. Alternatively, the ideological composition of the panels may matter. Since the panels are rearranged or reassembled each November, new combinations of policy outlooks or judicial preferences emerge, producing new patterns among the panels in how often they grant leave and to what kinds of cases.

A SUMMING UP AND BRIEF CONCLUSION

The selection of appeals for judicial review by the Supreme Court of Canada occurs through a process shaped by institutions and norms that differ in many respects from what exists in the United States. The Canadian process is more decentralized and perhaps less influenced by strategic considerations among the justices when they decide leave questions. The process, finally, is less politicized than its American counterpart. Placing leave decisions largely in the hands of the justices and their clerks on the leave panels reduces the number of participants in the process. It may lead to different standards or criteria for leave among the panels unless the justices share a common perspective of what cases should be granted leave. If such a common perspective existed, the rates at which leave was granted by the panels would be roughly similar. This is not the case, however. Acceptance rates varied widely across the panels. A decentralized system granting leave at different rates could also be corrected or modified at conference when all the justices can voice their opinions about applications granted or denied leave. The data also do not suggest that this occurs. It is important to remember, however, that further study of the process is required in order to test alternative hypotheses before accepting this finding as conclusive.

Strategic voting by the justices at the leave stage may be less prevalent than in the United States. The possible absence or infrequency of strategic voting reflects the Canadian norm of variable coram sizes for the merits bench. If all nine justices sat to review the merits of cases granted leave, strategic voting would probably occur more often. One of the central puzzles, which my future larger project will try to solve, is whether the justices on the panels seek to represent the interests or concerns of those justices not on the panels. In other words, do the justices strive to take the Court's interests into account when they select cases for review?

Organized interests in the United States have contributed to the politicization of the process. Newspapers and the electronic media pay attention to certiorari petitions and speculate on the legal or policy implications of cases that are denied cert or granted cert. In no small part, the involvement of organized interests by filing amicus curiae briefs during the agenda setting crystallizes the policy and legal stakes of cases for the media. Organized interests pervade the agenda setting process in the United States. This is not true in Canada, where the leave to appeal process is practically devoid of interest group activity. Justices may be able to anticipate whether there will be interveners in a case based on their experience, the lower court record, and the nature of the issues, but they do not know what arguments the interveners might have made about the public importance of the case, had there been an intervener.

ENDNOTES

1.   Research for this chapter was supported in part by the National Science Foundation in the United States (Grant SBR-9515025) and by grants from the Canadian Studies Grants Program. This discussion of the leave to appeal process describes the proce-

dures as they existed in 1993–95. Since 1996, after the field work was completed, several changes have taken place that eliminated the law clerks from the process, increased the size of the legal services staff in the Registrar's Office, and further restricted the right to appeal in criminal cases. An earlier version of this chapter was presented at the Conference on the Scientific Study of Judicial Politics, Emory University, Atlanta, Georgia, November 14–15, 1997. Jennifer Schwank provided skilful and diligent assistance during the revision of this chapter for publication.

2.   Useful surveys of the American literature can be found in Doris Marie Provine, *Case Selection in the United States Supreme Court* (Chicago: University of Chicago Press, 1980) and H.W. Perry, Jr., "Agenda Setting and Case Selection," in *The American Courts*, ed. John B. Gates and Charles A. Johnson (Washington, D.C.: CQ Press, 1991).

3.   An omnibus bill passed by Parliament in 1996 included a provision placing some limits on "appeals as of right" by giving the Court the latitude to dismiss criminal appeals based on lower court dissents on the law after an oral hearing.

4.   The reform eliminated monetary thresholds on the Court's jurisdiction and required leave to appeal in civil cases. In criminal cases, the right to appeal was retained in criminal cases involving indictable offences when either a court of appeal overturned an acquittal or a court of appeal was divided on an issue of law. More detailed discussions of the amendment can be found in Brian A. Crane and Henry S. Brown, *Supreme Court Practice 1996* (Scarborough, ON: Carswell, 1995) and John Sopinka and Mark A. Gelowitz, *The Conduct of an Appeal* (Toronto: Butterworths, 1993). Other proposals under consideration at the time of the reform are discussed by W.R. Lederman, "Current Proposals for Reform of the Supreme Court," *Canadian Law Review* 55 (1979): 687. The political background of the amendment is described by James G. Snell and Frederick Vaughan in *The Supreme Court of Canada: History of the Institution* (Toronto: Osgoode Society and University of Toronto, 1985), 238–40, and by Ian Bushnell in *The Captive Court: A Study of the Supreme Court of Canada* (Montreal and Kingston: McGill-Queen's University Press, 1992), 404–7, as well as by Peter H. Russell in *The Judiciary in Canada: The Third Branch of Government* (Toronto: McGraw-Hill Ryerson Limited, 1987), 344–49.

5.   Roy B. Flemming, John Bohte, and B. Dan Wood, "One Voice Among Many: The Supreme Court's Influence on Attentiveness to Issues in the United States, 1947–1990," *American Journal of Political Science* 41 (1997); Roy B. Flemming, John Bohte, and B. Dan Wood, "Attention to Issues in a System of Separated Powers: The Macro-Dynamics of American Policy Agendas," *Journal of Politics* 61 (1999, forthcoming).

6.   Crane and Brown, *Supreme Court Practice 1996*, 23.

7.   H.W. Perry, Jr., *Deciding to Decide: Agenda Setting in the United States Supreme Court* (Cambridge, MA: Harvard University Press, 1991), 27.

8.   Reprinted with permission. *Supreme Court Rules, 1995 Revisions*, page 27, by Robert L. Stern, Eugene Gressman, Stephen M. Shapiro, and Kenneth S. Geller. Copyright © 1995. The Bureau of National Affairs, Inc., Washington, DC 20037. For BNA Books publications call toll free 1-800-960-1220.

9.   H.W. Perry, Jr., "Certiorari, Writ of," in Kermit L. Hall, ed., *The Oxford University Companion to the Supreme Court of the United States* (New York: Oxford University Press, 1992), 132. One indication of the difficulties in deciphering what "public importance" means to the Canadian legal community is that during interviews with attorneys and clerks "national importance" was often used in place of "public importance." The two phrases are not necessarily the same, and some attorneys would correct themselves.

10. Lee Epstein and Jack Knight, *The Choices Justices Make* (Washington, D.C.: CQ Press, 1998).

11. Crane and Brown, *Supreme Court Practice 1998* (Scarborough, ON: Carswell, 1997), 24.

12. Sopinka and Gelowitz, 167. Justice Sopinka offered a slightly different, more detailed explanation that included his suggestions to the new clerks in a 1997 speech that is reprinted in Brown and Crane, *Supreme Court Practice 1998*, 306–16.

13. Stern et al., 165.

14. Bernard Schwartz, *A History of the Supreme Court* (New York: Oxford University Press, 1993), 25.

15. It is interesting to note that, at its very first sitting in 1876, the first matter put to Canada's Supreme Court was a reference from the Senate requesting the Court's opinion on a private bill dealing with a divisive religious issue. Brian A. Crane and Henry S. Brown, *Supreme Court Practice 1998* (Scarborough, ON: Carswell, 1997), 306.

16. Technically, only the federal government has the authority to submit a reference question directly to the Supreme Court. The provinces, however, have passed enabling legislation so that the provincial governments can refer questions to their respective courts of appeal. Since there is an automatic right of appeal to the Supreme Court for these matters, the effect is that the provinces have the same privilege as the federal government to submit reference questions to the Court.

17. Peter W. Hogg, *Constitutional Law in Canada* (Scarborough, ON: Carswell, 1996), 204.

18. This was the fee in 1995. There is a discrepancy in Crane and Brown, *Supreme Court Practice 1996*, who report a fee of $30 at p. 219 but $50 at p. 244; the latter amount is used since it is listed under the "Tariff of Fees." This error was corrected in the 1998 edition.

19. Lee Epstein et al., *The Supreme Court Compendium: Data, Decisions, and Developments* (Washington, D.C.: CQ Press, 1996), 85.

20. Supreme Court of Canada, *Bulletin of Proceedings: Special Edition* (Ottawa: Supreme Court of Canada, 24 March 1995). Data from the *Bulletin* with regard to case volumes, appeals heard, and leave applications do not agree with the information published annually in the *Supreme Court Law Review*, which is the source for Figures 3.1 and 3.2. The latter does not provide information on total cases or appeals heard, but because the *Supreme Court Law Review* information covers a much longer period of time, I have relied on it when making comparisons with the U.S. Supreme Court.

21. Gregory A. Caldeira and John R. Wright, "Organized Interests and Agenda Setting in the U.S. Supreme Court," *American Political Science Review* 82 (1988): 1109; Gregory A. Caldeira and John A. Wright, "The Discuss List: Agenda Building in the Supreme Court," *Law and Society Review* 24 (1990): 807; Gregory A. Caldeira and John A. Wright, "Amici Curiae Before the Supreme Court: Who Participates, When, and How Much?" *Journal of Politics* 52 (1990): 782; Kevin T. McGuire, "Amici Curiae and Strategies for Gaining Access to the Supreme Court," *Political Research Quarterly* 47 (1994): 821.

22. Charles Epp, *The Rights Revolution: Lawyers, Activists, and Supreme Courts in Comparative Perspective* (Chicago: University of Chicago Press, 1998); Ian Brodie, "The Court Challenges Program," in F.L. Morton, ed., *Law, Politics, and the Judicial Process in Canada* (Calgary, Alta: University of Calgary Press, 1992), 251–55; Sharon Lavine, "Advocating Values: Public Interest Intervention in Charter Litigation," *National Journal of Constitutional Law* 2 (1992): 27.

23. Crane and Brown, *Supreme Court Practice 1996*, 168.

24. The data for the United States come from the American Bar Foundation's *Preview of United States Supreme Court Cases*, which are published monthly during the Court's term.

Every fourth case was sampled from the *Previews*, and the information on the presence of amicus curiae briefs and what groups were involved in them was coded. Comparable data for Canada come from the data set of cases collected as part of the larger research project.

25.   David M. O'Brien, *The Storm Center: The Supreme Court in American Politics* (New York: Norton, 1996), 225.

26.   Prior to this time, leaves to appeal were relatively infrequent and decided by a single justice. The change was introduced in 1956 after considerable criticism of a justice who denied leave in 1954 in a highly publicized criminal case. Crane and Brown, *Supreme Court Practice 1996*, 6.

27.   David M. O'Brien, "Join-3 Votes, the Rule of Four, and *Cert*. Pool, and the Supreme Court's Shrinking Plenary Docket," *Journal of Law and Politics* 13 (1997): 779.

28.   Arthur D. Hellman, "The Shrunken Docket of the Rehnquist Court," in Dennis J. Hutchinson, David A. Strauss, and Geoffrey R. Stone, eds., *The 1996 Supreme Court Review* (Chicago: University of Chicago Press, 1996), 403–38.

29.   Peter H. Russell, "The Supreme Court in the 1980s: A Commentary on the S.C.R. Statistics," *Osgoode Hall Law Journal* 30 (1992): 777.

30.   Russell, 772; Epstein et al., 212.

31.   Supreme Court of Canada, 3.

32.   Epstein et al., 164.

33.   Justice Sopinka did not mention this change in his book on the appeal process. Oral hearings are no longer a routine part of the process. The Court may conduct hearings under certain circumstances at its discretion, but they are rare.

34.   Lorne Sossin, "The Sounds of Silence: Law Clerks, Policy Making and the Supreme Court of Canada," *University of British Columbia Law Review* 30, no. 2 (1996): 286.

35.   Neither leave applications nor petitions for writ of certiorari arrive in the Courts in this kind of evenly distributed manner. They arrive in clusters and irregularly. These averages are purely illustrative and designed to make the comparisons clear.

36.   Sossin reported the average length was 15 pages. Sossin, 290.

37.   Kirk Makin, "Binnie Quotes the Sundown Rule," *The Globe and Mail*, 28 November 1998, sec. A.

38.   Justice Sopinka was vague on this point in his book on appellate practice. He and his coauthor wrote: "The panel seized of the application processes it with each member of the panel voting either to grant leave or dismiss." Sopinka and Gelowitz, 171.

39.   Crane and Brown, *Supreme Court Practice 1998*, 307.

40.   A recent article by McCormick points to various groups and divisions on the Court with regard to merits decisions. While unanimity is common on the Court, it is not as pervasive as the leave votes recorded in the *Bulletin* would suggest. Peter McCormick, "Birds of a Feather: Alliances and Influences on the Lamer Court 1990–1997," *Osgoode Hall Law Journal* 36 (1998): 339.

41.   Glendon A. Schubert, "The Study of Judicial Decision-Making as an Aspect of Political Behavior," *American Political Science Review* 52 (1958): 1007; Glendon Schubert, "Policy Without Law: An Extension of the Certiorari Game," *Stanford Law Review* 14 (1962): 284; S. Sidney Ulmer, "The Decision to Grant Certiorari as an Indicator to the Decision 'On the Merits'," *Polity* 4 (1972): 429; Donald R. Songer, "Concern for Policy Outputs as a Cue for Supreme Court Decisions on Certiorari," *Journal of Politics* 41 (1979): 1185.

42.   Perry, *Deciding to Decide*, 198–207; Robert L. Boucher, Jr. and Jeffrey A. Segal, "Supreme Court Justices as Strategic Decision Makers: Aggressive Grants and Defensive Denials on the Vinson Court," *Journal of Politics* 57 (1995): 824; Jeffrey A. Segal, Robert Boucher, and Charles M. Cameron, "A Policy-Based Model of Certiorari Voting on the U.S. Supreme Court," *Journal of Politics* 57 (1995).

43. Russell, 772.

44. For reasons known only to the Court, there is no "Appendix A."

45. Crane and Brown, *Supreme Court Practice 1998*, 311.

DEMOCRACY, LEGITIMACY, AND CONSENT

PART 2

JUDICIAL REVIEW AND ELECTORAL LAW

Jennifer Smith and
Herman Bakvis

In any country, the electoral-law regime lies at the heart of the democratic process, for it governs the manner of the election of the members of the legislature and the political executive. Depending in good part on the nature of the electoral regime, that process can vary enormously in terms of fairness—fairness from the standpoint of the candidates and the political parties, and fairness from the standpoint of citizens generally. In the Canadian context, the concept of fairness is the leitmotif of the ongoing debate about the electoral-law regime.

In this chapter we review the role of the Canadian courts in the development of public policy on fairness in the financial conduct of elections. Campaign finance is a critical feature of elections that typically is governed by electoral law. It includes the issues of financial contributions to the political parties and the candidates, allowable expenditures made by the parties and the candidates, and who is and who is not authorized to incur such expenditures on their behalf. It is not too much to state that campaign finance lies at the heart of electoral law, and the development of public policy in relation to it is a textbook example of the kind of give-and-take between legislators, Charter plaintiffs, and the judiciary that was prompted by the adoption of the Canadian Charter of Rights and Freedoms[1] in 1982. The process is sporadic, full of twists and turns, and seemingly unending. And it is not without various problems, among them the capacity of judges to engage social science issues within the confines of a judicially structured format. But it is also a public process that commands the attention of interested parties and generates discussion among a wide array of groups and individuals. Finally, and perhaps most importantly, the ongoing discussion serves to crystallize the issues and clarify the points in contention among the participants in a manner more rigorous than is sometimes found on the political hustings. Indeed, in the case of campaign finance, there has been nothing less than the development of two competing visions of the very nature of electoral democracy.

We begin our examination of the development of public policy on the regulation of election expenditures by reviewing the pre-Charter origins of federal campaign-finance law as well as the relevant provisions of the law itself. The rationale behind the law is stressed because it has become the focus of dispute before the courts. Next we document the Charter-based challenges to the law, and outline the way in which the issues at the core of the challenges have been framed. The cases culminate with the Supreme Court of Canada's ruling in 1997 in *Libman v. Attorney General of Quebec*.[2] Given the importance of the case in settling the constitutional viability of the Quebec government's approach to the regulation of electoral spending, and by extension the federal government's, we consider closely the Court's argument. The responses of the federal government and the Quebec government to the decisions of the courts during the period under review are noted. In the conclusion, we evaluate the current state of public policy in this area, as well as the significance of the judicial contribution to its development.

THE FEDERAL ELECTION-EXPENSES REGIME, 1974

During election campaigns, the most important instrument that parties and candidates have available to them is advertising, primarily paid advertising in the broadcast media. The general impact of the broadcast media on life generally, let alone the conduct of election campaigns, is incalculable. However, by the 1960s there was one effect that was all too easy—and painful—to calculate, and that was its growing cost in elections. Everyone understood the advantages of advertising on television, but the costs were steep and rising. In the 1963 general election campaign, the Liberal party promised to take action on the matter if elected, which it was, and a year later the Liberal government appointed an Advisory Committee to Study Curtailment of Election Expenditures that was chaired by Alphonse Barbeau. Barbeau had worked on the reforms made to Quebec's election laws in 1963, which included limits on election expenditures, the first in Canada.

The Barbeau committee tackled the problem of election costs by zeroing in on the main cause, media advertising expenditures, and recommending that limits be placed on both the time frame and the total of such expenditures. Further, it urged that the limits apply not only to the expenditures made by the candidates and the parties in order to maintain fair competition between them, but also to the expenditures made by other individuals and groups as well. This was necessary, the committee explained, because otherwise the unregulated spenders would become the financial surrogates of their preferred candidates and parties, in effect doing the spending for them and thereby nullifying the whole point of the regulatory exercise.[3]

Two more elections were to pass before Parliament looked into the issue again with the establishment of a special committee of the House of Commons in

October 1970. The Chappell committee, named after the chairman, Hyliard Chappell, recommended that the idea of limits on election spending be expanded to include not only advertising on the broadcast media but the routine "election expenses" of candidates and parties as well, such as organizational and travel expenses.[4] When Parliament finally adopted the Elections Expenses Act in 1974, it chose the comprehensive regulatory route, the main features of which were, and still are: (1) limits on the amount of money that candidates and registered parties can spend on specified election expenses; (2) limits on the amount of money that individuals and groups can spend; and (3) rules governing the use of broadcast media by the candidates and the parties.

It is worth noting here that the direction Parliament chose to take—limits on expenses—was entirely different from the one ultimately taken in the United States at the federal level, where limits are placed on the permissible size of donations to the candidates and the parties, in part as a way of controlling overall the amount of money spent in elections. Initially, Congress, also concerned about the rapid rise in campaign costs, sought to limit them by capping permitted media expenses in the Federal Election Campaign Act adopted in 1971. The act also contained provisions for the comprehensive disclosure of campaign expenditures and donations to the candidates, the political committees acting on behalf of the candidates, and the political parties. In three major amendments to the act in 1974, ceilings were imposed on the costs of presidential and congressional campaigns, a system of public financing of presidential elections was added, and limits were placed on allowable contributions to the candidates, the political committees, and the political parties. For example, the contributions by individuals to congressional or presidential candidates may not exceed more than $1000 per election.[5] The 1974 amendments were tested almost immediately in the courts, with the result that in 1976 the Supreme Court of the United States threw out the spending limits on the grounds that they constituted impermissible restrictions on the freedom of speech, although it made an exception in the case of limits on presidential campaigns because of the public-funding component of them.[6] Therefore, with the exception of the presidential campaigns, federal law in the United States relies—ineffectively—on limits on donations to counter the rise in campaign costs.[7]

On a worldwide scale of democratic systems, however, the American regime, with its focus on limiting contributions rather than expenditures, stands as the exception. Most countries have chosen to limit expenditures as a means of ensuring a degree of equality between the competing parties and the candidates. Expenditure limits can be imposed by means of rules that explicitly stipulate how much can be spent on what kinds of items, as in Canada, or indirectly as in France, where advertising in the broadcast media is restricted to the political parties, in set time slots. Britain directly limits the expenditures of the candidates, and has done so since 1883, and allows only the political parties to use the broadcast media. State subsidies to the political parties, particularly to offset the costs of advertising, are also a common practice in many countries, including Canada.[8]

In its exegesis of the election spending regime in Canada, the Royal Commission on Electoral Reform and Party Financing (the Lortie commission), established in 1989, appraised it from the standpoint of political equality, which it defined as the "equal opportunity [of citizens] to exercise meaningful influence over the outcome of elections."[9] As the commission argued, Canadian election law can be read as a series of steps taken over the years to establish the conditions of political equality. And one of the most important conditions, it continued, is fairness. As far as election spending is concerned, fairness requires that inequalities in the marketplace not be imported holus-bolus into electoral competition.[10] In other words, the playing field needs to be as level as is practicable when it comes to that great weapon of electoral warfare—money. But who plays on the field? Here matters become somewhat controversial, as others, using rather different conceptions of fairness, have contended that the playing field as defined by the commission is too restrictive, excluding legitimate participants.

According to the Lortie commission, in the Canadian system of parliamentary democracy the key players are the political parties and the candidates. To say this does not mean that the voters are eased off the field. It means that they were never on the field because they are instead sitting in the stands. They watch the play, discuss it, and vote. Some may participate more actively but, if they do, it is as partisans. In the words of the commission, the "principal means whereby Canadians *actively* [our emphasis] participate in elections is as supporters of candidates and members of political parties."[11] One of the essential conditions under this conception of fairness, then, is that the key players—the political competitors, themselves—have more or less the same financial resources at their disposal, which is possible only if campaign budgets are capped.

The adjective, "principal," that was used in the preceding quotation does not connote "exclusive." In the electoral universe there is another category of participants that is comprised of individuals and groups who choose to spend money during election campaigns. The easiest way for them to do this, of course, is to donate money to the candidates and/or the political parties. Indeed, they can donate as much as they want, because the Canadian system pursues the value of fairness by limiting the election expenditures of the candidates and the parties, not the amount of money that donors can contribute to them. Obviously this undermines, and was intended to undermine, the effectiveness of a big-money contribution, since the recipients have to bank what they cannot use—hardly an immediate return on the investment. Nor under the legislation is there an alternative in the form of independent spending, which is sometimes referred to as third-party spending. As indicated earlier, this too is restricted. The restriction is held to be a second essential condition of fairness, a point that needs amplification.

As the Barbeau committee had maintained at the outset, there is little sense in limiting the expenditures of the candidates and the political parties if others can spend unlimited amounts of money on their behalf—or alternatively on campaigns targeted against them. Accordingly, under the spending regime launched in 1974, the others—individuals or groups other than the candidates and the registered parties—were simply prohibited from incurring election expenses, that is, from making expenditures designed to promote or oppose the candidates and the parties. They could spend to publicize their position on particular issues (advocacy spending), but not on the candidates and the parties (partisan spending). However, if in the course of advocacy spending they were to slide into partisan spending and thereby be subject to prosecution for violating the law, they were permitted a "good faith" defence. In other words, they could try to maintain that the slide was inadvertent.

What is important to emphasize is that under this kind of regime the primary participants are the political parties and the candidates. Those outside the circle—interest groups and ordinary individuals—are essentially prevented from participating directly, that is, from paying for advertisements targeted at specific parties or candidates. This limitation on the role of third parties necessarily entails a restriction of the rights of free speech and possibly freedom of association. Of course, interest groups and individuals can always choose to participate as parties or candidates. However, those not wishing to participate in this fashion felt aggrieved by the restriction of basic rights. Out of this sense of grievance has come, then, a different, competing conception of fairness, one which sees it as perfectly legitimate for third parties to participate in election campaigns, not merely as voters or as financial contributors to the political parties and the candidates, but as players themselves, and in particular as players who direct advertising at the electoral competitors. Third-party players also make the argument that their participation in the process provides voters with additional, important information to be used in making electoral choices.

To return to the record of events, in 1983, not long after the arrival of the Charter, Parliament removed the good-faith defence, a decision based on evidence that the defence was turning into a mere pretext for ever-larger amounts of independent spending directed at the candidates and the political parties.[12] However, this legislative line in the sand was too much for one organization, the National Citizens' Coalition (NCC). Armed with the Canadian Charter of Rights and Freedoms, in January 1984 it launched the opening challenge to the federal restrictions on third-party spending in the Alberta Court of Queen's Bench. Thus ensued the judicial round of the policy process, to which we now turn. It should be stressed here that no one yet has gone to court to fight the restrictions on the election expenses of the candidates and the political parties. The issue is the restrictions on third-party or independent spending, that is, spending by individuals and interest groups that takes place outside of the activities of the candidates and the parties.

THE COURTS AND THIRD-PARTY SPENDING

The NCC made the claim that the restrictions on independent spending were breaches of sections 2(b) and 3 of the Charter. Under section 2(b) everyone possesses the fundamental "freedom of thought, belief, opinion and expression, including freedom of the press and other media communications." Under section 3 every Canadian citizen has the "right to vote in an election of members of the House of Commons or of a legislative assembly and to be qualified for membership therein." The federal government denied the NCC's claim. However, it also argued that if the restrictions in question were found to be limitations of these rights and freedoms, then they were justifiable limitations designed to secure equality and fairness in the conduct of elections. Under section 1 of the Charter, the so-called "reasonable limits" clause, the rights and freedoms guaranteed under the Charter are subject to "such reasonable limits prescribed by law as can be demonstrably justified in a free and democratic society."

Judge Medhurst agreed with the NCC that the restrictions in question were indeed a limitation of the fundamental right of expression, although not of the democratic rights outlined in section 3. Further, he could not agree with the government that the limitation was reasonable because, he stated, there was insufficient evidence that third-party spending was an abuse of the spending regime that needed to be curtailed. "There should be actual demonstration of harm or a real likelihood of harm to a society value," he advised, "before a limitation can be said to be justified."[13]

The Canadian government declined to appeal the Alberta court's decision. In other words, at this stage it deferred to the court. The reasons remain a matter for speculation, although they are not entirely obscure. Hiebert notes that the media, which paid considerable attention to the case, took a negative view of the spending restrictions, and she suggests that this might well have undermined the resolve of the federal government to appeal the court ruling, even though it continued to defend the legislation in public. She also points out that the decision was handed down at a time when the governing Liberals were preoccupied by a change in the party's leadership and heading into a general election under the new leader.[14] Technically, the decision covered only Alberta during the subsequent general election, although in practice it had nation-wide application because the Chief Electoral Officer of Canada (CEO) decided not to prosecute interest groups that defied the spending restrictions in the 1984 federal election campaign.[15] The record of election expenses during the campaign subsequently revealed no unauthorized or partisan spending on the part of advocacy groups.[16]

The Progressive Conservative Party, which won the election, declined to deal with the issue at all during its first term of office, thus setting the stage for the second election in which advocacy groups effectively were free to spend what they wished in support of, or in opposition to, the candidates and the political parties. This time, however, there was third-party spending on a massive scale, at least by Canadian standards. In the 1988 election, the government's proposals for free trade with the United States were hotly contested, and advocacy groups weighed in, spending an estimated $4.73 million on advertising in the print media alone, advertising that was easily and directly related to the candidates and the parties because their respective positions on the proposed free-trade agreement were so clear.[17] According to W.T. Stanbury's calculations, this figure of $4.73 million was equivalent to 40 percent of the money spent on advertising by the three main parties in the election.[18]

As a result of their election win, the governing Conservatives remained in office, and the following year established the aforementioned Lortie commission, equipping it with a broad mandate to examine electoral matters.[19] On the issue of third-party spending, the Lortie commission accepted the need to limit third-party spending as well as the spending of the candidates and the parties.[20] However, it took the view that to prohibit third parties from any and all spending to support or oppose the candidates and the parties was to deny them freedom of expression in any meaningful sense. Issue advocates, it argued, could only express fully their views in relation to the known positions of the candidates and the parties, not in a vacuum.[21] Accordingly, and on the basis of the pattern of the donations made to the candidates and the parties in the 1988 election, it recommended that individuals and groups other than the candidates and the parties be permitted to spend up to $1000, be it for advocacy or partisan purposes, but that they be prohibited from pooling what they could spend, a dodge that would obviously defeat the purpose of the regulatory exercise.[22]

The government accepted the recommendation of the $1000 limit on partisan spending (but not advocacy spending, thereby letting third parties continue to spend as much as they like to advertise their views on policy matters only). It also accepted the prohibition on pooling resources. The changes took effect in May 1993, at which point the NCC, finding the $1000 spending limit as objectionable as the initial blanket prohibition on third-party spending, returned to court. The Alberta Court of Queen's Bench was once again the choice of venue, and the court did not let the NCC down.

The NCC argued, as it had in 1984, that the $1000 limit offended the Canadian Charter of Rights and Freedoms, in particular section 2(b), the freedom of expression, and section 3, the right to vote. It also argued that the ban on pooling resources offended these sections and section 2(d), the freedom of association.[23] Judge MacLeod agreed, and then asked whether the legislative provisions could be regarded as reasonable limits of the specified freedoms and the right to vote, and thereby saved. To this end he applied the *Oakes* test,[24] which requires, first, that the purpose or objective of the limits in question be compelling, pressing, or of great significance.

Counsel for the federal government reminded the court that the purpose of the scheme of spending limits was to promote fairness in the electoral process by equalizing the financial resources of the main participants, and then argued that the spending limits on third parties were an essential part of the scheme, without which the limits on the candidates and the parties could not be maintained.[25] Judge MacLeod could not agree that the limits on third-party spending were essential because, like Judge Medhurst in 1984, he could find no evidence to convince him that third-party spending matters. According to the *testimony* on the only two quantitative studies on the point before the court, he wrote, one of the studies was inconclusive, while the other study determined that third-party advertising had no effect on voter intentions.[26] Moreover, the comments of the federal minister responsible for the legislation seemed to indicate that money was not an important factor in elections anyway.[27] Since the provisions failed in terms of their objective, there was no need to deal with the second part of the *Oakes* test, which assesses the proportionality of the limits placed on the rights in accordance with three standards: whether there is a rational connection between the limits and the achievement of the legislative objective; whether the limits impair the right (or rights) as little as possible; and whether the costs imposed by the limits are proportional to the benefits gained by the objective. However, Judge MacLeod indicated that had such an assessment been made, the provisions would have failed there, too.[28]

The pattern of the 1984 round seemed set to repeat itself. The court's ruling was followed by a general election in October 1993, and once again the Chief Electoral Officer declined to enforce the third-party spending provisions anywhere in the country. According to Hiebert, the spending by individuals and groups other than the candidates and the political parties was puny in 1993 by comparison to the 1988 figure. She calculated the total figure for newspaper advertising, the pre-ferred choice of independent spenders, to be $235,000, of which the NCC accounted for $80,000, much of that being devoted to advertisements against Progressive Conservative incumbents in the Calgary area.[29] Hiebert's research also disclosed that almost all of the independent advertising in 1993 was partisan rather than issue-oriented, a notable contrast to the situation in 1988.[30]

In the meantime, however, the government had appealed the trial court's decision to the Alberta Court of Appeal, which dismissed the appeal in a ruling handed down in June 1996.[31] Elsewhere we have examined the rationale of the ruling at some length.[32] The point to stress is that in it Justice Conrad[33] under-took to supply what the two trial judges had not, namely, a theoretical position sustaining the legal finding that the restrictions on third-party spending were impermissible breaches of Charter rights and freedoms. She reached that position after rejecting the objectives of the restrictions as cited by counsel to the federal government, namely, (1) to instil public confidence in the electoral system as a whole by discouraging the notion that third parties endorsing particular candi-dates or parties might benefit later in the form of government patronage; and (2) to prevent the candidates and the parties from escaping the limits on their own spending by colluding with third parties who want to spend on behalf of the par-ties and the candidates.[34]

Finding no compelling empirical evidence before her to support positively the idea that the restrictions were necessary to meet these objectives, Justice Conrad determined that the *real* purpose of the spending restrictions on third parties was to maintain an electoral system that "gives a privileged voice to [regis-tered] political parties and official candidates within those parties."[35] And she found this to be inconsistent with the Charter which, she noted pointedly, is meant to guarantee the rights of citizens, not political parties. She conceptualized the individual voter who, she imagined, faced with advertising from the candi-dates and the parties, wants a counterweight in the form of information and inde-pendent advice on the politicians from interest groups or community and religious leaders. She conceived these commentators to be objective, or at least "without the self-interest involved in candidate and party advertising."[36] From this standpoint, she found the noncumulative limit of $1000 on independent spending too slight to sustain any meaningful counterweight.

In the electoral model presupposed by the very spending regime at issue before the court, the individual voter is thought to be best served by a competitive political-party system. And a key condition of competitiveness is a financially level playing field. In her thoroughgoing renunciation of third-party spending restrictions, Justice Conrad constructed an alternative electoral model of "open democracy"[37] that challenges the central position of the political parties in the party-democracy model. She constructed a rival to the model that is in place in most democratic systems around the world, that is, the prevailing model in which safeguards such as spending restrictions are held to be required to ensure that elections are contested on a level playing field, and that the competition between the contestants is not thwarted or undermined by external forces.

It would not be too much to say that Justice Conrad's exercise of the power of judicial review packed a punch. On hearing the news, David Somerville, the president of the NCC, was reported to have said: "They just picked up on all the arguments we've used for years to argue against the gag law. This is beyond all our expectations."[38] Press reports of the decision were favourable, often pointing out that the spending restrictions were condemned by a wide array of interest groups and in editorial opinion across the country. Even the federal government was loathe to defend the provisions at this stage. Indeed, the Minister of Justice at the time, Allan Rock, said they were "not defensible," and would not be reinstated.[39] The federal government decided not to appeal the decision, which might have been the end of the matter, except that Canada is a large country in which there is always the province of Quebec to consider.

THE SUPREME COURT OF CANADA, QUEBEC, AND THIRD-PARTY SPENDING

In Quebec there is a scheme to restrict expenditures that is in place during provincial general elections *and* referendums. The general purpose of the Quebec scheme is the same as that of the federal scheme, namely, to ensure that fairness, as conceived of in terms of the competition between the candidates and the political parties, is maintained as a central value of the democratic electoral process.[40] As matters transpired, it was the spending provisions of the law governing referendums that were moving through the Quebec courts at roughly the same time that the corresponding federal provisions were moving through the Alberta courts. However, by contrast with the Alberta outcome, both the Quebec Superior Court[41] and the Quebec Court of Appeal[42] sustained the validity of the spending provisions, which meant that the trial and appellate courts in the two provinces were at odds with one another. Since the plaintiff in the Quebec case chose to appeal the Quebec Court of Appeal's ruling to the Supreme Court of Canada, the judicial conflict was bound to be resolved one way or the other. Before turning to the Supreme Court's decision, it is helpful briefly to outline the relevant features of the spending provisions at issue.

Under Quebec's referendum law,[43] a national committee is established in favour of each of the options presented to the voting public in a referendum—say, a "yes" committee and a "no" committee in the case of a referendum question on sovereignty that permits either one of two answers/options—and each committee is responsible for the expenditures that are made in its name. In this way expenditures are controlled in terms of the overall amount and the type of expense permitted. The total amount that each committee is allowed to spend is calculated at one dollar per registered voter, and the state provides a subsidy to each committee in the amount of 50 cents per registered voter. In the 1995 referendum, the two committees spent just over $5 million apiece, half the total of which was a state subvention and the other half contributions from individuals and the political parties.[44]

Anyone who wishes to participate in the campaign in support of one of the options can join the appropriate committee. Further, any group (but not an individual) that wishes to participate to support an option but disagrees with the strategy pursued by the national committee or prefers not to be identified with the national committee for whatever reason can *affiliate* with the committee, which permits the group to conduct a parallel campaign using funds dispensed by the committee. Finally, any individual or group that chooses not to affiliate with a committee but to participate in the referendum campaign anyway is confined to a list of activities, the cost of which is unregulated because it is expected to be minimal. An example is the cost of writing a letter to the editor of a newspaper in the hope that it will be published. But one qualifying activity that is not as low cost is holding a public meeting at a cost not to exceed $600, so long as the meeting is not used to support or oppose one of the options in the referendum.

The appellant, Robert Libman, was the president of the Equality Party and an elected member of the National Assembly at the time that he and the party brought the action before the trial court. He had objected initially to the very concept of the committee structure, as well as the whole of the spending-limits scheme, as a violation of the rights and freedoms guaranteed under the Charter. However, by the time the case reached the Supreme Court, he was making the narrower claim that the restrictions on nonaffiliated individuals and groups violated the Charter freedoms of expression and association. He thought that they ought to receive some funding and be eligible to make the same sort of expenditures that the committees were permitted to incur. And the Supreme Court had some sympathy for his point of view.

In a powerful unsigned, unanimous decision, the full Court of nine judges agreed that the impugned spending provisions infringed the appellant's freedoms of expression and association.[45] Then it asked whether the provisions could be construed as reasonable limits of these freedoms in accordance with the tenets of the *Oakes* test. The referendum law passed the first step of the *Oakes* test with flying colours, the Court agreeing with counsel for the Quebec government that the objective of the law is to promote the value of fairness within a democratic, electoral process. Parsing this objective, the Court stated that in providing for the control and the use of money, and thereby minimizing the impact on the referendum process of its uneven distribution among the members of the society, the legislation was egalitarian, and had the effect of keeping debate open and inspiring public confidence that the process is not dominated by the "power of money."[46]

Having accepted the objective of the referendum law in general, the Court turned to the next step in the *Oakes* test, namely, the proportionality between the legislative objective and the legislative means (the spending limits), beginning with an appraisal of the rationality of the connection between them. Aided in its considerations by the report of the Lortie commission, which Quebec had adduced in evidence, the Court accepted completely the commission's argument that fairness in elections hinges on the democratic principle of political equality, which in turn requires attention to the financial factor. As a result, it approved of the limits placed on referendum expenditures by the authorized committees, and the limits placed on the expenditures of third parties, like Libman, who wanted to participate and spend independently of the committees. Moreover, the Court accepted the commission's argument that third-party spending needs to be restricted more than the spending of authorized committees (in a referendum in Quebec) or the spending of the candidates and the parties (in general elections). Otherwise, it stated, third-party spending might have a disproportionate impact on the process and thereby threaten the very purpose of instituting a spending regime at all.

At this point in the decision, the Supreme Court referred to the view of third-party spending limits entertained by the Alberta Court of Appeal, namely, that they are meant to entrench a privileged position in the process for the candidates and the political parties over others. The Supreme Court rejected this view, and then emphasized its own very different view "that the [fairness] objective of Quebec's referendum legislation is highly laudable, as is that of the *Canada Elections Act*."[47] The Court stated that it accepted "the need to limit spending both by the principal parties (the national committees in the case of a referendum) and by independent individuals and groups in order to preserve the fairness of elections and, in the present case, referendums."[48] Next it assessed the relationship between the legislative objective (fairness) and the means chosen (spending limits) in terms of "minimal impairment," which simply suggests that the limits chosen should impair rights and freedoms as little as possible. It was immediately obvious that something was up because, in a great display of deference to the Quebec legislature, the Court emphasized that its expertise lay in the protection of liberty and the interpretation of legislation, especially criminal justice legislation, but *not* in the realm of policy making, a role properly assigned to the elected representatives of the people.[49] Ironically, this was a signal that the policy-making realm was exactly where the Court planned to move, however gingerly.

Discussion ultimately landed on the unregulated expenses open to those who choose not to join or affiliate with the national committees. Predictably, the Court found them too meagre to pass the minimal-impairment prong of the proportionality test and immediately latched on to the federal alternative as a better one—the $1000 spending limit for third parties that was recommended by the Lortie commission, adopted by the federal government, and dismissed by the Alberta Court of Appeal. Surely nothing could have been more devastating to the Alberta Court of Appeal than the Supreme Court's warm embrace of the $1000 limit except, possibly, its equally warm consideration of the need for the ban on the pooling of resources. In case anyone chose to be obtuse about the matter, the Court cited in full the provisions of the Canada Elections Act that limit the advertising expenses of the third parties to $1000, noted the Alberta court's dismissal of them, repeated its disagreement with that court, and again recommended the federal model to the Quebec government.[50] It was unnecessary for the Court to consider the third and final prong of the proportionality test, that is, whether the deleterious effects of the limits on rights overwhelm the advantages gained by the limits, and in fact it declined to do so, although not before emphasizing its recognition that the "laudable" objective of electoral fairness necessitates some restrictions on freedom of political expression.[51]

POLICY MAKING POST-*LIBMAN*

Robert Libman won his case. The Supreme Court struck down the particular restrictions on third-party activity in Quebec's referendum law. On the other hand, the Quebec government—and by implication the federal government— scored the real victory because the Court also upheld the constitutional validity of such restrictions as part of an overall regime of spending restrictions designed to promote fairness in electoral contests. Indeed, the Court stated explicitly that while referendums and general elections are different events, the "same principles underlying election legislation" in general are applicable to both.[52] No one recognized this more clearly than David Somerville. Although no longer the president of the NCC, he was reported to have called the decision "dangerous, bad law" and then to have stated: "The decision essentially, gratuitously, advises [Quebec Premier Lucien] Bouchard, [Prime Minister Jean] Chrétien and others how they can construct an election gag law which the court will find acceptable."[53] In the same newspaper on the same day, an unhappy editorial writer echoed the theme: "The Supreme Court killed only the most extreme provisions of this ludicrously restrictive law. Worse for freedom of expression, it effectively revived a federal election-spending law that is nearly as bad as Quebec's."[54]

Politically speaking, the *Libman* case was highly sensitive because it was heard within the horizon of the current Quebec government's sovereignty project. The rules governing a referendum on sovereignty obviously are of the greatest moment to the Quebec government and to Canadians generally. The Quebec government initially was lukewarm to the decision, appearing not to understand the Court's sympathetic approach to its legislation. It is a matter for speculation, of course, but there might well have been division within the government on how best to exploit the decision, whether to emphasize the flattering passages about the province's law while quietly proceeding to amend the offending sections, or whether to treat the Court's rejection of those sections as a provocative gesture to Quebec. There was talk about invoking the override provision of the Charter, which allows Parliament and the provincial legislatures to protect legislation from the reach of some of the rights and freedoms of the Charter, including the fundamental freedoms of expression and association.[55] However, in May 1998 the Quebec government tabled amendments to the referendum law to bring it into line with the Court's requirements, and also amendments to the election law, since it was affected by the decision as well, and a general election was thought to be in the offing before any referendum on sovereignty.

Beginning with the amendments made to the Election Act, one change to notice is that anyone, including a group or an individual, is now entitled to organize public meetings at a cost not exceeding $200, so long as the meetings are not organized on behalf of a candidate or a political party. Any person or group that chooses to do this need not register as a private intervener. The other, more significant change is the introduction of this new and important category of "private intervener" to cover the individuals and groups who want to engage in election activities independently of the candidates and the political parties, and do more than hold a public meeting. These individuals and groups must register with the local election authorities as private interveners, following which they are entitled to incur advertising expenses in an amount not exceeding $300 for issue advocacy purposes or to recommend voter abstention or ballot spoiling. No pooling of resources is permitted. A private intervener must file a receipted statement of expenses with the Chief Electoral Officer within thirty days of polling day.[56]

The concept of the private intervener is also used in the amendments to the Referendum Act. Under the act anyone can continue as before to spend a maximum of $600 to hold public meetings so long as the meetings are not organized to promote one of the options in contention in the referendum. However, there are two new provisions, one of which permits individuals who are registered as private interveners and therefore not affiliated with a national committee to incur up to $1000 worth of advertising expenses to promote or oppose an option in contention in the referendum. The other new provision permits individuals *and/or groups* who are registered as private interveners to incur publicity expenses not exceeding $1000 to advocate abstention or the spoiling of ballots, without at the same time supporting or opposing a referendum option. Again, no pooling of resources is permitted, and the registered private interveners must file expense statements as is required in general elections.[57]

The changes to the Referendum Act appear to be in line with the Supreme Court's notion of a reasonable approach to third-party expenditure limits, although the need to register as a private intervener and to file expense statements might act as a deterrent to some prospective participants. On the other hand, the new third-party expenditure provisions in the Election Act are puzzling, and not just because the amounts involved seem trifling, falling far short of the benchmark $1000 figure. They are puzzling as well because they restrict third-party spending to advocacy purposes only. In this respect, the provisions stand in contrast to the Court's statement of agreement with the Lortie commission that any distinction between partisan and advocacy spending is unsustainable in practice.[58] Moreover, it cannot be overlooked that, as noted above, one of the amendments to the Referendum Act does permit third-party spending *directly on the options in contention*—which is not the same as partisan spending, true, but certainly is relevant spending in the context of a referendum. It is not stretching matters too far to conclude that the Quebec government is being a little provocative, challenging the Supreme Court to strike down the revised provisions in the Election Act. If so, the *Libman* decision is unlikely to be the end of the matter.

CONCLUSION

As has been noted, the *Libman* case unfolded in the shadow of the prospect of another referendum being held on the question of Quebec sovereignty. It is not improbable that the Supreme Court's decision was influenced by judicial sensitivity to a matter of such high politics. And it would be interesting to speculate what the outcome might have been had the case in which the same issues were raised originated in a non-Quebec jurisdiction—in other words, if the *Somerville* decision had been appealed instead to the Supreme Court. However, it was *Libman* that wound up there, and whatever the impact of the Quebec political situation, the fact remains that *Libman* has important implications for electoral law in Canada as a whole, implications that are worth pausing to consider.

In *Libman*, the Supreme Court affirmed the legislative choice to limit election expenses in general, and third-party advertising expenses in particular, in the effort to promote fairness in the electoral arena. It thereby accepted the model of party democracy with which this election-expenses regime is consistent. Under the model of party democracy, the electoral contest is chiefly between the candidates and the political parties, as the Lortie commission argued. Thus, under this conception, fairness requires the imposition of limits on the expenses of both the contestants and third parties, not to ensure that each of the contestants (the candidates and the political parties) spends the same amount of money, but instead to ensure that no one of them is completely overwhelmed by the resources of a particularly well-heeled opponent. There is an element of balance in this conception of a fair political competition.

At the same time as it accepted the party-democracy model, the Court, we argue, explicitly rejected the alternative model of open democracy advanced by Justice Conrad, a model in which ordinary citizens and interest groups are free to spend as much money as they like for advocacy or partisan purposes—in other words, a model in which fairness means *not* placing restrictions on third parties, a model in which fairness means "privileging" money under the banner of free speech. Obviously, if such an alternative model were in effect in federal elections today, it would produce a situation in which the expenditures of some (the candidates and the parties) were limited while the expenditures of others (individuals and interest groups) were not limited. This would be untenable, and in all likelihood resolved by the removal of the limits on the candidates and the parties. Indeed, this is exactly what David Somerville had suggested to the Alberta Court of Appeal, arguing that the limits on the candidates and the parties are as unconstitutional as the limits on third parties.[59] Thus the open-democracy model would have every chance of becoming the open-spending model. In rejecting Justice Conrad's model, then, the Supreme Court made a deep policy choice about the conduct of politics. It upheld the traditional party model in the face of the challenge of a more freewheeling model that brings into question the legitimacy of organized partisan politics.

In addition to the underlying policy choice, the Supreme Court also had something to say about the particulars when it enthusiastically endorsed the example of the $1000 limit on third-party spending that is part of the federal spending regime. This has the effect of making the $1000 limit a kind of benchmark figure against which the limits used in spending regimes in other jurisdictions may be measured. It can be concluded, then, that in terms of the development of Canada's electoral law, and specifically campaign finance, the judicial branch has been more than a minor player. Ultimately, the Supreme Court sustained the critical legislative choices first made by Parliament back in 1974, and then modified them on the basis of the research and recommendations of the Lortie commission in 1991. But it did so in the full knowledge of the alternative that was set out by the Alberta Court of Appeal.

Ironically, the Supreme Court's affirmation of the logic of the Canadian election-expenses regime puts the federal government in something of a quandary. The government realizes that the so-called gag law is not popular among free-speech enthusiasts, in the media and elsewhere. Certainly it is an easy target for the media. In any event, the government has not enforced the third-party spending provisions since 1984, a rather startling state of affairs given the importance of these provisions, but at the same time one that could at least be defended on the ground that the courts in Alberta had ruled the provisions invalid. Now, however, there is something of a conundrum. On the one hand, the Supreme Court has held out the spending provisions of the existing federal law as a model for the Quebec government to follow and, consistent with this suggestion, has indicated its disapproval of the view of the provisions taken by the Alberta Court of Appeal. On the other hand, disapproval of the Alberta court's decision *in another case* is not the same thing as overturning that decision on appeal. The Supreme Court was dealing with the *Libman* appeal, not the *Somerville* appeal.[60] The conundrum would become all too real if an aggrieved candidate or a political party or an ordinary citizen, for that matter, were to launch a court action demanding that the federal government enforce the existing law.

One course of action would be for Ottawa to take the middle ground and revise the law, possibly by raising the third-party spending limits in an effort to assuage those who find the current $1000 too confining for the effective expression of their views. In British Columbia, for example, the figure is $5000. And, indeed, in March 1999 there was talk in the press that Ottawa was considering restricting expenditures by individuals and interest groups to $3000 per riding and $200 000 nationally.[61] In contemplating revisions, however, the government is constrained by the Supreme Court's ruling in *Libman* on what is necessary to ensure a fair campaign-finance regime. In other words, the government is constrained by its own objective of electoral fairness as conceived in the party democracy model, an objective affirmed by the Court.[62] It is hard to see how the government could back away from this value of fairness, except by radically redefining it, which in all likelihood would point Canada in the direction of the free-spending American campaign-finance model.

ENDNOTES

1. Canadian Charter of Rights and Freedoms, Part 1 of the Constitution Act, 1982, being Schedule B of the Canada Act 1982 (U.K.), 1982, c.11.

2. *Libman v. Quebec (Attorney General)*, [1997] 3 S.C.R. 569.

3. *Report of the Committee on Election Expenses* (Ottawa: Queen's Printer, 1966), 50.

4. *Report of the House of Commons Special Committee on Election Expenses* (Ottawa: Queen's Printer, 1971).

5. See Herbert E. Alexander's review of these developments in his "The Regulation of Election Finance in the United States and Proposals for Reform," in *Comparative Issues in Party and Election Finance*, Volume 4 of the Research Studies for the Royal Commission on Electoral Reform and Party Financing, ed. F. Leslie Seidle (Toronto and Oxford: Dundurn Press, 1991), 3–56.

6. *Buckley v. Valeo* (1976) 424 U.S. 1.

7. The restrictions on donations were an attempt to address the problem of the large contributor rather than the rising cost of campaigns. See Alexander, 10.

8. See Jane Jenson, "Innovation and Equity: The Impact of Public Funding," in Seidle, *Comparative Issues in Party and Election Finance*, 111–77.

9. The commission, established by the federal Conservative government, was chaired by Pierre Lortie. See *Reforming Electoral Democracy*, Volume 1 (Ottawa: Minister of Supply and Services Canada, 1991), 322.

10. Ibid., 324.

11. Ibid., 325.

12. See Janet Hiebert, "Fair Elections and Freedom of Expression under the Charter," *Journal of Canadian Studies* 24 (1989–90): 73.

13. *National Citizens Coalition, Inc. v. Canada (Attorney General)* (1984) 11 D.L.R. (4th) 496. The issue of harm has been taken up most recently by A. Brian Tanguay and Barry J. Kay in their "Third-Party Advertising and the Threat to Electoral Democracy in Canada: The Mouse that Roared," *International Journal of Canadian Studies* 17 (1998): 57–79. They study two interest groups in two elections, and conclude: "Since 1984, when the legislative restraints on third-party spending were first struck down, interest groups have remained, in electoral terms, a mere mouse, albeit one with a ferocious roar and a tendency to boast about its ability to 'knock off' parties and their candidates." Ibid., 72.

14. See Hiebert, "Fair Elections and Freedom of Expression under the Charter," 77–78.

15. Ibid., 79.

16. Ibid.

17. The governing Conservatives obviously supported the agreement they had negotiated with the United States, while both of the main opposition parties, the Liberal Party and the New Democratic Party, opposed it. The $4.73 million figure is based on Janet

Hiebert's calculations in her "Interest Groups and Canadian Federal Elections," in *Interest Groups and Elections in Canada*, Volume 2 of the Research Studies of the Royal Commission on Electoral Reform and Party Financing, ed. F. Leslie Seidle (Toronto and Oxford: Dundurn Press, 1991), 20.

18.   "Regulating the Financing of Federal Parties and Candidates," in A.B. Tanguay and A.-G. Gagnon, eds., *Canadian Parties in Transition*, 2d ed. (Scarborough: Nelson Canada, 1996), 396.

19.   *Reforming Electoral Democracy*, Volume 1, 3.

20.   Ibid., 352.

21.   Ibid., 351.

22.   Ibid. The commission found that 98 percent of the contributions of individuals to the candidates and the parties were below $1000. For the contributions of businesses, the figure was 72 percent.

23.   The NCC also tackled the so-called black-out provision, which prohibited advertising between the day the election writ is dropped and the twenty-ninth day before polling day and the day before and the day of polling. It argued successfully that the provision was an impermissible infringement of the freedom of expression and the right to vote.

24.   The test was developed by Chief Justice Dickson in *R. v. Oakes* [1986] 1 S.C.R. 138–40. The first step of the test is to consider whether the objective of the legislation is sufficiently compelling and substantial to justify restrictions on rights and freedoms. If it is, then the next stage of the test is to determine whether the restrictions used (the means) are rationally and proportionally connected to the objective (the end).

25.   *Somerville v. Canada (Attorney General)* Calgary, oral judgment, 25 June 1993, unreported, 14–15.

26.   The NCC called political scientist Neil Nevitte as an expert witness, and Professor Nevitte cited two studies, R. Johnston et al., *Letting the People Decide: Dynamics of a Canadian Election* (Montreal: McGill-Queen's University Press, 1992) and B.I. Page et al., "What Moves Public Opinion?" *American Political Science Review* 81, no. 1 (1987): 23–43. For a discussion of this aspect of the case and how the courts treated the two quantitative studies, see Herman Bakvis and Jennifer Smith, "Third-Party Advertising and Electoral Democracy: The Political Theory of the Alberta Court of Appeal in *Somerville v. Canada (Attorney General)* [1996]," *Canadian Public Policy* XXIII, no. 2 (1997): 164–78.

27.   The judge quoted from the Hon. Harvey Andre's testimony before the special committee of the House of Commons that was considering the $1000 limit on third-party spending: "I can't think of an election anywhere that was altered by somebody spending too much and so on." *Somerville v. Canada*, 1993, 20.

28.   Ibid., 20–22.

29.   "Money and Elections: Can Citizens Participate on Fair Terms amidst Unrestricted Spending?" *Canadian Journal of Political Science* XXXI, no. 1 (1998): 96–97.

30.   Ibid., 98.

31.   *Somerville v. Canada (Attorney General)* [1996], 136 D.L.R. (4th) 205.

32.   Bakvis and Smith, 164–78.

33.   Three judges heard the appeal, with Justice Conrad writing for herself and Harradence J.A., and Kerans J.A. stating his general agreement with them in a separate opinion.

34.   *Somerville v. Canada (Attorney General)* [1996], 225–32.

35.   Ibid., 233.

36.   Ibid., 235–36.

37.   Ibid., 225.
38.   *The Globe and Mail,* 6 June 1996, A1.
39.   Ibid., 10 October 1996, A8.
40.   The Supreme Court quoted the words of Professor Peter Aucoin, who served as the Quebec government's expert witness: "The purpose of spending limits in an election or a referenda [*sic*] campaign is to promote fairness as a primary value or objective of the democratic process." See *Libman v. Quebec (Attorney General)* [1997], 596.
41.   *Libman c. Quebec (Procureur general)* [1992] R.J.Q. 2141 (C.S.Que.).
42.   *Libman c. Quebec (Procureur general)* [1995] R.J.Q. 2015 (C.A.Que.).
43.   Referendum Act, R.S.Q. (1978) c. C-64.1.
44.   The financing of the "no" and "yes" committees breaks down as follows:

Committee	State Subvention	Sums Received from Political Parties	Contributions of $200 or Less	Contributions over $200	Total Spending	Public Funding as a Percentage of Actual Spending
NON	$2 543 490	$2 590 000	$700	$51 300	$5 186 680	49.04%
OUI	$2 543 490	$2 650 108	$2608	$10 620	$5 224 377	48.69%

Source: Le Directeur Général des Élections du Québec, *Sommaires des rapports de dépenses réglementées: Référendum du 30 octobre 1995* (Quebec City: DGE, 1996), 15, 18.

As the table makes clear, the majority of nonstate funding came from political parties rather than individual contributors. The latter are limited to contributions of $3000 or less. The names of those who donate $200 or less are not reported. Although the subvention should total 50 percent of the amount spent by each of the committees, the somewhat lower percentages reflect slight overspending by them.
45.   *Libman v. Quebec (Attorney General),* [1997], 594–95.
46.   Ibid., 597.
47.   Ibid., 604.
48.   Ibid.
49.   Ibid., 606.
50.   Ibid., 618–20.
51.   Ibid., 621.
52.   Ibid., 598.
53.   Graham Fraser, "'Gag-Law' Ruling Infuriates Citizens Coalition," *The Globe and Mail,* 13 October 1997, A4.
54.   "New Life for the Gag Law," Ibid., A20.
55.   Under section 33 of the Charter, the override can be invoked in relation to the rights and freedoms guaranteed in section 2 and sections 7 through 15. The override is valid for five years, after which it dies, unless the legislature explicitly renews it.

56.   Bill 450 (1998, chapter 52), An Act to amend the Election Act, the Referendum Act and other legislative provisions in *Gazette Officielle du Québec*, 4 November 1998, Vol. 130, No. 45, Part 2, 4328–4351.

57.   Ibid., 4352–4364.

58.   *Libman v. Quebec (Attorney General)* [1997], 600.

59.   *Somerville v. Canada (Attorney General)* (1996), 213–14.

60.   Janet Hiebert argues that the decision of the Alberta Court of Appeal in *Somerville* stands despite the Supreme Court's disapproval of it. See her "Money and Elections," 105. As a result, she thinks that third-party spending will continue not to be regulated unless new, and presumably modified legislation is introduced for that purpose. She concludes that the Alberta Court of Appeal "has been able to exercise considerable influence on what the norms will be for federal election competition." Ibid., 110.

61.   "Ottawa Tries Again to Limit Campaign Spending," *National Post*, 29 March 1999, A1.

62.   The concept of electoral fairness was affirmed most recently by Riche J. of the Supreme Court of Newfoundland, trial division in *Robert Hogan et al. v. Newfoundland (Attorney General) and Canada (Attorney General)* [1998]. The case involved the amendment made to Term 17 of the Terms of Union, agreed to between Newfoundland and Canada in 1948 and incorporated in the Newfoundland Act (British North America Act, 1949), to eliminate denominational education in the province. The plaintiffs alleged that the amendment, and the steps taken to procure it, were unconstitutional. One of the steps was a referendum on the issue that the provincial government held on September 2, 1997. The judge agreed with the plaintiffs that the referendum was unfair because the government spent money to support one side (the "yes" side), provided no money for opponents on the "no" side, and imposed no spending limits at all. See unreported decision, paras. 24, 14.

THE SUPREME COURT'S RULING ON QUEBEC'S SECESSION:

LEGALITY AND LEGITIMACY RECONCILED BY A RETURN TO CONSTITUTIONAL FIRST PRINCIPLES

José Woehrling

On August 20, 1998, the Supreme Court of Canada handed down its long-awaited decision on the possible secession of Quebec.[1] The decision was an advisory opinion given in response to questions submitted by the Canadian government in September 1996. I will first recall the circumstances under which the issue was referred to the Court, and briefly review the manner in which it was heard and the arguments raised. Then I will summarize and analyze the judgment itself, and attempt to ascertain its political impact.

PROCEDURE AND ARGUMENTS RAISED

In the October 1995 referendum, held by the Parti Québécois government, 49.44 percent of the electorate voted in favour of Quebec's sovereignty, along with a formal proposal to the rest of Canada for "a new economic and political partnership." One of the consequences of this referendum was the federal government's decision to refer to the Supreme Court certain legal questions raised by Quebec's possible secession, by asking for an advisory opinion. The reference procedure enables the federal Cabinet to obtain directly from the Supreme Court, without having to pass through the first instance and appeal levels, a ruling on any type of constitutional issue.[2] The three questions referred to the Court were the following:

1. Under the Constitution of Canada, can the National Assembly, legislature or government of Quebec effect the secession of Quebec from Canada unilaterally?
2. Does international law give the National Assembly, legislature or government of Quebec the right to effect the secession of Quebec from Canada unilaterally? In this regard, is there a right to self-determination under international law that would give the National Assembly, legislature or government of Quebec the right to effect the secession of Quebec from Canada unilaterally?
3. In the event of a conflict between domestic and international law on the right of the National Assembly, legislature or government of Quebec to effect the secession of Quebec from Canada unilaterally, which would take precedence in Canada?

The statutory provisions applicable to the reference procedure[3] grant the right of intervention to every provincial Attorney General who expresses an interest in the matter. As well, the Court can authorize any interested person or group to participate in the proceedings. Furthermore, the Court may, on its own initiative, appoint a lawyer (amicus curiae) to speak in favour of an interest which, in the Court's opinion, would not otherwise be represented in a satisfactory manner. These various interventions bring an adversarial character to the proceedings despite the fact that, strictly speaking, there is no legal dispute to resolve, and thus ensure that the Court is well-informed on every aspect of the issues raised. In this case, some thirteen interveners participated in the proceedings: the Attorneys General from two provinces, Saskatchewan and Manitoba; the Ministers of Justice from the Northwest Territories and Yukon; organizations representing a number of Aboriginal peoples living in Quebec or elsewhere in Canada; the Ad Hoc Committee of Canadian Women on the Constitution and the Minority Advocacy and Rights Council; and, finally, a number of private citizens who, from a personal standpoint, argued either in favour of or against Quebec's right to secede from Canada. As for the government of Quebec, it adopted the stance that "Quebec's accession to sovereignty was and would remain a political and democratic matter that could only be decided in a valid and legitimate manner by the people of Quebec." It chose, accordingly, not to be represented before the Supreme Court. The Court therefore appointed an amicus curiae, a lawyer mandated to reply to the federal government's brief and to present the arguments that, in the Quebec government's absence, would not be sufficiently put forth by the other interveners. The Court insisted that the appointed lawyer not be a representative of any government or group. Instead, the appointed lawyer would present arguments related to the case that other parties would not, thus expanding the range of views heard by the justices.

THE CANADIAN GOVERNMENT'S POSITION

In general, the federal government's position was that neither Canadian domestic law nor international law permit the Quebec people or the provincial representative authorities to effect a unilateral secession. Secession of a province could only be properly achieved by amending the Canadian Constitution, which would require the consent of federal authorities and of a number of provinces, possibly all ten.[4] The federal government was thus admitting that the Canadian Constitution can be modified in its entirety and that one of its amending formulas must implicitly permit a province to secede, since no express provisions are set out in this respect. The government then called on the Supreme Court to declare that secession by a province entails a constitutional amendment that exceeds the powers of the provincial authorities acting unilaterally. In accordance with the provisions for constitutional amendment found in sections 38 to 49 (Part V) of the Constitution Act, 1982,[5] the only amendments allowed by unilateral provincial action are those that apply to certain aspects of the internal provincial constitution. Finally, the federal Attorney General strongly insisted that the Court abstain from specifying which of the other amending formulas might allow Quebec to legally secede under the Constitution.

Such a federal government position can probably be explained by its wish to have unilateral independence ruled out without the specification of a legitimating alternative. According to most experts, secession of a province would indeed require the agreement of both chambers of the Canadian Parliament and of all ten provincial legislative assemblies (amendment by unanimous consent). Some of the interveners forcefully pleaded this argument. There was a fear that if the Court adopted such a view, many Québécois might conclude that the sovereignty of Quebec would, in practice, be impossible to achieve lawfully. The failure of the Meech Lake Accord in 1990, still fresh in everyone's memory, was caused by the opposition of only two small provinces that together represented less than 8 percent of the Canadian population, even though the other eight provinces had given their consent. Furthermore, it is now generally held outside of Quebec that the consent of Aboriginal peoples is required for any constitutional amendment bearing on their interests. Some experts even assert that the same is true regarding the three northern territories. Finally, taking into account the precedent set by the referendum on the Charlottetown Accord, it is also widely believed that any major constitutional amendment must now be authorized—politically, if not legally—by a popular referendum. Three provinces (British Columbia, Alberta, and Saskatchewan) have already legislated this requirement; it would not be surprising if other provinces followed suit in the future. Given these circumstances, insisting on compliance with such an onerous and laborious amending formula would have been tantamount to denying outright the Québécois' right to self-determination. The government of Quebec could then have easily claimed that the Canadian Constitution has become a prison for the Québécois people. As well, it must be remembered that the Constitution Act, 1982, in which the present amending formula is contained, was imposed on Quebec's representative authorities against their will; no Quebec government, whether separatist or federalist, has since given it its political consent. As we shall see, the Supreme Court appears to have been sensitive to the political risk involved in demanding that the Québécois comply with the 1982 amending formula, since it ruled that the legitimacy—and even the legality—of Quebec's possible secession ought to be assessed in light of certain fundamental constitutional principles rather than in consideration of the specific provisions governing the constitutional amendment procedure.

As for international law (this was the subject of the second question referred to the Court), the federal government stated that it does not confer on Quebec any right to *external* self-determination, that is, a right to secession. This assertion was based on an analysis of international instruments and practices over which a general consensus exists. Indeed, it is almost unanimously accepted that the right to external self-determination is restricted to colonial peoples and to very rare situations of foreign occupation or repressive regimes. Only in the case of obvious oppression, clearly not the situation in Quebec, can it be said that a noncolonial people has the right to separate from the state in which they are contained. However, while international law does not confer on peoples who are not in a colonial situation, or in a situation of grave oppression, the *right* to accede to independence, it does not *forbid* them from claiming and gaining independence either. Should they then succeed and secession become effective, international law would recognize the new state's existence. The Canadian government, in its factum, did not explore the hypothesis of a successful unilateral secession which, on the basis of the effectivity principle, would produce a new state despite the failure to respect Canadian domestic law. On the other hand, as we shall now see, this matter was raised by the amicus curiae appointed by the Court.

THE AMICUS CURIAE'S POSITION

André Joli-Cœur, the lawyer appointed by the Court to act as amicus curiae, first raised preliminary objections to the Court's reference jurisdiction. As well, he argued that the Court should exercise its power to refuse to answer the questions submitted by the federal government because these were speculative, purely political, and not ripe for judicial decision. On the substantive issues, Joli-Cœur was of course defending the secessionist point of view, which would not otherwise have been correctly presented before the Court.[6] Respecting international law, his main argument rested on the effectivity principle, under which secession, even when unilateral and illegal, would be recognized at international law if it became an effective political reality. The success of Quebec's unilateral secession from Canada would therefore be established by the secessionist government's effective control over the Quebec territory. However, the amicus curiae admitted that the right to self-determination recognized at international law does not confer on the Québécois a *right* to secession.

Second, the amicus argued that the effectivity principle—founded on the notion that a de facto situation, even if illegal in its origin, will eventually be recognized by law if it persists for a sufficiently long period of time—is accepted as well in British law, and was introduced into Canadian law by the preamble to the Constitution Act, 1867.[7]

The criticism to which this argument based on effectiveness was open—and such a criticism was properly made by the Attorney General of Canada in his reply—is that it confuses the existence of a right with that of a de facto situation. The issues of effectivity and of the right to secession arise at different moments in time and relate to the different stages of an attempt to secede. The effectivity principle does not confer on Quebec the *right* to begin the process of unilateral secession, nor does it impose on Canadian authorities, as a result, the correlative obligation to approve or tolerate it. The effectivity principle is only likely to come into play once the outcome of a secession attempt is known, that is, if Quebec authorities, after a unilateral declaration of sovereignty, were to succeed in exercising all public authority over the territory being claimed, and if the Canadian government, willingly or not, renounced the exercise of its own authority. It would then be a matter of acknowledging an established fact, rather than of implementing a right. To the extent that no right to secede exists in Quebec's case, federal authorities clearly have no obligation either to recognize the existence of such a right or to allow its exercise. On the contrary, international law would allow them to actively oppose an attempted secession by any legitimate means. State practice has shown that when the government of the predecessor state opposes an attempt to secede, other states appear very reluctant to recognize the secessionist entity. Recognition by the international community is thus delayed until the predecessor state has accepted the fact of secession.

THE ABORIGINAL INTERVENERS' POSITIONS

On the whole, the Aboriginal interveners' positions followed closely the one adopted by the federal government, but several interveners went further on certain issues. The four Aboriginal groups (the Grand Council of the Crees, the First Algonquin Nation, the Makivik Corporation, which represents the Inuit from northern Quebec, and the Chiefs of Ontario) argued that the participation of Aboriginal peoples and their consent would be necessary for Quebec to secede legally. In light of its fiduciary obligations toward Aboriginal peoples, not only must the federal government refuse any constitutional amendment that has not met with Aboriginal approval, but it must also actively and strongly resist any attempt by the Quebec government to secede unilaterally. It was also maintained that Aboriginal peoples living in Quebec (mainly in the province's North) could demand that their traditional lands remain a part of Canada, should secession occur; this would entail the partition of Quebec's territory.

THE COURT'S DECISION

THE ISSUE OF JUSTICIABILITY

The Supreme Court began by rejecting the amicus curiae's arguments that it should refuse to answer the submitted questions because they were speculative, of a political nature, and not ripe for judicial consideration (para. 4–31).[8] The Court acknowledged that it could, indeed, exercise its discretion to interpret or to amend the submitted questions if these were too vague, and even to decline altogether to answer on account of their "non-justiciability." This last situation would arise if, in answering the question, the Court exceeded what it considers its proper role within a democratic framework or if the question did not have a sufficient legal component to warrant the intervention of the judicial branch. Neither of these two situations applied in the present case. The submitted questions did not request that the Court usurp any democratic decision that the Québécois could be called on to make. They were strictly limited to some of the aspects of the legal framework in which that democratic decision must be taken. Furthermore, the questions were clearly directed to legal issues, and as such, the Court was in a position to answer them. Finally, it could not be said that the questions were too imprecise or ambiguous, nor that the Court was not provided with sufficient information about the context in which the questions arose. In the circumstances, the Court was thus duty bound to provide its answers.

THE ANSWER TO THE FIRST QUESTION (UNILATERAL SECESSION UNDER THE CANADIAN CONSTITUTION)

The first question asked the Court to ascertain whether the Canadian Constitution allowed unilateral secession of a province. As I have already stressed, the federal Attorney General had called on the Court to respond by limiting the scope of its inquiry to an examination of the specific provisions that set out the procedures for constitutional reform. Even more specifically, he had requested that the Court state merely that secession was not permitted under the unilateral power of amendment provinces may exercise in regard to certain aspects of their internal constitution. The federal government thus hoped that the Court would restrict itself to establishing the *illegality* of a unilateral act of secession without questioning the *political legitimacy* it might acquire if supported by a majority of Québécois in a referendum. It was improbable, however, that the Supreme Court would adopt such a position. First, the Court would want to protect its credibility and its legitimacy by avoiding any suggestion that it was only meeting the federal government's expectations. Second, it would seek to provide answers that could not be interpreted as a denial of the Québécois' *political* right to determine their future; otherwise, its decision could very well have served to strengthen sovereignist sentiments and support for secession in Quebec, rather than the contrary.

As a matter of fact, the Court announced at the outset that it would examine the issue from a much wider perspective, that of the underlying principles embodied in the Constitution: "In our view, there are four fundamental and organizing principles of the Constitution which are relevant to addressing the question before us ... : federalism; democracy; constitutionalism and the rule of law; and respect for minorities" (para. 32). The Court then reviewed Canada's constitutional history (paras. 33–48) in order to show how those principles have guided the evolution of the Canadian union and how "[i]n our constitutional tradition, legality and legitimacy are linked" (para. 33).

ANALYSIS OF THE CONSTITUTIONAL PRINCIPLES

The Court then analyzed the nature of the four constitutional principles on which its answer to the first question would be based (paras. 49–82). The principles underlying the written Constitution "inform and sustain the constitutional text: they are the vital unstated assumptions upon which the text is based" (para. 49). Above all, the four principles most germane to the issue of secession—federalism, democracy, constitutionalism and the rule of law, and respect for minority rights—"function in symbiosis"; one principle cannot "... trump or exclude the operation of any other" (para. 49). This assertion is crucial. As we shall see, it would allow the Court to deliver a ruling that gave cause for satisfaction to each protagonist: the federal government and the other provinces, who gained the assurance that a possible secession by Quebec could be achieved only in accordance with existing principles of Canadian law, as well as in keeping with the interests of other Canadians and minorities within Quebec; the Québécois, to the extent that the Court recognized, in deference to the democratic principle, the legitimacy of the secessionist project and imposed on the rest of Canada the obligation to negotiate should the Québécois ever opt for secession in a sufficiently clear manner.

The Court next looked into the relationship that should exist between the unwritten constitutional principles—its role being to elucidate them—and the Constitution's written text. This passage evidently aims at establishing the legitimacy of the Court's decision. Although the underlying principles do not appear in written form, they are nevertheless the Constitution's "lifeblood" (para. 51). They must assist the courts not only in interpreting the text, but also in supporting the ongoing evolution and development of the Constitution, but without being taken by the judiciary "as an invitation to dispense with the written text of the Constitution" (para. 53). While a written constitution "promotes legal certainty and predictability, and [it] provides ... a touchstone for the exercise of constitutional judicial review," the underlying principles permit "the filling of gaps in the express terms of the constitutional text" (ibid.). Moreover, these very principles can give rise to genuine legal obligations, "very abstract and general" in some cases, "more specific and precise" in other circumstances (para. 54). "The principles are not merely descriptive, but are also invested with a powerful normative force, and are binding upon both courts and governments" (ibid.).

In twenty-seven long paragraphs (55–82), the Court then proceeded to analyze the content and meaning of the four constitutional principles it had put forward. Since these, except federalism, are fundamental principles shared by all liberal democracies, one would have hoped for the Court to retrace their evolution within liberal philosophy and Western constitutionalism. Instead, it repeatedly cited excerpts from its own precedents, undoubtedly to suggest that only the courts have the power to determine the meaning of the principles that underlie the Constitution and are its "lifeblood." As a result, this part of the ruling, which could have benefited from a broader perspective, is generally dry. Fortunately, some passages are more inspired, such as the one that considers the relationships between democracy, viewed as the expression of the will of the people, and the rule of law, seen as the framework in which this will must be exercised; or again, the relationships between the legitimacy of institutions, founded on the consent of the governed, and their legality, founded on the respect of established rules (paras. 67–68). The democratic principle creates the obligation, incumbent on all partners in the federation, to begin constitutional talks in response to the desire for change expressed by a province's population (para. 69); however, a majority vote in a provincial referendum could not allow the Constitution to be circumvented (para. 75). In the Court's view, and with respect to amending the current Constitution, democracy can be harmonized with constitutionalism "[b]y requiring broad support in the form of an 'enhanced majority'" (para. 77) as a means of guaranteeing that minority interests be addressed before the adoption of any changes that would affect them. One of the minority interests requiring protection is Aboriginal rights, mentioned by the Court but not discussed at any great length (para. 82).

OPERATION OF THE CONSTITUTIONAL PRINCIPLES IN THE CONTEXT OF SECESSION

The Court began by summarily dismissing the notion, as expressed by a few commentators, that the Constitution simply does not authorize a province to secede because this would "destroy," rather than amend, it. The fact that profound changes would follow a possible secession does not negate their nature as constitutional amendments: "The Constitution is the expression of the sovereignty of the people of Canada. [A]cting through [the] various governments duly elected and recognized under the constitution, [it can] effect whatever constitutional arrangements are desired within Canadian territory, including, should it be so desired, the secession of Quebec from Canada" (para. 85).

The Court then defined the meaning that it believed should apply to the term "unilaterally" in reference to the first question submitted by the federal government, which had asked if, under the Constitution, Quebec could secede "uni-laterally." This passage represents one of the ruling's turning points, since the Court gave the term "unilaterally" a meaning markedly different from that attrib-uted to it by the federal government, which had drafted the question. As shown by the arguments presented during the hearings, the government considered seces-sion to be unilateral if it did not comply with the specific provisions set out in the Constitution for constitutional amendment (Part V, sections 38–49, Constitution Act, 1982). In the Court's opinion, however, secession would be unilateral if effected "without prior negotiations with the other provinces and the federal gov-ernment" (para. 86). This change in meaning would allow the Court to analyze the question not exclusively nor even mainly in the perspective of Part V of the Constitution Act, 1982, but rather in light of the underlying principles of the Constitution. Without excluding the application of the Part V provisions to a pos-sible secession, the Court would emphasize the subordination of these written provisions to the unwritten constitutional principles.

Even though, under written constitutional provisions, a referendum would not have any direct legal impact and could not in itself bring about unilateral secession, the democratic principle, the Court said, "would demand that consid-erable weight be given to a clear expression by the people of Quebec of their will to secede from Canada" (para. 87). The Court added that "[t]he referendum result, if it is to be taken as an expression of the democratic will, must be free of ambiguity both in terms of the question asked and in terms of the support it achieves" (ibid.). The principle of federalism, in conjunction with the democratic principle, requires that the clearly expressed desire of a province's population to effect secession "give rise to a reciprocal obligation on all parties to Confederation to negotiate constitutional changes to respond to that desire" (para. 88). This principle is then generalized: "The corollary of a legitimate attempt by one par-ticipant in Confederation to seek an amendment to the Constitution is an oblig-ation on all parties to come to the negotiating table" (ibid.). In other words, when a province or the federal government (who are the "participants in Confed-eration") takes the initiative in proposing a constitutional amendment of any sort,[9] the federalism and democratic principles place an obligation on other par-ticipants to negotiate in good faith. This obligation applies even if the proposed amendment pertains to the secession of a province: "The clear repudiation by the people of Quebec of the existing constitutional order would confer legitimacy on demands for secession, and place an obligation on the other provinces and the federal government to acknowledge and respect that expression of democratic will by entering into negotiations and conducting them in accordance with the underlying constitutional principles already discussed" (ibid.).

The Court emphasized that the principles just stated led it to reject "two absolutist propositions." The first proposition would confer on Quebec an abso-lute right to secede, and on the federal government and the other provinces, the obligation to consent to an act of secession whose terms would be dictated by Quebec. The second would require that a clear expression of self-determination by the people of Quebec impose no obligations on the other provinces or the federal government (paras. 90–92). On the contrary, "[t]he negotiation process precipitated by a decision of a clear majority of the population of Quebec on a clear question to pursue secession would require the reconciliation of various rights and obligations by the representatives of two legitimate majorities, namely, the clear majority of the population of Quebec, and the clear majority of Canada as a whole, whatever that may be" (para. 93).

The Court acknowledged that negotiations would be very difficult, and that no one could predict the course they might take nor their outcome. With respect to the possible partition of Quebec, it only mentioned that "[a]rguments … regarding boundary issues" had been raised before it, without discussing the matter any further (para. 96). In this way, the Court was perhaps trying to suggest that the boundaries of a secessionist Quebec would be open to negotiation, but without actually saying so, for fear of provoking a strong reaction from the Québécois. The Court also referred to linguistic and cultural minorities "including aboriginal peoples," again without further consideration of the matter (ibid.). Consequently, given the vast number of very difficult issues that would have to be resolved, "[i]t is foreseeable that even negotiations carried out in conformity with the underlying constitutional principles could reach an impasse" (para. 97).

Should negotiations fail, how would the courts sanction the constitutional obligations described by the Supreme Court? Although these obligations are legally binding, and do not derive from conventions of the Constitution, which carry only political sanctions, the Court nevertheless considered that it could not compel their respect. In order to support this statement, it invoked the theory of "non-justiciability," linked to the notion of "judicial restraint." It is unlikely that the judicial branch would assess the various actors' behaviour during negotiations, as "[t]he reconciliation of the various legitimate constitutional interests … is necessarily committed to the political rather than the judicial realm, precisely because that reconciliation can only be achieved through the give-and-take of the negotiation process" (para. 101). The Court added: "Where there are legal rights there are remedies, but … the appropriate recourse in some circumstances lies through the workings of the political process rather than the courts" (para. 102).

Moreover, the same principles apply to the circumstances that would give rise to the obligation to negotiate, "namely a clear majority on a clear question in favour of secession." These are fundamental issues, for "[a] right and a corresponding duty to negotiate secession cannot be built on an alleged expression of democratic will if the expression of democratic will is itself fraught with ambiguities." However, these questions are not justiciable, and it is not up to the Court to specify what constitutes either a "clear question" or a "clear majority." "Only the political actors would have the information and expertise to make the appropriate judgment as to the point at which, and the circumstances in which, those ambiguities are resolved one way or the other" (para. 100). In this way, the Court clearly suggested that the conditions for the next referendum in Quebec—particularly the wording of the question and the decisive threshold of support—would have to be accepted by rest-of-Canada actors for the referendum outcome to create on their part an obligation to negotiate.

With regard to constitutional matters, a distinction has traditionally been made in Canada between the *conventions* of the Constitution, subject only to political sanctions, and constitutional *law*, characterized by the fact that it is subject to legal sanctions, applied by the courts. It seems that the Court has now introduced a new category that lies between the two preceding ones and whose principles are, on the one hand, truly legal, yet, on the other hand, subject only to political sanctions because of their "non-justiciability." Why did the Court not choose to say, instead, that in the case of a positive referendum in Quebec, the obligation to negotiate would follow from a convention of the Constitution based on the democracy and federalism principles?[10] Presumably for three reasons. First, because even though not justiciable, a *legal* obligation to negotiate nevertheless carries more weight than the purely *political* obligation that would arise by constitutional convention. Second, because albeit conventions can, in practice, neutralize the application of legal rules, they cannot trump them in the judicial arena. A simple convention would thus have maintained the complete application of the provisions found in Part V of the Constitution Act, 1982, while legal principles, even though they cannot be sanctioned by the courts, can modify the operation of these provisions. Third, the Supreme Court requires three constituent elements to be present to give rise to a constitutional convention[11]: the existence of precedents; the recognition by those who created these precedents (the "political actors") that the rule is obligatory; and finally, a reason for the rule, that is, an important constitutional principle that justifies the emergence of a convention. In order to support the existence of a constitutional convention that would oblige the federal government and the governments of the nine other provinces to negotiate the secession with Quebec, one could refer to the two precedents set by the 1980 and 1995 referendums in Quebec. The federal government participated in these processes, but did not attempt in any way to contest their validity. The democratic principle could clearly have provided the reason for the rule. However, it would have been much more difficult, if not impossible, to prove the recognition by all political actors, especially those from the other provinces, that the rule is binding.

By asserting that the legal obligation to negotiate secession would be subject to political sanctions only, the Court was undoubtedly aware that it was weakening the persuasiveness of its ruling. Perhaps in order to counterbalance this effect, before even broaching its answer to the second question, it established a link between considerations pertaining to constitutional law and those regarding international law. In fact, it stated that the failure to respect the obligation to negotiate, to the extent that it would undermine the legitimacy of a party's actions, could have important ramifications at the international level. If the government of Quebec were found in breach of the obligation to negotiate in good faith, its chances of obtaining recognition by the international community would diminish. Conversely, the probability of gaining such recognition would increase if Quebec negotiated in conformity with the principles and was facing unreasonable inflexibility on the part of the other provinces or of federal authorities: "In this way, the adherence of the parties to the obligation to negotiate would be evaluated in an indirect manner on the international plane" (para. 103). The Court thus lent an international dimension to a question that could have been considered strictly domestic. It must be emphasized that such recourse to the international community's judgment is necessarily restricted to the matter of secession only, which would inevitably be projected onto the international scene (because other states would have to take positions on recognizing or not recognizing the secessionist entity). Any other proposed constitutional amendment supported by referendum, such as Senate reform, for example, would also give rise to a constitutional obligation to negotiate; however, the conduct and results of these negotiations clearly would remain a purely domestic matter and be of no concern to the international community.

The Court further stated that, as the situation currently stands, it would abstain from specifying which constitutional amending formula would apply to Quebec's secession. No doubt this means that one of the formulas will have to be followed at the appropriate moment (para. 105). Remarkably, however, nowhere in this passage, nor anywhere else in the ruling, does the Court even mention the provisions contained in Part V of the Constitution Act, 1982. In this way, the Court suggests that, even if compliance with Part V is necessary to ensure the conformity of a possible secession with the Constitution, the specific written provisions will have to be subordinated to unwritten constitutional principles and to the ensuing obligation to negotiate.

How is the primacy of those principles over the specific provisions for amendment likely to be established? The principles could conceivably provide a framework for the exercise of powers accorded to the various constitutional actors by the provisions set out in Part V, in particular the right of veto that is given to federal authorities and to each province (if the unanimous consent formula set out in sec. 41 is indeed applicable). Before the Court's decision was known, it made sense to think that the veto could be exercised in a discretionary manner, since each holder of this right was absolutely free to determine whether to approve or reject any proposed constitutional amendment. This view no longer holds: the whole mechanism of the amending formula, in particular the use of the veto, must now conform to the underlying principles of the Constitution and to the obligation to negotiate in good faith.

Is it possible to go further, and consider that those principles might allow the application of the provisions of Part V to be circumvented altogether in some situations? Let us imagine, for example, that following a positive referendum in Quebec, negotiations with federal authorities and the other provinces resulted in an agreement on the conditions for secession. The formal mechanism for constitutional amendment would still need to be implemented, the consent of the federal authorities and of each province being necessary. What happened with the Meech Lake Accord could repeat itself: the opposition of a single legislative assembly could derail the whole amending process. Such opposition might be founded, for example, on the negative results of a referendum held in that particular province. Could it then be considered that the recalcitrant province is not respecting the underlying principles of the Constitution, democracy and federalism in particular? If these principles are to take precedence, they could render the provisions of Part V inapplicable and allow the amendments necessary to carry out secession despite the provincial veto. Failing such a solution, Quebec could declare sovereignty unilaterally, based on the conditions that had been agreed. Such a course of action could be justified before international public opinion by invoking the incoherence and paralysis of the "rest of Canada" brought on by a complex and unwieldy amending procedure. We have seen how the Court clearly implied that Quebec could attempt a unilateral declaration of independence, and that international public opinion would then judge whether the protagonists were acting in good or in bad faith, or whether their actions were coherent. Along the same lines, it bears reminding that, while the Court declared that a unilateral secession would be illegal, it defined the latter as an act of secession effected "without prior negotiations with the other provinces and the federal government" (para. 86), rather than as an act of secession in breach of Part V. In this light, an act of secession that would have been the object of a negotiated agreement therefore would not be unilateral nor illegal, even if it did not respect the provisions contained in Part V.

In emphasizing the obligation to negotiate and to respect the underlying constitutional principles, the Court relegated the specific procedures set out in Part V to a mere formality. It thus also "bilateralized" relations between Quebec and the "rest of Canada." Under Part V, Quebec would have to negotiate separately with federal authorities and each of the nine other provinces, because each of these actors' consent would be necessary. Such negotiations with ten different parties would obviously leave the Quebec government in a weak position. Under the obligation to negotiate that was defined by the Court, federal authorities and the other provinces would be required to speak with one voice. This is strongly suggested by the following passage from the ruling: "[t]he negotiation process precipitated by a decision of a clear majority of the population of Quebec on a clear question to pursue secession would require the reconciliation of various rights and obligations by the representatives of two legitimate majorities, namely, the clear majority of the population of Quebec, and the clear majority of Canada as a whole, whatever that may be" (para. 93).

THE ANSWER TO THE SECOND QUESTION (UNILATERAL SECESSION UNDER INTERNATIONAL LAW)

The part of the Court's ruling relating to international law is considerably briefer than that concerned with constitutional law. It requires less comment, since the Court dealt rather unimaginatively with the topic. As a matter of fact, the Court was content to record the existing consensus on the question. It began by establishing that international law does not recognize a right to secession, nor does it specifically prohibit it, even though it clearly favours the principle of territorial integrity for existing states. As to the existence of a people's right to self-determination, it is now so widely acknowledged that this principle can be considered as a general principle of international law (paras. 113 and 114). After passing in review the main international instruments—conventions and resolutions— whereby the right of peoples to freely determine their political status (or, the right of peoples to self-determination) is recognized (paras. 115–121), the Court established that this right must normally be exercised within the framework of existing sovereign states and in a manner consistent with the maintenance of the territorial integrity of those states (internal self-determination), and that the right to secession (external self-determination) arises only in exceptional circumstances.

But first of all, a group that invokes the right to self-determination must be a "people." During the hearings before the Court, the following issue was raised: Does the Québécois population constitute one or several peoples, and could certain groups, such as the anglophones or the Aboriginals residing in Quebec, invoke the right to self-determination in order to separate from a sovereign Quebec and maintain their integration with Canada? The Court was cautious not to be drawn into this highly charged debate, yet it suggested that there may, indeed, exist more than one "people" in Quebec:

> While much of the Quebec population certainly shares many of the characteristics (such as a common language and culture) that would be considered in determining whether a specific group is a "people," as do other groups within Quebec and/or Canada, it is not necessary to explore this legal characterization.…
> Similarly, it is not necessary … to determine whether, should a Quebec people exist within the definition of public international law, such a people encompasses the entirety of the provincial population or just a portion thereof. Nor is it necessary to examine the position of the aboriginal population within Quebec. As the following discussion of the scope of the right to self-determination will make clear, whatever be the correct application of the definition of people(s) in this context, their right to self-determination cannot in the present circumstances be said to ground a right to unilateral secession (para. 125).

Under current international law, a state is entitled to the protection of its territorial integrity if its government represents the whole of the people or peoples resident within its territory, on the basis of equality and without discrimination, and respects these peoples' right to internal self-determination (para. 130). The only clear cases in which the right to self-determination of peoples can be exercised "externally" (by way of secession) are those in which the people is either colonized or subject to alien subjugation, domination, or exploitation outside a colonial context (paras. 131–133). A number of commentators have further asserted that there is a third case, namely, when a people is blocked from the meaningful exercise of its right to internal self-determination. In the Court's view, it remains unclear whether this third situation actually reflects an established international legal standard. But in any case, even assuming that this third circumstance is sufficient to create a right to unilateral secession under international law, its conditions are clearly not met in the context of Quebec (paras. 134–135). One cannot plausibly claim that the Québécois are denied access to Canadian political institutions (para.

136), or that the failure to reach an agreement on constitutional amendments to the satisfaction of Quebec's government amounts to a denial of the Québécois' right to internal self-determination (para. 137). In summary, none of the exceptional circumstances that give rise to the right to external self-determination apply to Quebec's case in the existing context. Consequently, neither the population of Quebec nor its representative institutions possess a right, under international law, to secede unilaterally from Canada (para. 138).

Finally, the Court dealt with the argument based on the effectivity principle advanced by the amicus curiae, that a unilateral secession would be recognized internationally if it led to effective control by the secessionist government over the territory of what is presently the province of Quebec. The Court acknowledged the existence of this principle and recognized "that international law may well, depending on the circumstances, adapt to recognize a political and/or factual reality, regardless of the legality of the steps leading to its creation" (para. 141). However, "international recognition ... does not relate back to the date of secession to serve retroactively as a source of a 'legal' right to secede in the first place. Recognition occurs only after a territorial unit has been successful, as a political fact, in achieving secession" (para. 142). The Court at this point took up the distinction that the Attorney General of Canada had drawn in his reply to the amicus curiae, between the existence of a right and that of a de facto situation. The question to which the Court had to reply asked whether there exists a *right* to unilateral secession, not whether a unilateral secession can create a de facto situation that would eventually be recognized under international law. However, one must remember that, in its response to the first question, the Court stated that the attitude of other states could constitute a form of sanction with regard to the obligation to negotiate that Québécois and Canadian actors are under. This takes us back to the effectivity principle, to the extent that the effective success of a unilateral act of secession would, in good part, depend precisely on the attitude of the international community. And the foreign states' decision either to recognize or not to recognize the secessionist unit would depend, among other things, on the legitimacy of the process by which secession has been effected or attempted (para. 143). In this regard, the Court referred to the *European Community Declaration on the Guidelines on the Recognition of New States in Eastern Europe and in the Soviet Union.*[12]

Hence, the Court's argumentation has come full circle. The obligation to negotiate under Canadian law would be sanctioned by the attitude of other states at the international level. And their attitude would be determined in particular by the legitimacy of the process of secession, that is, by the respect of the constitutional obligation to negotiate imposed on the secessionist unit as well as on the authorities of the state from which secession is sought. The Court hereby succeeded in demonstrating that the principle of effectivity that applies at the international level would reinforce the constitutional principles, instead of contradicting them as the amicus curiae claimed.

As Canadian constitutional law and international law both provide the same answer, namely that Quebec does not have the right to secede unilaterally from Canada, there is no conflict between the two legal orders. The Court, therefore, did not consider it necessary to answer the third question, concerning whether domestic or international law would take precedence in the event of a conflict (para. 147).

THE RULING'S IMPACT AT THE POLITICAL LEVEL

The Supreme Court's decision was hailed as a victory by both federal government and Quebec government representatives alike. Where the latter were concerned, it was a spectacular about-face since, in the months preceding the decision, the Parti Québécois government had expended great energy attempting to discredit the Supreme Court and undermine beforehand the legitimacy of a decision it clearly expected to be completely opposed to its interests.[13]

In fact, each protagonist can find a measure of satisfaction in the ruling. The federal government has the satisfaction of hearing the Court declare that the Canadian Constitution does not allow unilateral secession and that, under international law, the right of peoples to self-determination amounts to a right to secession only in the case of colonial or oppressed peoples, which is not the situation in Quebec. Consequently, a unilateral declaration of sovereignty would clearly be unconstitutional. Furthermore, the ruling recognizes that the federal authorities' and the other provinces' obligation to negotiate would only arise, following a positive referendum on sovereignty in Quebec, if the outcome reflected a "clear expression of a clear majority of Quebecers that they no longer wish to remain in Canada." This implies that rest-of-Canada political actors will be able to exercise some control over the respect of these two conditions. By its acceptance of and satisfaction with the ruling, the Quebec government is thus renouncing certain claims it has made in the past, most notably that a positive referendum in Quebec would suffice to achieve independence, and that only Quebec authorities are able to appreciate the valid conditions of a referendum on sovereignty. More generally, the government of Quebec recognizes, albeit after the fact, the legitimacy of the Supreme Court's intervention; in the future, it will not be able to attack its credibility so readily should the Court be called upon once again to pronounce itself on the question of secession.

The ruling also contains a certain number of points that the federal government obviously did not wish for and that strengthen the sovereignist position. The most important one is the constitutional obligation to negotiate that, according to the Court, derives from the unwritten principles underlying the Constitution, and that would be imposed on the rest of Canada in the aftermath of a positive referendum in Quebec. It is true that, especially at times when the level of support for sovereignty seemed to render this possibility more theoretical than real, federal authorities and some of their provincial counterparts have recognized that a successful referendum in Quebec would create a situation in which it would be *politically* difficult to refuse to negotiate secession. Nonetheless, since the 1995 referendum, which nearly saw the sovereignist vote exceed the fifty percent threshold, this attitude no longer finds such a clear expression. One could even hear, in the rest of Canada, academics and politicians claiming that there would be no negotiation whatsoever. The Court's decision now renders this position unfeasible, all the more so since the obligation to negotiate established by the Court not only exists at the political level, but is also of a *constitutional* nature. This part of the ruling is likely to reassure a certain number of anxious Québécois voters who may be less reluctant to vote in favour of sovereignty, knowing that a positive referendum result will necessarily entail negotiations; some of them may even hope that the negotiations will lead to reforms within the federal system rather than to separation.

In its decision, the Court clearly rejected two extreme arguments: the first, sometimes advanced by the Parti Québécois government, holds that a positive referendum suffices to create for the rest of Canada an obligation to accept Quebec's secession; the second argument, increasingly raised in English Canada since 1995, holds that a positive referendum would have no consequences, whether political or legal. Thus, the Court is obliging the two parties to return to the more moderate playing field of discussions and negotiations.

Even as it defines the fundamental principles framing a possible secession, the Court's decision leaves numerous questions unanswered. Some of these, for example, the specific constitutional amending formula that may serve to formalize the results of a negotiated agreement between Quebec and the rest of Canada, may be submitted once again in the future, at a time when they are "ripe" for judicial consideration. With regard to some other questions, as we have seen, the Court asserted that they are by nature nonjusticiable and must, consequently, be left to political actors. The Court notably included within this second category the conduct of negotiations following a potential positive referendum outcome in Quebec, as well as the nature of the conditions to be fulfilled—"a clear answer to a clear question"—in order that the obligation to negotiate incumbent on federal authorities and the other provinces follow the said referendum. Not surprisingly, since the Court handed down its decision, the debate between sovereignists and federalists has centred on these two issues: the wording of the question to be put before the voters and the appropriate threshold of support the sovereignty option would require in a future referendum.[14]

ENDNOTES

This chapter was translated from the French by Diane Roussel.

1. *Reference re Secession of Quebec*, [1998] 2 S.C.R. 217. The judgment, delivered on August 20, 1998, is available on the Internet at the following site: www.droit.umontreal.ca/quebec.

2. Even before the federal government decided to obtain an advisory opinion from the Supreme Court, private citizens had already initiated court proceedings in order to prevent the Quebec government from holding a referendum on secession. Some of these were still in progress at the time of the reference and were stayed pending the Supreme Court's decision. In fact, as of August 1995, Guy Bertrand, a Quebec lawyer and former sovereignist

who is now an adamant advocate of Canadian unity, had filed an action for declaratory judgment and permanent injunction in the Superior Court of Quebec in order to prevent the government of Quebec from organizing the referendum projected for October 1995. The Attorney General of Canada refused his invitation to join the proceedings. The Attorney General of Quebec withdrew from the case after the Superior Court rejected his motion to dismiss. He thus refused to argue on the merits of the matter (for the same reasons he decided not to appear before the Supreme Court in the reference on secession). On September 8, 1995, Mr. Justice Lesage of the Superior Court of Quebec rendered his judgment: *Bertrand c. Bégin*, [1995] R.J.Q. 2500 (C.S.). Although he determined that the means employed by the Quebec government to organize the referendum on secession violated the Constitution, Judge Lesage nevertheless refused to grant an injunction forbidding that the referendum be held, on the ground that the injunction might cause a wrong greater than the one being prevented. As we know, the referendum was indeed held on October 30, 1995. On January 3, 1996, Mr. Bertrand filed another action for declaratory judgment and permanent injunction in order to prevent the preparation of a third referendum, which the Premier of Quebec, Lucien Bouchard, had just promised to organize. Once more, the Quebec government responded with a motion to dismiss, arguing that the issue raised was not triable "because the process leading to the sovereignty of Quebec was fundamentally democratic" and that, consequently, "the timeliness of this process need not be debated before the courts." This time, the federal government decided to intervene alongside Bertrand and to contest the Quebec government's motion to dismiss; it declared, however, that it would withdraw once again from the debate when substantive issues were to be raised. On August 30, 1996, Mr. Justice Pidgeon of the Superior Court of Quebec rejected the motion to dismiss submitted by the government of Quebec, which then announced, as it had when Bertrand first took the matter to court, its decision to withdraw from the matter and not defend itself on the merits of the case. In other words, it seemed that, as on the previous occasion, the issue would continue without the participation of the two governments, at the sole initiative of a private citizen. It was at this time, on September 26, 1996, that the federal government decided to ask the Supreme Court for an advisory opinion on the matter, evidently in order to regain control over strategy in the fight against secession before the courts.

3.   Supreme Court Act, [1985] R.S.C., c. S-26. Section 53 (1).

4.   In his factum, however, the Attorney General of Canada emphasized that "in no way did he question either the government of Quebec's power to hold a public consultation or the Québécois' right to express themselves by this means."

5.   Constitution Act, 1982, Schedule B of the Canada Act, 1982, R.-U., c.11; R.S.C. (1985), app. II, no. 44.

6.   At least not in an effective manner. As a matter of fact, among the private citizens authorized to intervene was Yves Michaud, a partisan of Quebec's sovereignty. Michaud had, however, filed an essentially political factum in which he requested that the Court refuse to pronounce itself on the issue, most notably because this would create a conflict of interest, since its preservation and the scope of its jurisdiction depended on the answers brought to the questions asked.

7.   Constitution Act, 1867, (1985) R.S.C. app. II, no. 5. The effectivity principle was invoked by the British courts in reference to issues that were determined in the context of Southern Rhodesia's unilateral declaration of independence in 1965. See especially *Madzimbamuto v. Lardner Burke*, [1969] 1 A.C. 645. In this matter, the Judicial Committee of the Privy Council had asserted that the success or efficacy of a change in the constitutional regime constitutes the principal means of determining whether the constitution in

force in a country has come to an end. The new constitutional regime's efficacy will then be considered as established from the moment that the former political regime no longer contests the validity of measures taken by the new political authorities. Even in cases in which the former political regime refuses to recognize the validity of the so-called usurping regime's actions, it may appear obvious, in certain circumstances, that this usurper has acquired effective control over the territory. In such circumstances, the courts must acknowledge that the new political regime has supplanted the former one. It must be certain, however, that the supplanted political regime will not be able to regain control over the contested territory.

8.   Excerpts from the decision will be cited by paragraphs. The amicus curiae also argued against the constitutional validity of the Court's reference jurisdiction. However, this argument was not very serious, since the validity of the reference procedure had already been unsuccessfully contested in the past.

9.   In accordance with section 46(1) of the Constitution Act, 1982, the procedures for amendment may be initiated either by the Senate or the House of Commons, or by the legislative assembly of a province. It should be noted that the Court's ruling does not mention this provision.

10.   Conventions of the Constitution are generally unwritten rules. Although not sanctioned by the courts, they are considered binding at the political level. They complete and clarify constitutional law in some cases, and neutralize or contradict it in other cases (without, however, bringing about formal amendments). Some of the most fundamental rules underlying the Canadian constitutional regime are unwritten conventions. For example, the principle of "responsible government," according to which no government may exercise power unless it enjoys the confidence of a majority of elected members of Parliament, will not be found in any formal constitutional document: It is an unwritten constitutional convention.

11.   Re: *Resolution to Amend the Constitution,* [1981] 1 S.C.R. 753.

12.   (1992) 31 *International Legal Materials* 1485.

13.   Spokespeople for the Quebec government used the image of the Tower of Pisa, which "always leans toward the same side."

14.   The November 30, 1998, provincial election brought the Parti Québécois back to power. The Prime Minister of Quebec, Lucien Bouchard, stated the following day that a new referendum would be organized as soon as "winning conditions" could be met.

DELGAMUUKW v. BRITISH COLUMBIA:

REDEFINING RELATIONS BETWEEN ABORIGINAL PEOPLES AND THE CROWN

Peter Clancy

Chief Justice Antonio Lamer has suggested that Aboriginal rights litigation may pose the toughest test to the courts in years to come, and that *Delgamuukw* should be seen as a beginning rather than a conclusion to this process.[1] This view is widely shared by Aboriginal peoples across Canada, who may be more conversant with the force of *Delgamuukw* than is the Canadian public at large.

In fact, the judicial process, and the Supreme Court in particular, have long been important to Canada's First Nations. Their life prospects have to a great degree been circumscribed by laws—including treaties, proclamations, statutes, and constitutional terms—enacted by the British government and by the federal and provincial governments in Canada. If many of the governing instruments could not be effectively influenced in their design, they might be better influenced through judicial action. In other words, the courts offer a prospective avenue of political redress at times when executive and legislative processes prove unresponsive. This is not to say that the Canadian courts have always rewarded Aboriginal plaintiffs, but that landmark cases have many times dislodged political deadlocks at both the federal and provincial levels, thereby paving the way for new policy initiatives. This has particularly been the case in the past thirty years, and the Supreme Court's ruling in *R. v. Delgamuukw*, released in December 1997, is the most recent decision in this line of landmark judgments. Whether the courts might have figured more prominently in earlier times is a question rendered moot by the fact that a 1927 amendment of the Indian Act by federal authorities prohibited any person from raising funds (without government permission) to prosecute Indian claims.[2] This was rescinded only in 1951.

THE FACTS OF *DELGAMUUKW*

The Gitxsan and Wet'suwet'en tribal territories lie in northern British Columbia, east of Prince Rupert in the Bulkley, Babine, and Skeena River watersheds.[3] Here Aboriginal people have lived since prehistoric times, with archaeological sites dating activities back 3500 to 6000 years. Both tribes were organized socially into a number of clans and houses led by hereditary chiefs. The first contact of these peoples with Euro-Canadians came through the fur trade in the early nineteenth century. Immigrant pressures intensified with the founding of the Dominion of Canada, and the Gitxsan and Wet'suwet'en stiffened their resistance accordingly. In the 1860s, crews cutting telegraph trails were blocked from crossing tribal lands. The British mainland and island colonies on the Pacific were united in 1866, and the province of British Columbia was established in 1871.This was followed by the Skeena Rebellion of 1872, in which the Gitxsan fought miners pushing north in search of claims. Since then, tribal leaders have continued to vigorously defend their lands.[4]

Today the Gitxsan number some 5000 people and the Wet'suwet'en another 2000; members of both tribes belong to 71 houses in all. In 1984 the two tribes launched legal action, seeking a judicial declaration of ownership of their traditional lands, and jurisdiction over them, including the confirmation of the hereditary chiefs as paramount authorities. The lands in question covered about 58 000 square kilometres, which is equal to 6 percent of B.C. provincial lands or, put another way, the equivalent of an area the size of Nova Scotia. The Gitxsan and Wet'suwet'en asserted that the provincial Crown had no basis to assert jurisdiction over lands that had never been surrendered. (Treaties were never negotiated between the two tribal groups and the Crown in British Columbia.)

The lead name among the Gitxsan and Wet'suwet'en plaintiffs was Delgamuukw (also known as Earl Muldoe), who sued for both himself and the members of the houses of Delgamuukw and Haaxw. Even though many additional Gitxsan and Wet'suwet'en houses were involved, the case became known as *Delgamuukw v. British Columbia.* After several years of legal preparation, the case went to trial in 1987, before Chief Justice Allan McEachern of the B.C. Supreme Court. Lasting more than three years, with 374 days of evidence and argument presentation, it ranks as the most extensive hearing in the annals of Aboriginal litigation. In March 1991, Chief Justice McEachern dismissed the Gitxsan and Wet'suwet'en case.[5] On the question of ownership, he acknowledged that there were traditional subsistence harvesting activities in the time prior to the assertion of British sovereignty (1846 in the case of British Columbia). However, he was not persuaded that the Indians possessed or controlled the *lands* in question (except for their villages) in any organized sense. On the issue of Indian jurisdiction (construed as a claim to government), McEachern ruled that the Gitxsan and

Wet'suwet'en legal system amounted to a most uncertain and highly flexible system of rules, frequently not followed and thus failing to constitute lawful jurisdiction. McEachern then explored the possibility that the plaintiffs held Aboriginal rights other than those sought. These he found in the form of "non-exclusive aboriginal sustenance rights" for hunting, fishing, and gathering, but not for fur trapping or other land-based commercial activities. However, these Aboriginal rights to land, McEachern found, had been extinguished before Confederation by colonial acts related to settlement, whose implied purposes were incompatible with a continuing Aboriginal interest. Despite this, he ruled that the Crown has a fiduciary duty (held in trust), arising out of this extinguishment, which affects the administration of Crown lands and resources. Justice McEachern concluded by dismissing the Gitxsan–Wet'suwet'en action, while granting a declaration entitling them to use unoccupied or vacant Crown land subject to the general laws in force.

This judgment drew impassioned reactions from both sides. It was celebrated by mainstream British Columbia commercial and governmental interests, for disposing (once again, it was said) of exaggerated Indian claims. McEachern's dismissal of Aboriginal ownership, jurisdiction, and rights claims eliminated a potentially massive legal burden on Crown lands and resource development leases. It also confirmed the province's traditional position that Aboriginal title did not exist in British Columbia. For the same reasons the trial decision was condemned by First Nations groups, and by the Aboriginal solidarity movement, as anachronistic thinking and shaky jurisprudence. Moreover, these groups felt that the Chief Justice's characterizations of traditional Gitxsan life seemed shatteringly ethnocentric for the 1990s.

Significantly, the *Delgamuukw* trial judgment triggered extended debate in British Columbia, with many voices in the white majority rejecting as unacceptable its "colonial" social and political assumptions. Indeed, the McEachern decision is one of those rare Canadian trial decisions to become the subject of an entire book of essays.[6]

Not surprisingly, the tribal chiefs appealed this ruling to the British Columbia Court of Appeal, where it was heard in 1992. Here the trial ruling was upheld, but the trial order was varied (modified) by a 3–2 margin, with two judgments offered on each side.[7] While this gave rise to a myriad of subtle differences, the basic thrusts can be summarized. All judges agreed, contrary to McEachern, that certain Aboriginal rights survived the colonial period. There were differences, however, on the nature of these rights. The majority view, expressed by Justice MacFarlane, held that the rights involved sustenance but not ownership or proprietary interests in land, or rights of jurisdiction. The minority found continuing Aboriginal rights to extensive parts of traditional lands and rights of self-regulation encompassing at least some powers over lands. The majority were not willing to substitute their own findings of fact in place of McEachern's, while the minority would have substituted. The majority granted a declaration for the existence of unextinguished Gitxsan and Wet'suwet'en rights, but not the Gitxsan's desired declarations for ownership and jurisdiction. The minority would have granted declarations on title, sustenance, and jurisdictional rights.

Given such broad differences of finding, an appeal to the Supreme Court of Canada seemed inevitable. After the papers were filed, however, the appellants sought and obtained an adjournment in 1994. For eighteen months, they participated in treaty negotiations with the governments of British Columbia and Canada (under what was then the recently established B.C. treaty process[8]). However, once the province suspended the negotiations in early 1996, the Supreme Court action was resumed. The case was argued over two days in July 1997. This featured the Gitxsan and Wet'suwet'en appeal, with British Columbia and Canada responding, and a British Columbia cross-appeal of MacFarlane's finding that the provincial Crown lacked the jurisdiction, after 1871, to extinguish common law Aboriginal rights. Additional interveners included the First Nations Summit (an Aboriginal coalition involved in the B.C. Treaty process), the Musqueam and Westbank First Nations, and two corporations operating in the Gitxsan–Wet'suwet'en territories (Alcan Aluminum Ltd. and Skeena Cellulose Inc.). The majority judgment, written by Chief Justice Antonio Lamer, overturned the lower courts and ordered a new trial. By way of clarification, the Supreme Court spoke extensively on the nature of Aboriginal title, the evidence required to establish title in particular cases, and the Crown's obligations in administering lands with a continuing Aboriginal interest. These points will be developed at greater length in later sections of this chapter.

TABLE 6.1 Summary of *Delgamuukw* Proceedings

Jurisdiction	Dates	For the Court
Trial: B.C. Supreme Court	1987–1990: Trial proceeding March 1991: Judgment	McEachern
Appeal: Appeal Court of B.C.	May–July 1992: Appeal heard June 1993: Judgment	MacFarlane, Taggart, and Wallace (concurring); Lambert, Hutcheon (dissenting)
Appeal: Supreme Court of Canada	July 1997: Appeal heard December 1997: Judgment	Lamer (for Cory, McLachlin, and Major); La Forest (for L'Heureux-Dubé) (concurring)

THE SUPREME COURT'S IMPACT ON ABORIGINAL RIGHTS

While the common law, statutory, and constitutional bases of Aboriginal rights and title are far from unassailable, the fact remains that judicial rulings have conferred significant leverage on the interests of Aboriginal peoples in their political struggles with the state. An impressive number of these cases originated in British Columbia, which for several reasons offers strong potential for test cases. The process of treaty making, which advanced across Canada in the late nineteenth and early twentieth centuries, stalled as it moved west across the Rocky Mountains. Successive B.C. governments displayed studied indifference or entrenched hostility to Aboriginal land claims, and the federal government often deferred to this position. This left little opportunity for political solutions.[9] It did, however, encourage Native peoples to press the courts, beginning in the 1960s, for confirmation of first common law (case law based) and later constitutional rights, which were being denied in the legislative and executive realms. The most prominent of this impressive string of cases (reviewed below) reached the Supreme Court of Canada, forming the policy-setting edge of a far wider front of Aboriginal litigation. On this basis, individuals, bands, tribal councils, and others have claimed Aboriginal rights and title in a wide variety of settings.[10]

Some key Supreme Court rulings since 1970 are now briefly explored. They cover the tenures of the three most recent Chief Justices: Bora Laskin (1973–84), Brian Dickson (1984–91), and Antonio Lamer (1991–99). The Court has travelled a remarkable distance over a quarter of a century, moving from a restrained response on doctrines of common law title, to a more forceful recognition of title based on traditional occupancy and use, and, most recently, to an expansive embrace of the Aboriginal rights provisions in the Constitution Act, 1982. Names such as Calder, Baker Lake, Guerin, Sparrow, Van der Peet, and finally Delgamuukw, denote the Aboriginal plaintiffs in these cases.[11]

It is important to remember that, as recently as 1969, the Trudeau government proposed to rescind the Indian Act and dismantle the Department of Indian Affairs in an effort to make the legal status of Native peoples level with that of Euro-Canadians.[12] While this plan was abandoned in the face of near-unanimous Indian opposition, the government continued to deny the existence of Aboriginal (as distinct from treaty) rights.[13] Then, in 1973, the Supreme Court of Canada ruled in the *Calder* case, which pertained to the existence of Nisga'a land rights to their traditional territories in northwestern British Columbia. While the Nisga'a lost their particular request for a declaration of unextinguished title, by a 4–3 margin, six of the judges accepted the concept of an Aboriginal title existing in law.[14] Moreover, they found that it derived from prior occupancy, independent of the Royal Proclamation of 1763 (although only the minority found the title to be still intact at the time of trial). The minority decision written by Justice Hall is one of the most influential opinions in modern Aboriginal title law; its reasoning influenced many future Supreme Court cases. Hall declared that in order to extinguish Aboriginal title, the Crown's intention must be "clear and plain."

Furthermore, the onus for proving this intention lies with the Crown, not the Aboriginal claimants. Despite its victory (strictly speaking) in the case, the federal government soon announced a policy of negotiating the settlement of any unextinguished ("comprehensive") land claims, thereby reversing its longstanding position.[15] While a further string of Aboriginal cases arose during the 1970s, the Laskin Court tended to avoid where possible making explicit declarations on the character of Aboriginal title.[16]

The 1982 constitutional amendment transformed the field dramatically by way of two key provisions. Section 35(1) gave constitutional recognition to "existing treaty and aboriginal rights" and section 25 protected these rights from challenges based on other charter guarantees. These clauses were secured in the face of considerable governmental resistance, and only after intense lobbying by the Canadian Aboriginal movement.[17] Once entrenched, however, it was left to the Dickson Court to begin the job of elucidating their meaning. The cases were not long in coming, and three deserve special comment. In *Guerin v. The Queen*, the court elaborated on the Crown's "fiduciary duty" to protect Aboriginal interests, particularly in situations in which their rights to land were being surrendered.[18] Here the Musqueam band in Vancouver sought damages from the disposal of a 1958 lease of reserve lands to the Shaughnessy Golf Course. Federal Indian Affairs staff altered the terms of the proposed lease already approved by the band, resulting in a long-term contract for less than market value. The Supreme Court confirmed the damages awarded at trial, while enunciating a new legal principle. It found that the Crown's broad discretion under the Indian Act is subject to a fiduciary obligation in managing the land on the band's behalf, especially when dealing with third parties. In characterizing the nature of the Indian title conveyed to the Crown, Chief Justice Dickson introduced an important new concept. The Aboriginal interest, he said, was *sui generis* (of its own kind, or unique). It was "personal in the sense that it cannot be transferred to a grantee, but it is also true, as will presently appear, that the interest give rise upon surrender to a distinctive fiduciary obligation on the part of the crown to deal with the land for the benefit of the surrendering Indians."[19] Since *Guerin*, the Supreme Court has clarified the character of "sui generis" several times.

In *Simon v. The Queen*, the constitutional status of Mikmaq hunting rights were in question. This judgment, delivered in 1985, was one of the first to address the scope of s.35(1) *treaty* rights. *Simon* proved to be particularly important to the continuing force of colonial treaties in the Maritime provinces. Chief Justice Dickson ruled that the treaty hunting clauses remained in effect, contrary to provincial government arguments that maintained that they had been extinguished. Dickson also took the opportunity to comment on the appropriate standards for treaty interpretation, holding that "Indian treaties and statutes relating to Indians should be liberally construed and uncertainties resolved in favour of the Indians."[20]

The Dickson Court closed this string of rulings with the 1990 case of *R. v. Sparrow*.[21] This case turned on the interpretation not of treaty but of Aboriginal rights, with the particular question of whether federal Fisheries Regulations could be applied to an Aboriginal food fishery. This opened the more general question of how s.35 Aboriginal rights should be construed, and it is here that the enduring significance is found. In a unanimous judgment, Dickson and La Forest offered a purposive interpretation of s.35(1), such that the rights it recognizes and affirms must be generously interpreted but not treated as absolute. In effect, they confer a measure of protection, though not absolute immunity, from government regulation. Dickson and La Forest outlined a four-stage procedure: the first asks whether the activity in question falls within an Aboriginal right; the second asks whether the Aboriginal right continues to be in effect (i.e., has never been extinguished); the third determines whether a *prima facie* (on the surface) infringement of such a right existed (with the onus to prove lying with the claimant); while the fourth determines whether the infringement is justifiable, according to s.1 of the Charter (with the onus now resting with the Crown). A justifiable infringement requires both a valid legislative objective and a mode of implementation that accords with Ottawa's fiduciary duty (brought forward from *Guerin*), for example, with least possible infringement, with fair compensation, and with consultation. Dickson and La Forest advised that the courts should interpret the purpose of s.35(1) in a generous and liberal way, with awareness of the Aboriginal perspective on the meaning of the rights in question. In the case of *Sparrow*, the Court found an Aboriginal right to fish for food under s.35(1). At the same time that regulations pertaining to food fishing practices infringed on this right, valid conservation measures were found to be a justifiable interference. Furthermore, the ruling made the points that any extinguishment of an Aboriginal right had to be clearly and plainly intended (thereby "writing in" to this judgment the minority position from the *Calder* case), and that laws that regulate a right cannot be construed to extinguish it.

The *Sparrow* judgment is regarded by many legal commentators as a beginning for a generous and balanced approach to Aboriginal rights.[22] It acknowledged the legitimacy of government regulation in defence of important objectives, while also requiring them to be served by the least intrusive methods. *Sparrow* was favourably received by the Aboriginal bar, in part because it called for a flexible interpretation of Aboriginal rights to enable their evolution through time. Unlike the "frozen rights" approach, which ties title to proof of occupation and pattern of use prior to the assertion of Crown sovereignty, *Sparrow* takes a more "contemporary" approach. This "allows for the exercise of ancestral rights in a contemporary form that is not qualified by references to historical and customary uses of land."[23]

Long a key figure in Aboriginal jurisprudence, Chief Justice Dickson retired shortly after the *Sparrow* decision.[24] The considerable substance of these cases raised Native peoples' expectations of constitutionalized rights, while also underlining to governments, such as those of British Columbia and Canada, the virtues of negotiated agreements over extended litigation. It is not coincidental that the B.C. Treaty Claims Task Force was launched in 1990 to explore the prospects for negotiated settlements, and that a formal Treaty Negotiations Process based on the task force's findings began to be used in 1993.

The Lamer Court did not immediately address questions of treaty and Aboriginal rights. However, in the space of a single term in 1996, the Supreme Court considered nine related cases.[25] The centrepiece has become known as the "Van der Peet trilogy," because a common methodology was applied to three cases. The title case asked whether Fisheries Regulations prohibiting the sale and barter of fish obtained under a food fishing licence infringed on an Aboriginal right to sell fish. Writing for the majority, Chief Justice Lamer found that the purpose of s.35(1) is to acknowledge that Aboriginal peoples live on the land in distinctive societies with their own "practices, customs and traditions."[26] Furthermore, to be considered an Aboriginal right, an activity must be a practice, custom, or tradition "of central significance to the culture of the group claiming the right." Since Van der Peet failed to demonstrate that the exchange of fish for either money or goods was integral to the culture prior to European contact (it was judged instead to be "incidental" to the food fishery), there was no need to proceed further with the Sparrow test. Lamer did, however, declare that the evidentiary standards used to judge "integral" and "central" may be different from those in other (non-Aboriginal) legal contexts.

If the Sparrow case was warmly received by legal academics, then Van der Peet was roundly criticized for reviving a "frozen rights" approach. The "practices, customs and traditions" criteria focused attention on historical conditions at the time of contact and sovereignty, with the effect of narrowing the contemporary scope and meaning of these rights. Barsh and Henderson, for example, have described the Lamer Court's approach as "naive imperialism," since "the courts of the colonizer have assumed the authority to define the nature and meaning of Aboriginal cultures."[27] (As we saw above, Chief Justice McEachern was also engulfed in these difficulties in the Delgamuukw trial.) The logic of Van der Peet was soon evident in R. v. Pamajewon. Here the Shawanaga First Nation asserted a right of self-government in refusing to license its casino under Ontario regulations. This case was lost when the Supreme Court applied the Van der Peet test but failed to find a central custom, practice, or tradition integral to the distinctive culture. Bradford Morse has pointed out the evidentiary difficulties involved in meeting such a test when modern activities must be grounded legally in traditional practices. Furthermore, he sees the test tilting the prospects for success toward traditional activities and their derivatives, thus reinforcing a "museum-diorama vision of aboriginal rights."[28]

Brief mention must also be made of two other rulings, R. v. Adams and R. v. Côté. Each involved a defence based on an Aboriginal fishing right, with the Côté case also claiming a treaty right. Here Justice Lamer distinguished between Aboriginal rights from Aboriginal title, thereby enabling rights to be claimed even in cases in which title had been extinguished. Lamer outlines a "spectrum of rights" in terms of their relation to land, with title at one end and practices, customs, and traditions integral to a culture at the other. The possibility of "freestanding rights" was a signal development in Aboriginal law—one which carried important implications for rights of self-government.

DELGAMUUKW IN LAW

Delgamuukw came before the Supreme Court of Canada at a tantalizing moment. Arguments were heard in July 1997, almost a year after the flurry of Aboriginal cases beginning with *Van der Peet.* This time, however, the subject was squarely a *title* question, as distinct from one of Aboriginal *rights* related to traditional activities. Thus, while elements of *Guerin, Sparrow, Van der Peet,* and others would have a bearing, there was room for considerable uncertainty as to their combined impact on a B.C. Aboriginal title dispute. This was magnified by the complexity of the issues arising from the lower courts. To clarify the leading themes, the discussion below will reflect the five questions set out by Chief Justice Lamer in his majority ruling of December 1997.[29] (The concurring judgment by Justice Gerard La Forest is described briefly in Table 6.2 on pages 118–19.)

A. DO THE PLEADINGS PRECLUDE THE COURT FROM ENTERTAINING CLAIMS FOR ABORIGINAL TITLE AND SELF-GOVERNMENT? LAMER: NO.

The first question was whether the form of pleadings (legal contentions) should prevent the court from addressing the claims being pursued. In the initial trial action, the Gitxsan and Wet'suwet'en peoples sought "ownership and jurisdiction" over traditional lands, and it was in these terms that the marathon case was argued. However, on appeal, the tribal groups altered the terms to "aboriginal title and self-government." Furthermore, the individual and house claims from the trial were amended into two communal claims on appeal. British Columbia argued that this constituted a "defect" in the pleadings that both impaired their defence strategy and should prevent a decision from being rendered. The Court responded by ordering a new trial on the merits of the case, but nevertheless answered the questions of title law.

B. WHAT IS THE ABILITY OF THE COURT TO INTERFERE WITH THE FACTUAL FINDINGS MADE BY THE TRIAL JUDGE? LAMER: THE FACTUAL FINDINGS CANNOT STAND. A NEW TRIAL IS ORDERED.

Lamer repeated his caution from *Van der Peet* that appellate courts should refrain from interfering with the facts of trial proceedings, except in the face of "palpable and overriding error." He acknowledged, however, that misapprehensions of material evidence constitute one such exception, and concluded that the trial judge failed to appreciate the evidentiary difficulties of Aboriginal title cases, especially those involving oral histories. Given that the Dickson Court addressed this need as early as the *Simon* case of 1985, McEachern's effective dismissal of such materials posed an obvious problem. Lamer took pains to establish the principle of weighing the oral history evidence on a case-by-case basis, to assess its character as factual material. He did not contend, as has sometimes been described, that it must always be taken into account at face value. However, he did rule that it cannot be excluded or downplayed categorically in an area of law in which the absence of written records poses heavy burdens on Aboriginal litigants. Finally, since McEachern was working before, and without the benefit of, the *Van der Peet* decision (in which Lamer held that ordinary rules of evidence must be adapted), and given the unusual complexity of the trial record, the Chief Justice ordered a new trial in which the evidence could be differently viewed.

C. What Is the Content of Aboriginal Title, How Is It Protected by s. 35(1) of the Constitution Act, 1982, and What Is Required for Its Proof? Lamer: As below.

These questions go to the heart of the judgment and make up its largest and most complex discussion. Here the Court breaks new ground in the law of Aboriginal title. It fills in the substance of the sui generis interest, placing it somewhere between fee simple (private property) and Aboriginal rights of activity (e.g., hunting or fishing) on a tract of Crown land. Furthermore, Aboriginal title entails the right to use land for various purposes related to the traditional attachment to the land, but is subject to the limitation that these use rights not be incompatible with the traditional attachment. Chief Justice Lamer offered the example of paving a tract of land as an incompatible use.

On the nature of the s.35(1) protection, the "spectrum" concept of Aboriginal rights is invoked from the *Adams* case. Aboriginal title sits at one end, with practices, customs, and traditions of an Aboriginal group at the other, and activities related to a *particular* piece of land in the middle. Thus, it is clearly possible to assert free-standing Aboriginal rights or activity-based rights, even when title has been extinguished. This carries important and positive implications for Aboriginal groups that signed land-cession treaties after Confederation, but who may still hold certain rights on Crown land. The influence of academic analysts of Aboriginal law is clearly evident in this discussion of the impact of s.35 on common law, as Lamer several times cited some seminal commentaries.[30]

On the question of proof, Lamer held that a claim of Aboriginal title must show that the land was occupied prior to settlement—a) in a continuing fashion (if present occupation is part of the evidence), and b) exclusively at the time when sovereignty (as distinct from contact) was asserted. Since Aboriginal title is not an absolute right, it may be infringed in a justifiable fashion (building on the *Sparrow* precedent) under the following conditions: First, the legislative objective being pursued by the state must be pressing and substantial. Second, the infringement must be consistent with the Crown's fiduciary duty to Aboriginal peoples. This requires that they be notified (of administrative intention), consulted in advance (in a meaningful way), provide their consent (in certain situations), and receive compensation (for loss of interest). Clearly, this imposes a new level of rigour in weighing infringement, and it places a significant responsibility on the Crown.

D. HAS A CLAIM TO SELF-GOVERNMENT BEEN MADE OUT BY THE APPELLANTS? LAMER: THE NEED FOR A NEW TRIAL MAKES IT IMPOSSIBLE TO MAKE OUT THIS QUESTION.

The issue of self-government attracted relatively little comment from the litigants on appeal. However, Lamer referred to his judgment in *Pamajewon* on the point that rights to self-government cannot be "phrased in excessively general terms" (i.e., that specific rather than blanket assertions of self-government activities are necessary). For this reason, Lamer concluded that the Gitxsan case for self-government is not cognizable under s. 35(1).

E. DID THE PROVINCE HAVE THE POWER TO EXTINGUISH ABORIGINAL RIGHTS AFTER 1871, EITHER UNDER ITS OWN JURISDICTION OR THROUGH THE OPERATION OF S.88 OF THE INDIAN ACT? LAMER: NO TO ALL PARTS.

This question was posed by the province's cross-appeal of Justice MacFarlane's ruling in the Court of Appeal that British Columbia lacked the jurisdiction, after entering Confederation in 1871, to extinguish Aboriginal rights in common law. Chief Justice Lamer upheld MacFarlane, on the basis of division of powers. Since s.91(24) conferred on Ottawa the jurisdiction for "Indians, and Lands Reserved for Indians," it held the exclusive power to extinguish Aboriginal rights (including title). Thus, any attempt by a province to extinguish title by explicit law, or by necessary implication from laws of general application, or by s.88 of the Indian Act (which imports into Indian application provincial laws not mentioning Indians) would be *ultra vires* (beyond its jurisdiction).

LAMER'S CONCLUSION AND DISPOSITION: THE GITXSAN–WET'SUWET'EN APPEAL IS ALLOWED IN PART, WHILE THE BRITISH COLUMBIA CROSS-APPEAL IS DISMISSED AND A NEW TRIAL IS ORDERED.

In a memorable phrase, the Chief Justice closed his judgment by encouraging non-judicial settlements for both Aboriginal rights and title questions: "Ultimately it is through negotiated settlements, with good faith and give and take on all sides, reinforced by the judgments of this Court, that we will achieve ... 'the reconciliation of the pre-existence of aboriginal societies with the sovereignty of the Crown.'"[31]

THE POLITICAL IMPACT OF THE *DELGAMUUKW* RULING

Aftershocks began the morning after the Supreme Court release, as the key players began to explore its significance. The outcome touched a wide range of interests—enhancing some, inhibiting others, altering all of their strategic outlooks. These can be pictured as a succession of concentric circles extending outward from the litigants.

THE EPICENTRE

The Gitxsan and Wet'suwet'en peoples did not gain their particular objectives for a declaration of ownership, since a new trial (with new pleadings) would be required to settle this. However, the McEachern trial and MacFarlane appeal rulings were set aside, thereby erasing the setbacks that had occurred in the British Columbia courts in the early 1990s. Furthermore, the Supreme Court of Canada decision clarified several key legal questions arising in the *Delgamuukw* litigation, involving the nature of Aboriginal title, its relationship to Aboriginal rights, its status under s.35(1) of the Constitution, the tests for justifiable infringement by state policy, and the provincial crown's capacity to extinguish Aboriginal title after 1871. While the Court did not accept the Gitxsan and Wet'suwet'en arguments on all major points, it did provide the tribal groups, and B.C. Aboriginal groups in general, with important new sources of jurisprudential leverage. This shifted the coordinates for future litigation, and set the context for a possible new trial. It was in this sense that the appellants' lawyers characterized the judgment as "a complete victory for us."[32] However, the Court also stressed the advisability of negotiating rather than litigating such disputes, and it invited all governments and Aboriginal parties to explore alternative settings for dispute settlement.

Measured against its courtroom arguments, the British Columbia government fared far less well. Its narrow view of Aboriginal title was rejected, and the arguments about prior extinction, which had been accepted in the lower courts, failed to persuade the Supreme Court of Canada. At the same time, the Court confirmed the possibility that state policy could be justified, under certain conditions, even as it infringed on existing Aboriginal title. Of particular importance here was the discussion of consultation and compensation for encroachment on Aboriginal interests in Crown (and certain private) lands. This offered guidance both for future litigation (given that the province continues to be party to a variety of legal actions involving title questions) and for future negotiations. Indeed, for British Columbia, the implications of *Delgamuukw* for the broader legal domain were crucial. Within only months of the decision, the province was answering new challenges in its courts. Future litigation seems inevitable, given the need to further define the limits and balances of new key terms such as consultation, compensation, and consent.

Looking beyond claims litigation, the *Delgamuukw* decision forced a fundamental review of two extraordinarily important provincial policy regimes: the B.C. treaty negotiation process; and the B.C. Crown lands and resources management system. Both were cast into doubt by this ruling, which was handed down on December 11, 1997. By the close of 1997, some forty-two First Nations groups were involved in the tripartite treaty negotiating process announced in 1994. The question arose as to whether the *Delgamuukw* decision had undercut this four-year-old treaty process as the leading path toward settlement of title claims.

In the days following the decision's release, a high-level civil service task force was struck to identify changes that might have to be made to the negotiating process.[33] Reporting six weeks later, it concluded that "the credibility of the treaty process is in question," and offered proposals to revitalize the process and prevent tribal groups from abandoning negotiations.[34] Indeed, the First Nations Summit presented a formal statement to federal and provincial ministers that outlined a new, post-*Delgamuukw* relationship. Central to this was an immediate freeze on the further alienation of land and resources, and the negotiation of "interim measures" to protect the integrity of Aboriginal rights and title, pending the achievement of final settlements. Otherwise the Summit predicted the breakdown of the treaty process.[35] In March 1998, a tripartite review of the treaty process was announced. Among the issues addressed were ways to streamline and accelerate negotiations on land, resource, and cash settlement. These talks continued over the next four months; agreement, however, proved elusive.

In 1998, treaty talks and land and resource management regimes became inextricably tied. All treaty parties recognized the explosive implications of Lamer's ruling for the continued exercise of property rights in the forest, mining, real estate, and other sectors. The central fact was the continuing existence of Aboriginal title interest in virtually all B.C. lands. While the Court recognized that the provincial Crown could infringe on this interest in certain circumstances, the justificatory test outlined new standards for consultation and compensation that existing policy did not meet. This prompted a wide spectrum of political initiatives as the year progressed.

A number of tribal groups launched or threatened court actions for recognition of their Aboriginal interest in Crown lands. The Sechelt band, considered quite moderate since it negotiated a self-government deal with Ottawa in 1986, began a case for co-sovereignty over Crown lands along the Sunshine Coast. The Tsilhqot'in of the Interior Tribal Council called for a moratorium on new Crown tenure decisions by provincial departments, warning civil servants that they would be held professionally and privately accountable for any transactions contrary to the *Delgamuukw* standards.[36] In its January statement, the First Nations Summit insisted on "full and informed consent" for any infringement of Aboriginal title. This represented a significant stretch of the Supreme Court's requirement for genuine consultation in all cases and consent in some. Soon the debate was centred on the possible existence of a "veto power" over Crown land applications, with Premier Clark firmly dismissing this possibility (though it was obviously not his decision to make).[37] Local actions continued to mount across the province in succeeding months. The Gitanyow people from the Nass Valley made a statement of claim for traditional occupation of 94 percent of the Nisga'a tribal territory, which was already under settlement negotiation. In the northeast of the province, the Takla Lake and Tsay Keh Dene bands sought to halt development of the Kemess mine, on the grounds that environmental assessments infringed on Aboriginal title.[38]

One of the first cases to come to court involved the Kitkatla Band's opposition to International Forest Products' plan to clearcut one hundred acres of old-growth forest near Prince Rupert. The band obtained an interim injunction (to block the cut), which it sought to make permanent in June 1998.[39] Several *Delgamuukw* findings were at issue, including whether the band had been adequately consulted before logging began, and what degree of consultation was appropriate to the level of Aboriginal interest at stake. The band argued that IFP's effort at consultation was merely token, while the company contended that it had made great efforts to contact and consult. The Kitkatla also argued that the area may have special cultural significance as a burial ground.[40] After Justice Mary Southin denied the permanent injunction in B.C. Supreme Court, the case moved to the provincial Court of Appeal.[41] Here a panel of three judges upheld the denial, finding that the level of consultation had been adequate. (IFP, it was found, had consulted with the Laxkwalaams First Nation, whose claims included the forest area in question. When the Kitkatla Band signalled an overlapping claim, additional talks were held, but without resolution. On the degree of Aboriginal interest, the Court of Appeal was influenced by the fact that the Kitkatla did not occupy the land.)[42]

These events were paralleled by a sustained campaign by non-Aboriginal (business and municipal) interests that expressed grave concerns about the sudden uncertainty over their existing tenure rights. Business associations pressed the Clark NDP government to resolve the confusion quickly and decisively. While warning that it would "defend forest industry tenure rights if litigation continues," the B.C. Council of Forest Industries declared itself "encouraged by the Court's new parameters for infringement which give enhanced opportunities for forestry and other development to proceed unimpeded."[43] Uncompromising proposals also circulated among business audiences.[44] This hardened attitude was reflected in the positions of the provincial Liberal and federal Reform Parties. The Liberals insisted that any negotiated treaty rights be contingent on the surrender of

Aboriginal title. Their response to *Delgamuukw* was aligned with a wider insistence on finality, certainty, and the protection of the public interest, declaring that "[i]t's time we had one law and one set of rights that applies equally to all British Columbians."[45] The federal Reform Party also took up the critique, pressing for Parliamentary action in response to the uncertainty following *Delgamuukw*. Its approach was modelled on the Australian Native Title Act, which was passed by the Australian lower house in 1996, but blocked by the Senate.[46] The Reform Party accelerated its campaign in Parliament in June 1998, as Preston Manning demanded legislation to pare down the scope of Aboriginal title and end a potential federal–provincial crisis over resource jurisdiction.[47]

The government of British Columbia responded to this vortex of controversy by developing a comprehensive set of *Consultation Guidelines* for decisions involving Aboriginal title.[48] Setting aside the question of whether and where Aboriginal title exists, these norms were designed to assist B.C. officials in fulfilling the spirit of consultation under *Delgamuukw*. They were outlined and the text of the guidelines distributed in training sessions to administrative staff over a month-long period.

INTERMEDIATE IMPACTS

The other party to the title negotiations, and the respondent in the *Delgamuukw* case, was the government of Canada. Ottawa played several special roles. The federal Crown was the only authority to whom Aboriginal title could be surrendered. It also bore significant liabilities for the compensation due to Aboriginal people through the process of surrender and was subject to the fiduciary obligations set out by the Court. These points ensured that Canada, no less than British Columbia, faced higher standards of performance as a result of the ruling. While the tripartite treaty review continued into the summer of 1998, the federal Minister of Indian Affairs announced the formation of a "capacity panel," that would propose measures to enhance the organizational capacity of band and tribal groups in negotiating and implementing both treaty and land questions.[49]

Across Canada, Aboriginal peoples examined the *Delgamuukw* judgment closely. The Gitxsan had secured a declaration of ownership, with an elaboration of the rights this entailed. It had a powerful influence on other groups with unextinguished claims to title, underlining their conviction that they had an enforceable case in law. *Delgamuukw* spoke also to the concerns of Native peoples asserting land-related rights at other points on the Aboriginal rights "spectrum." In New Brunswick and Nova Scotia, for example, a growing number of Mikmaq have asserted, since 1995, a right to harvest logs on Crown land. Here the vanguard court action involved Thomas Peter Paul, a New Brunswick Mikmaq charged with illegal logging. His defence combined colonial treaty rights and Aboriginal rights. Released in the midst of the Peter Paul litigation, the Supreme Court ruling in *Delgamuukw* offered new and expanded grounds to assert an Aboriginal interest in lands and forests.[50] One year later, a similar political claim arose in northern Alberta, where Cree tribal authorities asserted a continuing interest in oil and gas resources on Crown lands. With the threat of litigation as a lever, industry interests were approached to negotiate "benefits" packages including training, employment, and subcontracting.[51] Cases such as these can be treated as harbingers of a new politics of Aboriginal title claims.

ASSESSMENT OF THE SUPREME COURT JUDGMENT IN *DELGAMUUKW*

Of its landmark status there can be no doubt. *Delgamuukw* provides new perspectives on Aboriginal title by specifying some of its sui generis features. An Aboriginal interest in land requires that the holders be consulted in meaningful ways over its regulation and use, and that they be compensated in certain cases. *Delgamuukw* also confirms a distinct set of evidentiary standards for future Aboriginal title and rights litigation. Furthermore, it clarifies the criteria by which Crown infringements on Aboriginal title must be justified, if law and policy are to be sustained in the face of encroachment. Finally, it urges the parties to Aboriginal title issues to resolve their disputes by negotiation rather than litigation.

One measure of the importance of the Supreme Court ruling in *Delgamuukw* is its impact on politics beyond the courts. Almost immediately, the government of British Columbia was forced to review its treaty negotiating process, and its Crown land and resource management regime. On the treaty front, the matter of "interim measures" (actions taken in anticipation of final agreements) assumed new importance, as did the question of negotiating parameters. In resource management, new arrangements for Aboriginal consultation, consent, and compensation were required on a systematic basis for Crown administration to remain intact. Ottawa also recognized its heightened responsibility for "capacity building" among Aboriginal groups. More generally, nontreaty peoples explored their changing legal prospects in the light of *Delgamuukw*, both in the province of British Columbia and beyond. Maritime Mikmaq asserted new ownership and commercial rights to exploit Crown timber resources in New Brunswick, Nova Scotia, and Quebec. In northern Alberta, the Cree asserted a new interest in the oil and gas industry, based on an extended view of Aboriginal title.

At the same time, the Supreme Court's *Delgamuukw* ruling opens as many question as it answers. The new thresholds of consultation, consent, and compensation seem destined for future court challenge. The "practices, customs and traditions" criteria and the culture-at-point-of-sovereignty assessments will also demand further review. Whether *Delgamuukw* has firmly altered the direction of Aboriginal title doctrine, as suggested here, will hinge on future words from the judicial oracle. It will only become clear as the Lamer Court and its successors address new disputes still latent in the fabric of Aboriginal–Crown relations.

TABLE 6.2   *Delgamuukw v. British Columbia, 1997—Summary of Supreme Court of Canada Ruling*

Lamer, C.J., for Cory, McLachlin, and Major*	La Forest for L'Heureux-Dubé*
A. Do the Pleadings Preclude the Court from Entertaining Claims for Aboriginal Title and Self-government? The defect in the pleadings prevent the Court from considering the merits of the appeal. New trial ordered.	In addition to the technical defect, there was a substantive defect to the pleadings: an absolute interest in land and jurisdiction requires proof of governance as opposed to occupation only.
B. What Is the Ability of the Court to Interfere with the Factual Findings Made by the Trial Judge? The trial judge's treatment of oral history did not satisfy the principles set by Chief Justice Lamer in *Van der Peet*. Oral histories may be considered in the new trial.	
C. What Is the Content of Aboriginal Title? How Is It Protected by S.35(1) of the Constitution Act, 1982, and What Is Required for Its Proof? Aboriginal title is *sui generis*, lying somewhere between fee simple and Aboriginal rights of activity. It is a right in land, conferring the right to use land for a variety of purposes, but subject to the limitation that they not be incompatible with the nature of the attachment to the land. Aboriginal title at common law is fully protected under s. 35(1). These rights fall along a spectrum—with practices, customs, and traditions integral to an Aboriginal group at one end, activities related to a particular piece of land in the middle, and Aboriginal title to the land at the other end. To make out a claim for Aboriginal title, the group asserting the title must show that: the land was occupied prior to settlement continually (where present occupation is offered as proof) and exclusively at the time sovereignty was asserted.	The *sui generis* interest is personal (alienable only to the Crown) and subject to a fiduciary obligation for fair treatment. Title is an Aboriginal right to occupy and possess, and should be distinguished from discrete rights to engage in an Aboriginal activity in a particular area. *Van der Peet* dealt with the latter. But the key features of *Van der Peet*—precision (of practices), specificity (of area), continuity (of occupation or use), and centrality (of importance)—are still central.

TABLE 6.2 *Delgamuukw v. British Columbia,* 1997—Summary of Supreme Court of Canada Ruling (cont.)

Like other Aboriginal rights asserted under s.35(1), Aboriginal title is not absolute. It may be infringed by the federal or provincial Crown, subject to the following test of justification: the infringement must be in furtherance of a compelling and substantial legislative objective, and the infringement must be consistent with the special fiduciary responsibility between Crown and Aboriginal peoples. This entails good-faith consultation and sometimes full consent, and compensation.

Under part two of the justification test the accommodation of Aboriginal peoples' interests is a broad obligation including notifying, consulting, and negotiating. Fair compensation is not equated with fee simple price but may vary by site and interdependence of traditional uses, in keeping with the good faith of the crown.

D. Has a Claim to Self-government Been Made out by the Appellants?
The need for a new trial makes it impossible to make out this question.

There is insufficient evidence for a determination.

E. Did the Province Have the Power to Extinguish Aboriginal Rights after 1871, Either under Its Own Jurisdiction or through the Operation of S.88 of the Indian Act?
Provincial governments are prevented, on jurisdictional grounds, from legislating extinguishment—directly, by laws of general application, or by s.88—since those rights form part of the core of Indianness in s.91(24).

The province has no authority to extinguish Aboriginal rights.

The best approach in these types of cases is a process of negotiation and reconciliation.

The appeal is allowed in part, the cross-appeal is dismissed, and a new trial ordered.

Allowed in part, cross-appeal dismissed, and new trial ordered.

*Justice Sopinka was present at the appeal but died before the decision was issued.

ENDNOTES

1. Kirk Makin, "Lamer Worries about Public Backlash," *The Globe and Mail*, 6 February 1999, A1.

2. For details, see Paul Tennant, *Aboriginal Peoples and Politics: The Land Question in British Columbia, 1849–1989* (Vancouver: University of British Columbia Press, 1990), Chapter 8. The amendment was a direct response to the work of the Allied Tribes of British Columbia, an Indian organization that subsequently collapsed.

3. In this chapter, I will use the spelling *Gitxsan*, following the lead of the tribal authorities. Many court documents and journalistic accounts also use the spelling *Gitksan*.

4. The authoritative account of Gitxsan and Wet'suwet'en society, from precontact days to the present, is Dara Culhane, *The Pleasure of the Crown* (Vancouver: Talon Books, 1997).

5. *Delgamuukw v. British Columbia*, [1991] 79 D.L.R. (4th) 185.

6. Frank Cassidy, ed., *Aboriginal Title in British Columbia:* Delgamuukw v. The Queen (Montreal: Institute for Research in Public Policy, 1992).

7. Court of Appeal for British Columbia, *Delgamuukw v. British Columbia*, [1993] 104 D.L.R. (4th) 470.

8. On the origins and design of the B.C. treaty process, see Christopher McKee, *Treaty Talks in British Columbia* (Vancouver, University of British Columbia Press, 1996).

9. For an interpretation of the political background and the litigation, see Tennant, *Aboriginal Peoples and Politics*.

10. For a comparison of the Nisga'a, the Nuu-chah-nulth, and the Gitxsan–Wet'suwet'en comprehensive claims, see Cassidy, "Aboriginal Land Claims in British Columbia," in Ken Coates, ed., *Aboriginal Land Claims in Canada* (Mississauga: Copp Clark Pitman, 1992).

11. A useful edited collection of prominent Supreme Court cases to 1990 is Peter Kulchyski, ed., *Unjust Relations: Aboriginal Rights in Canadian Courts* (Don Mills: Oxford University Press, 1994).

12. Sally Weaver, *The Making of Canadian Indian Policy* (Toronto: University of Toronto Press, 1974).

13. For a discussion of Aboriginal law to 1971, see Peter Cumming and Neil Mickenberg, eds., *Native Rights in Canada*, rev. ed. (Toronto: General Publishing, 1972).

14. *Calder v. Attorney-General of B.C.*, [1973] 1 S.C.R. 313–427. Justice Pigeon declined to address the substance of Aboriginal title, due to a technical deficiency. He found that, in the absence of a grant of fiat from the B.C. lieutenant-governor (a requirement for such litigation), the Supreme Court lacked the jurisdiction to hear the case.

15. The literature on comprehensive claims negotiation is vast. One useful survey of the issues, as they stood in the 1980s, can be found in the Task Force to Review Comprehensive Claims Policy, *Living Treaties, Lasting Agreements* (Ottawa: Department of Indian Affairs and Northern Development, 1985). For an analysis of one major settlement (the Nunavut claim) achieved under this process, see Peter Clancy, "The Politics and Administration of Aboriginal Claims Settlements," in M.W. Westmacott and Hugh Mellon, eds., *Public Administration and Policy* (Scarborough: Prentice Hall, 1999).

16. Bradford W. Morse, ed., *Aboriginal Peoples and the Law* (Ottawa: Carleton University Press, 1985), 81.

17. See, for example, Douglas Sanders, "The Indian Lobby," in R.E.B. Simeon, ed., *And No One Cheered* (Montreal: McGill-Queen's University Press, 1983).

18. *Guerin v. The Queen*, [1984] 2 S.C.R. 335–94.

19. Ibid., 382.

20. *Simon v. The Queen,* [1985] 2 S.C.R. 390–413.

21. *R. v. Sparrow,* [1990] 1 S.C.R. 1075–1122.

22. Not all analysts would agree with this appraisal of *Sparrow,* and the level of crit-icism may grow as the perspective shifts from the specifically legal context to the wider per-spective of power relations. Parmesh Sharma (in *Aboriginal Fishing Rights* [Halifax: Fernwood Publishing, 1998], 78) has argued, for example, that "[i]n both legal and prac-tical terms, *Sparrow* has not served the interests of aboriginal peoples. It has failed [them] in two significant ways: the legal decision itself has failed them and so has the state's response."

23. Catherine Bell, "New Directions in the Law of Aboriginal Rights," *Canadian Bar Review* 77 (1998): 42.

24. After departing the Court, Brian Dickson continued to be involved in Aboriginal issues. He was appointed by Prime Minister Brian Mulroney to serve as Special Representative, recommending the establishment of the Royal Commission on Aboriginal Peoples in 1991. Dickson's retired Supreme Court colleague, the Hon. Bertha Wilson, served as a commissioner, while Quebec Judge René Dussault co-chaired the inquiry. The commission issued its five-volume *Report of the Royal Commission on Aboriginal Peoples* (Ottawa: Supply and Services) in December 1996.

25. In order of release, the cases include: *R. v. Badger,* [1996] 1 S.C.R. 771–824; *R. v. Lewis,* [1996] 1 S.C.R. 921–961; *R. v. Nikal,* [1996] 1 S.C.R. 1013–1073; *R. v. Van der Peet,* [1996] 2 S.C.R., 507–661; *R. v. N.T.C. Smokehouse Ltd.,* [1996] 2 S.C.R. 672–721; *R. v. Gladstone,* [1996] 2 S.C.R. 723–820 (the last three collectively known as the *Van der Peet* trilogy); *R. v. Pamajewon,* [1996] 2 S.C.R. 821–841; *R. v. Adams,* [1996] 3 S.C.R. 101–138; and *R. v. Côté,* [1996] 3 S.C.R. 139–198.

26. *R. v. Van der Peet,* [1996] 2 S.C.R. 507.

27. Russel L. Barsh and James Y. Henderson, "The Supreme Court's Van der Peet Trilogy: Naive Imperialism and Ropes of Sand," *McGill Law Journal* 42 (1997): 1002.

28. Bradford W. Morse, "Permafrost Rights: Aboriginal Self-Government and the Supreme Court in *R. v. Pamajewon,*" *McGill Law Journal* 42 (1997): 1030.

29. In addition to being reported in the leading law reports, this judgment can be found in book form, in Stan Persky (Intro.), *Delgamuukw* (Vancouver: Greystone Books, 1998).

30. These include Kent McNeil, *Common Law Aboriginal Title* (Oxford: Clarendon Press, 1989) and "The Meaning of Aboriginal Title," in M. Asch, ed., *Aboriginal and Treaty Rights in Canada* (Vancouver: University of British Columbia Press, 1997); William Pentney, "The Rights of the Aboriginal Peoples of Canada in the Constitution Act, 1982, Part II – Section 35: the Substantive Guarantee," *U.B.C. Law Review* 22 (1988); Brian Slattery, "The Constitutional Guarantee of Aboriginal and Treaty Rights," *Queen's Law Journal* 8 (1982–83) and "Understanding Aboriginal Rights," *Canadian Bar Review* 66 (1987): 727–83.

31. *Delgamuukw v. British Columbia,* [1997] 3 S.C.R. 1010, para 186.

32. Robert Matas, "Natives Win on Land Rights," *The Globe and Mail,* 12 December 1997, A1.

33. Settlers in Support of Indigenous Sovereignty, "Leaked B.C. NDP Report Reveals Post-Delgamuukw Strategy: Achieve Certainty," Press Release, 10 February 1998, Victoria.

34. "Land Claim Case Fallout Seen," *Vancouver Sun,* 11 February 1998, A1.

35. First Nations Summit, "Statement to Minister Stewart and Minister Cashore," 31 January 1998, North Vancouver, B.C.

36. Stephen Hume, "Crown Land Lawsuit Looms," *Vancouver Sun*, 17 January 1998, B3.

37. Justine Hunter, "Clark Denies Aboriginal Veto Power," *Vancouver Sun*, 11 April 1998.

38. Jeffrey Simpson, "Consequences of Delgamuukw Decision Now Ticking in B.C.," *The Globe and Mail*, 26 May 1998, A22.

39. Jim Beatty, "Forest Industry Joins Interfor in Logging Fight," *Vancouver Sun*, 19 June 1998; Jim Beatty, "Decision Reserved in Logging Case," *Vancouver Sun*, 20 June 1998.

40. *Hill v. Minister of Forests*, McEachern, C.J., 24 June 1998; *Hill v. Minister of Forests*, Southin, J.A., 25 June 1998; and B.C. Superior Court's homepage: www.courts.gov.bc.ca.

41. Ina Bailey, "Special Court Hearing Set for Natives to Oppose Interfor Logging," *Canadian Press*, 1 July 1998; Greg Joyce, "Kitkatla Claim Moral Victory Despite Court Dismissal," *Canadian Press*, 6 July 1998.

42. *Hill v. Minister of Forests*, Court of Appeal for British Columbia, 6 July 1998, *B.C. Superior Courts Homepage*, ibid.

43. Council of Forest Industries, "Supreme Court Judgement on Delgamuukw v. British Columbia," News Release, 12 December 1997, Vancouver.

44. Melvin Smith, Speech to Vancouver Board of Trade, 10 February 1998.

45. B.C. Liberal Party, "Aboriginal Treaties: One Law for All"; "NDP Dithering on Delgamuukw: A Prescription for Economic Paralysis," Press Releases, 2 February 1998.

46. Ted White, M.P., "Confusion Reigns," Press Release, 25 March 1998.

47. Peter O'Neil, "Manning Asks Ottawa to Pare Down B.C. Land Claims," *Vancouver Sun*, 9 June 1998, A1, and "Who Owns B.C., Reform Asks Ottawa," *Vancouver Sun*, 10 June 1998, A4.

48. Government of British Columbia, *Consultation Guidelines*, Victoria, September 1998.

49. Canada. Indian and Northern Affairs. "Canada Demonstrates Commitment to Revitalizing B.C. Treaty Process," News Release, 7 July 1998, Ottawa.

50. Mikmaq loggers drew moral and legal inspiration from the Supreme Court's ruling in *Delgamuukw*. Although this decision was available to the New Brunswick Court of Appeal in its review of the Peter Paul case, the court found that the *Sparrow/Van der Peet* provisions were not met. See *R. v. Peter Paul*, [1998] N.B.C.A. *LawPost* N.B.C. No.4453.

51. See the following articles by Carol Howes: "Anger Over Oilpatch Deals with Bands," *National Post*, 4 February 1999, C1; "First Nations Sue Alberta Over Oil Exploration," *National Post*, 5 February 1999, D1; "Alberta Indian Chiefs, Oil Firms, Hold Closed-Door Talks," *National Post*, 8 February 1999; and "Alberta Blasts Bands Oilpatch Squeeze," *National Post*, 12 February 1999, C1.

PERSONAL AUTONOMY AND EXPRESSION

PART 3

LIBERALISM, FEMINISM, AND PORNOGRAPHY:

REGINA V. BUTLER

Richard Vernon and
Samuel LaSelva

In 1992, the Supreme Court of Canada handed down its landmark decision of *Regina v. Butler*.[1] Donald Butler, owner of an adult video store in Winnipeg, had been charged five years earlier with seventy-seven counts of selling or renting "hard core" material under the obscenity provision of the Criminal Code. At trial, he was convicted on eight counts; the Manitoba Court of Appeal subsequently entered convictions with respect to all the material. On further appeal the Supreme Court ordered a new trial on the grounds that both the trial judge and the Court of Appeal had failed to apply the proper test of obscenity. In so doing, the Court took several important steps in the interpretation of obscenity law and its relationship to freedom of expression under the Charter of Rights—steps that were widely regarded as path breaking and were particularly welcomed by many women's groups. Writing in *The Globe and Mail*, a well-known feminist was euphoric: "This is a stunning legal victory for women, this is of world historic importance."[2]

We will explain and comment on some of the choices faced by the Court in making its decision, especially in relation to obscenity, community standards, free expression, and harm. Our primary objective is to determine whether, in taking steps in the direction favoured by many feminist advocates of the restriction of pornography, the Supreme Court's ruling in the *Butler* case thereby abandoned the mode of liberalism embodied in the Charter. Our conclusion will be that it did not.

TWO TESTS FOR OBSCENITY

Obscenity is a difficult topic for liberal jurisprudence, partly because there is no consensus about what rights individuals should have, and partly because its suppression raises difficult questions about what kinds of objectives states can properly pursue. It is instructive, however, to examine from the perspective of liberal jurisprudence two of the most famous tests for obscenity—the Hicklin rule and the community standards test. Although both tests still enjoy varying degrees of support among judges and members of the public in general, neither test now occupies the pride of place it once did. Liberal jurisprudence has exposed difficulties in both tests. In doing so, it has contributed much to the development of more appropriate tests for obscenity, thus demonstrating the vitality of its own principles.

Developed by an English court in 1868 and subsequently used by Canadian judges until 1959, the Hicklin rule stipulates that "the test for obscenity is this, whether the tendency of the matter charged as obscene is to deprave and corrupt those whose minds are open to such immoral influences."[3] One difficulty with the Hicklin rule is that it is too open-ended, thereby putting at risk freedoms that people rightfully desire to exercise and creating the danger that judges will apply their personal beliefs about what is clean or dirty, right or wrong. An important function of free speech is to allow people to challenge traditional but repressive social taboos, yet the Hicklin rule can be used to defend even the most reactionary social order. Another difficulty is that it has the effect of reducing adults to the status of children. A famous American judge, Learned Hand, believed the Hicklin rule reduced the "treatment of sex to the standard of a child's library." The time would come, he hoped, when truth, beauty, and even sex "are too precious to society at large to be mutilated in the interests of those most likely to pervert them to base uses."[4] Finally, why should the law take an interest in depravity and corruption as such? In a classic defence of individual freedom and minority rights, John Stuart Mill argued that no punishment should attach to thoughts or tastes, precisely because the role of the state is to keep the peace among co-citizens whose thoughts and tastes are different. What Mill feared in *On Liberty* was that a community would think itself justified in imposing its own standards of propriety on individuals and minorities simply because they are its own standards, and would tolerate nothing that offended the beliefs of the majority.[5] The problem with the Hicklin rule is not that it attaches too little importance to freedom, but that it gives freedom no weight at all.

In 1959, a new era of Canadian obscenity law began with the enactment of a new definition in the Criminal Code that stipulates that "any publication a dominant characteristic of which is the undue exploitation of sex, or of sex and of any one or more of the following subjects, namely, crime, horror, cruelty and violence, shall be deemed to be obscene." It was under this provision that Donald Butler was charged. Although the new provision avoided some of the pitfalls of the Hicklin rule, it contained ambiguities and other difficulties. The second clause of the provision refers to the presence of such things as cruelty and violence, which are not only a good deal clearer than the obscure "depravity" of the Hicklin test, but can be established in a relatively uncontroversial way. The first clause, however, appeals to the idea of the "undue" exploitation of sex, a very open-ended and, potentially, a highly subjective criterion. In this regard the Code's new obscenity provision hardly makes progress in terms of precision, and seems to postulate two criteria, one of a factual kind, the other wholly open to interpretation.

In 1962, in the case of *Brodie v. The Queen*, the Supreme Court had striven to make sense of the "undueness" test and to mitigate its open-ended character. Principally the Court attempted to do so by importing a further test in terms of "community standards." Quoting an Australian decision, Justice Judson held: "There are certain standards of decency which prevail in the community.... What is obscene is something which offends against those standards." The community standards test, Judson acknowledged, had been criticized as unwarranted judicial legislation. But the criticism, he insisted, was not altogether valid. A judge or a jury can either apply personal opinions about what constitutes obscenity or can base the decision on the standards of the community. "Of the two," he reasoned, "... the second is the better choice."[6] In a sense, the appeal to community standards—like the appeal to the presence of cruelty or violence—is an appeal to fact: the community either does or does not have certain standards. However, community standards are majoritarian by definition and afford, as a result, even less protection for individual and minority rights than the ill-fated Hicklin rule.[7]

Eventually, the Supreme Court took several steps to blunt the objectionable force of the appeal to community standards. In 1985, in the *Towne Cinema* case, it was held that the "standards" in question must be taken as standards of *tolerance* and not of *taste*: that is, "what matters is not what Canadians think is right for themselves to see ... [but] what they would not abide other Canadians seeing because it would be beyond the contemporary Canadian standard of tolerance." There has to be an intervening judgment in addition to feeling offended or disgusted, before sexual depiction can be judged "undue." In a concurring opinion, Madam Justice Wilson made much the same point by insisting that judgments about undueness must be consequential ones; they must be based on some evidence about the undesirable effects of the material in question. Chief Justice Dickson went one step further—he said that exploitation of sex is undue if it has degrading or dehumanizing effects, and it would be undue even if the community were willing to tolerate such effects.[8]

Part of the significance of *Butler* is that it spells out the rationale hinted at by Chief Justice Dickson. In *Butler*, Justice Sopinka not only commented on the need to establish a norm for determining what amounts to an undue exploitation of sex, but also insisted that "courts must determine as best they can what the community would tolerate others being exposed to on the basis of the degree of harm that may flow from such exposure."[9] He then said that depictions that couple sex with violence or cruelty will "almost always" be intolerable; sexual depictions that, without being violent, are degrading and dehumanizing, will be intolerable "if the risk of harm is substantial"; other forms of explicit sexual depiction are generally tolerated.[10] This is a reasoned and moderate position. But does it owe anything to the "community standards" test? Pornography that combines sex with violence or cruelty is forbidden by the Criminal Code, and not by any appeal to community standards. And even if there are widely held views in Canadian society that coincide broadly with the Court's rejection of degradation and dehumanization, it is not their being widely held that makes them relevant. Rather, they are relevant because they embody, in the Court's opinion, a reasonable way of interpreting the Criminal Code. The community's own beliefs are not decisive in the process enunciated in the *Butler* decision. At the very least, it is misleading to disguise this process as an application of community standards. And if, from the standpoint of individual liberty, the community standards test is as oppressive as the Hicklin rule, then it would be better to let the community standards test share the same fate as the Hicklin rule, rather than to preserve it by judicial ingenuity.

CHARTER FREEDOM OF EXPRESSION GUARANTEES

In *Butler,* the Supreme Court had to confront the issue of how obscenity should be defined. But it also had to consider whether or not the obscenity provision of the Criminal Code violated the guarantees of freedom of expression in the Charter. Expression is an important value in Canada and other liberal societies, and it is closely connected with a large number of other basic social and political values such as personal autonomy, the pursuit of truth, social progress, and political democracy. Even if a publication were reliably known to be obscene, there still would be the issue of the importance of free expression. On what basis should liberal societies criminalize *any* form of publication, even one acknowledged to be obscene?

A possible and important line of argument, which the Supreme Court might have espoused, takes seriously the differences between the various kinds of expression. "Freedom of expression," it might be argued, is an imprecise phrase, and what is really valued is something narrower than "expression." *Some* forms of expression have socially important consequences; but obviously, such consequences cannot be ascribed to all the activities that we might call "expressive." We have already mentioned Mill, whose book *On Liberty* is a standard point of reference for liberal ideas. Mill's book contains an important chapter that makes a powerful case for what he calls the "absolute" liberty of "thought and discussion." He believes "discussion" should be absolutely free because of the benefits that it has in terms of "human progress," that is, the enlargement of our understanding of the world we live in and of our ability to shape it in advantageous ways. But nowhere does he defend anything so comprehensive as "expression." It is certainly doubtful, to say the least, that his argument could be made to cover the videotapes sold by Donald Butler.

Instead of defending "expression" generally, we might defend specific forms of expression, such as political debate or scientific inquiry or artistic creativity, that have nothing to do with pornography at all.[11] In *Butler,* that route was taken by the Manitoba Court of Appeal. Writing for the majority, Mr. Justice Huband appealed to the existence of something that he referred to as "meaning." Only forms of expression that communicated meaning were protected by section 2(b) of the Charter. The videotapes in question depicted "purely physical" activity that did not even attempt to convey a meaning. "It does not appear," he wrote, "that the obscenity provisions of the Code have thwarted or subverted anyone in conveying or attempting to convey a meaningful message."[12] An American political philosopher has made much the same point. "At its most extreme," writes Frederick Schauer, "hard core pornography is a sex aid, no more and no less." It is not speech or communication in any significant sense; and although it may be protected by a "free sex principle," it is not covered by the principle of free speech.[13]

The Supreme Court disagreed. All forms of nonviolent expression are covered by section 2(b) of the Charter, even if their content is objectionable. As the Court said in *Irwin Toy*: "Freedom of expression was entrenched ... so as to ensure that everyone can manifest their thoughts, opinions, beliefs ... however unpopular, distasteful or contrary to the mainstream."[14] The Court reaffirmed this principle in the famous *Keegstra* case decided two years before *Butler*, when what was at issue was the distribution of "hate literature" directed at a religious minority. Chief Justice Dickson acknowledged that the content of James Keegstra's opinions was offensive and demeaning in the extreme. But Keegstra's hate message undoubtedly conveyed a meaning, and was covered by section 2(b). The fact that his message was "invidious and obnoxious is beside the point."[15] Of course, Keegstra did not escape punishment; yet his conviction recognized the principle that even hate propaganda was covered by freedom of expression. The Court applied the same principle in the *Butler* case. Even the offensive and demeaning content of pornography, it held, was covered by section 2(b) of the Charter.

The Court's broad interpretation of the meaning of "expression" has several disadvantages. An absolute right to express anything at all would seem to rest on an understanding of liberalism that celebrates an atomistic view of the individual, and exalts personal freedom whatever its cost to other values. Not only does it seem likely that only a minority of Canadians would support a political philosophy of that kind, but putting the pornographer's freedom on the same level as the citizen's political freedom or the scientist's freedom of inquiry might weaken support for freedoms and rights of all kinds, and diminish the more valuable ones. Celebrating expression as such also risks increasing skepticism about "rights." Even before the Charter was adopted, many feared that rights discourse would lead to a fanatical absolutism incapable of acknowledging the importance of social and political compromise. Finally, a "right" is stronger than a "freedom." To have a right, according to an influential school of thought, is to have an interest that is in itself so compelling that it puts other people under a duty to respect it.[16] Surely any interest that one might have in selling or viewing pornography could hardly be *that* important?

On the other hand, the Court's approach also has an advantage. In a liberal society such as our own, the use of coercion requires justification precisely because individual freedom is regarded as a basic value. If this is so, then there is a presumption in favour of freedom, even though it can be overridden by powerful appeals to other values. The Charter of Rights recognizes the existence of this presumption under section 1, the reasonable limits clause. In *Regina v. Oakes,* the Supreme Court insisted that section 1 has two functions: it guarantees the rights set out in the Charter and states explicitly the justificatory criteria against which limitations must be measured. As the Charter acknowledges, Canada is a "free and democratic society," and these underlying values "are the ultimate standard against which a limit on a right or freedom must be shown."[17] We will say more about reasonable limits later in the essay. For the present, it should be emphasized that even though a right can be overridden by appeals to the public interest, the recognition of a "presumption of liberty" is important. To define something as a right is to elevate it to a position such that considerations of public interest must be compellingly shown. To maintain that section 2(b) of the Charter protects all forms of expression, then, is to compel those who favour censorship to demonstrate the justification for it in each case.

Is this a good thing? One reason for believing that it is relates to the institutional aspects of censorship. As one constitutional lawyer has suggested, "the most significant feature of systems of prior restraint [censorship] is that they contain within themselves forces which drive irresistibly toward unintelligent, overzealous, and usually absurd administration."[18] In fact, John Milton suggested in his famous essay, *Areopagitica*, that only the base and ignorant wanted to be censors. If this is so, then schemes of censorship require strict judicial scrutiny and should be upheld only if compelling justifications can be offered for them. Another and even deeper reason would be that society as a whole has an important interest in freedom of expression as part of an open and communicative public culture. Considered in this light, it stands together with prevailing views of politics as a democratic and competitive activity, with prevailing views about how knowledge of the natural and social world is acquired and transmitted, and prevailing views about the need to modify and refine the traditional and customary basis of shared social life. Those who hold such views will need to be given good reasons for acts of censorship, and will generally view would-be censors with suspicion.

If we are to understand the Court's position as a defence of an open and communicative public culture, then we may need to qualify the definition of "rights" that was offered earlier. At least in the case of some rights, it is not the interest of the person holding the right that is important; it is not some interest of the pornographer, for example, that makes it important to protect his or her freedom of expression, or to make its restriction difficult. Rather, it is an interest of Canadians in general, to the extent that they share some very broad views about how human society works, such as a belief about the importance of maintaining an open and communicative public culture. So one may have some rights, at least, for other people's sake rather than one's own. In suggesting that it is a public interest that lies at the root of some rights, at least, this interpretation has the further merit of helping to explain why, in some cases, other considerations of public interest may outweigh the rights' exercise, as section 1 of the Charter provides.

REASONABLE LIMITS AND THE BALANCING OF RIGHTS

Perhaps the most prominent element in the Court's decision was its ruling that the suppression of some kinds of pornography is a reasonable limit on freedom of expression. Briefly, the Court was called on to adjudicate between two views:

one, the view that exposure to obscene materials causes changes to people's attitudes that may lead in turn to socially harmful behaviour, such as the violent treatment of women or the willingness to subject women to discriminatory practices; two, the view that the censorship of pornography implies an archaic (and illiberal) view of the state as a sort of moral guardian empowered to make people better against their will. The Court affirmed the validity of the first view, yet denied that censorship necessarily casts the state in the role of an archaic moral guardian. After noting that the enforcement of morality as such was not defensible in view of the Charter, Justice Sopinka went on to say: "I cannot agree with the suggestion ... that Parliament does not have the right to legislate on the basis of some fundamental conception of morality for the purposes of safeguarding the values which are integral to a free and democratic society."[19] Not all restrictions based on moral grounds imply an objectionable view of the state. Many parts of the Criminal Code—such as the prohibition of murder—give legal force to moral prohibitions. Originally, perhaps, obscenity legislation had the illegitimate objective of punishing "moral corruption" on the sole ground that it was wicked; but in the context of our society, in which we must weigh the interests of a burgeoning pornography industry against the interests of women in regard to personal security and equal treatment, it is right to use the law as an instrument against "moral corruption of a certain kind."[20]

One important feature of this line of reasoning concerns the idea of "harm." That idea is particularly associated with Mill's *On Liberty*, which proposes that the law be confined to the task of preventing people from harming one another. Mill's claim has often been attacked on the grounds that "harm" is inseparable from moral judgments about what people really need; so to take "harm" as the criterion for adjudicating between conflicting claims is not to take up some neutral position, but to take up a position that will inevitably involve taking sides on different moral views about what is and is not essential to human lives. There is something in this objection; or at least there would be if it applied to Mill's argument. But it is far from clear that Mill intended judgments about "harm" to be separable from moral questions. After all, his argument makes significant "harm" depend on what rights we are said to have, and no one has ever supposed that we can settle on what rights people should have in isolation from moral considerations about the way in which people need respect. So in linking the definition of harm to the failure to act in accordance with the fundamental moral norms entrenched in the Charter, the Supreme Court was not guilty of verbal trickery, but provided fresh insights into the moral underpinnings of the concept of harm in Canadian society.

A second important feature of the Court's reasoning is its treatment of the conflict between, or the balancing of, rights. Fortunately, the Court did not attempt the nearly hopeless task of determining, in the abstract, whether the right to free expression was more or less important than the rights to personal security and to equality. Instead, the Court focused on particulars, weighed the available evidence, and refused to reify the rights protected by the Charter. As we noted earlier, the Court insisted that all forms of expression deserved some level of protection; but at this stage of its ruling, the different forms of expression once again assumed importance. "The values which underlie the protection of free expression," wrote Justice Sopinka, "relate to the search for truth, participation in the political process, and individual self-fulfilment."[21] He acknowledged that "good pornography" was integral to individual self-fulfilment because it celebrates erotic pleasure. However, there was also a type of pornography that portrayed women as mere sexual objects, as sexual worshippers of men, and as having personal value that depended entirely on their physical attributes. He concluded: "In my view the kind of expression which is sought to be advanced [by this kind of pornography] does not stand on an equal footing with other kinds of expression which directly engage the 'core' of the freedom of expression values."[22]

To complete the balancing process, the Court also took account of the fact that the pornography industry operated as a big business driven by the profit motive, that some kinds of pornography degraded and demeaned women, that the state had a reasonable basis for restricting this kind of pornography because of the identifiable harms associated with it. "Parliament," Justice Sopinka held, "was entitled to have a 'reasoned apprehension of harm' resulting from the desensitization of individuals exposed to materials which depict violence, cruelty, and dehumanization in sexual relations."[23] In *Butler*, the Court distinguished between kinds of expression, between kinds of harms, and between the kinds of interests asserted by women. By doing so, it was able to demonstrate its concern for freedom of expression while refusing to protect some types of pornography, and to protect the rights of women while taking seriously the guarantees of the Charter.

Many feminists were jubilant. Beginning in the 1970s, they had insisted on the distinction between erotica and pornography, and had urged that although erotica deserved constitutional protection, pornography did not. "Pornography," Gloria Steinem explained in an influential essay, "is not about sex. It's about an imbalance of male-female power that allows and even requires sex to be used as a form of aggression." Erotica is the word used "to differentiate sex from violence and rescue sexual pleasure."[24] The reasoning of many feminists had striking resemblances to that of Justice Sopinka, and they claimed *Butler* as a vindication of their position. Catharine MacKinnon praised the *Butler* decision for upholding the equality rights of women and criticized the American courts for failing to take seriously the harms of pornography. The awful message of pornography, she complained, is that "when you scratch us we get turned on; when you tickle us, we start to come; and when you kill us we orgasm until death."[25]

THE VIRTUES OF RECIPROCITY

Butler was not, of course, a perfect reconciliation of liberal and feminist concerns. Nor did all liberals or all feminists endorse its principles. Some radical feminists, such as Andrea Dworkin, believe that the defence of artistic merit should not be permitted in pornography trials.[26] But Justice Sopinka disagreed: without such defences obscenity legislation would be overbroad and excessively repressive. Even when freedom of expression can be justifiably limited, he held, the limitation must meet the test of "minimal impairment."[27] There were, as well, feminists who rejected *Butler* because they rejected censorship. They strongly disapproved of sexist pornography, but they believed that the appropriate remedies were a program of education about the pernicious effects of pornography and economic measures to improve the personal and social standing of women. They called themselves, as the title of an influential book reveals, women against censorship.[28] Justice Sopinka was aware of their concerns and attempted to respond to some of them. "Education and legislation," he wrote "are not alternatives but complements in addressing such problems [as obscenity]. There is nothing in the Charter which requires Parliament to choose between such complementary measures."[29]

Even if it is possible to defend *Butler* against many of its critics, how can a decision that gives weight to specific moral objectives still be called "liberal"? Above, we noted the fact that liberalism seeks recognition that various members of society hold different views about what is right, and proposes a political order in which people who disagree on moral grounds may nevertheless coexist politically. They can do so by respecting one another's rights, and by accepting the decisions of institutions that declare what is to be done when rights conflict. But how is this possible when moral considerations enter into what rights we have, and also into what we have to do when our rights conflict?

"Moral considerations" are not, of course, all of a kind; and the fact that liberals resist giving political weight to some of them does not mean they must refuse to give weight to all of them. They may—and if they are realistic they must—attach importance to the moral rules and political culture that are essential to the kind of institutions and practices they admire. If one is in any doubt, one might turn from Mill's *On Liberty* to his *The Subjection of Women*, which advocates not strict neutrality between all "moral" views, but a transformation of ways of thought and attitude. What Mill rejected and wished to eliminate was the "barbarism" that underlies sexual inequality. What he admired and wished to promote was the cultivation of the "virtues" of civilized reciprocity between men and women. It is open to "Charter liberals" to adopt the same kind of project. After all, many Charter liberals believe that rights do not stand alone, but are embedded in a matrix of beliefs, and insist that a key purpose of rights is to resist or even ameliorate the "barbaric" abuses of power that disfigure social and political life.

Promoting "reciprocity," to stay with Mill's example, is not to commit oneself to the kind of moralism that liberals find repellent. Liberals are repelled by attempts by some groups to impose their ideas about how to live on other groups. But a value such as reciprocity is not a possible way of life, like a religious faith or other kind of cause; it is a condition that governs and sets limits to ways of life that one may possibly choose. Naturally, these conditions and limits are likely to affect different political causes in different ways, and to favour some rather than others. In *Butler*, the Supreme Court determined that, in the case at hand, the underlying requirements of the Charter favoured "feminist" outcomes rather than "libertarian" ones. That does not mean that the Court allowed the Charter to be hijacked by feminists, but rather that it reflected on and rearticulated the moral priorities of liberalism itself.[30]

ENDNOTES

1. *Regina v. Butler*, [1992] 1 S.C.R. 452.

2. Catharine MacKinnon as quoted in Dany Lacombe, *Blue Politics: Pornography and the Law in the Age of Feminism* (Toronto: University of Toronto Press, 1994), 136.

3. *The Queen v. Hicklin* (1868) in Edward De Grazia, ed., *Censorship Landmarks* (New York: Bowker, 1969), 9.

4. *United States v. Kennerley* (1913) in De Grazia, 58.

5. See also H.L.A. Hart, *Law, Liberty, and Morality* (Stanford: Stanford University Press, 1963).

6. *Brodie v. The Queen*, [1962] S.C.R. 706.

7. *Report of the Special Committee on Pornography and Prostitution*, vol. 1 (Minister of Supply and Services Canada, 1985), 114–17; Bernard Williams, ed., *Obscenity and Film Censorship* (Cambridge: Cambridge University Press, 1981), 50–60.

8. *Towne Cinema Theatres Ltd. v. The Queen*, [1985] 1 S.C.R. 508, 524, 505.

9. *Regina v. Butler*, [1992] 1 S.C.R. 485.

10. Ibid.

11. Thomas I. Emerson, *Toward a General Theory of the First Amendment* (New York: Vintage Books, 1966), 3–15.

12. *Regina v. Butler* (1990), 60 C.C.C. (3d) 231.

13. Frederick Schauer, *Free Speech* (Cambridge: Cambridge University Press, 1982), 181, 184.

14. *Irwin Toy v. Quebec*, [1989] 1 S.C.R. 968.

15. *Regina v. Keegstra*, [1990] 3 S.C.R. 730.

16. Joseph Raz, *The Morality of Freedom* (Oxford: Clarendon Press, 1986), 166.

17. *Regina v. Oakes*, [1986] 1 S.C.R. 136.

18. Thomas I. Emerson, "The Doctrine of Prior Restraint," *Law and Contemporary Problems* 20 (1955): 658.

19. *Regina v. Butler*, [1992] 1 S.C.R. 493.

20. Ibid., 494.

21. Ibid., 499.

22. Ibid., 500.

23. Ibid., 504.

24. Gloria Steinem, *Outrageous Acts and Everyday Rebellions* (New York: New American Library, 1986), 250.

25. Catharine MacKinnon, "Pornography and the Rights of Women," in Elizabeth Smith and H.G. Blocker, eds., *Applied Social and Political Philosophy* (Englewood Cliffs, N.J.: Prentice Hall, 1994), 308. See also Catharine MacKinnon, *Only Words* (Cambridge: Harvard University Press, 1993), 100–7.

26. Andrea Dworkin, "Against the Male Flood: Censorship, Pornography and Equality," *Harvard Women's Law Journal* 8 (1985): 1.

27. *Regina v. Butler*, [1992] 1 S.C.R. 505.

28. Varda Burstyn, ed., *Women Against Censorship* (Vancouver: Douglas & MacIntyre, 1985).

29. *Regina v. Butler*, [1992] 1 S.C.R. 508–9.

30. Richard Vernon, "John Stuart Mill and Pornography: Beyond the Harm Principle," *Ethics* 106 (1996): 629–31.

THE SUPREME COURT OF CANADA ON REPRODUCTION:

PRIVATE MATTERS AND CONFLICTING INTERESTS

Laura Shanner

Whether to have children or not, and under what circumstances, are deeply personal and life-altering decisions. Reproduction also has important consequences for whole communities. Accordingly, the Supreme Court of Canada has been requested on multiple occasions to clarify how the Canadian Charter of Rights and Freedoms affects reproductive choices. Although the case law in reproductive matters is patchy, and little exists prior to the introduction of the Charter, the Court has gradually developed a body of rulings that protect certain reproductive rights while acknowledging a legitimate state interest in healthy offspring.

The phrase "reproductive rights" may mean many things in different contexts. A right to *avoid* reproducing would ensure the availability of contraception and abortion. When pregnancies are continued, difficult questions arise regarding the legal status of fetuses prior to birth. The appropriate limits of state intervention in the bodies or lives of pregnant women in order to protect fetuses or future children are far from clear. A "right to reproduce" might also be a positive claim of entitlement to bear children. Forced sterilization raises the question of whether having children is a specific human right that has been denied, or whether the injury in sterilization is simple bodily intrusion without consent. Infertile people who request access to infertility treatments also often claim a right to reproduce. The law, particularly at the level of the Supreme Court of Canada, has not fully caught up to medical and social developments in reproduction.

CONTRACEPTION

The Supreme Court of Canada has not specifically addressed the voluntary use of contraception, likely because contraception was medically and socially common prior to the adoption of the Canadian Charter of Rights and Freedoms. However, language from several U.S. Supreme Court contraception cases is echoed in Canadian rulings on other reproductive topics. *Griswold v. Connecticut*[1] (1965) concerned a state law that outlawed the use or provision of contraceptives. Although the U.S. Constitution does not specifically identify a right of privacy in personal decisions, several amendments do address certain limited aspects of privacy.[2] In the "penumbras" of those amendments, in their shadows and fuzzy edges, Justice Douglas found a "zone of privacy" that extends to the general protection of individual choices from state intrusion. In his words, "would we allow the police to search the sacred precincts of marital bedrooms for telltale signs of the use of contraceptives? The very idea is repulsive to the notions of privacy surrounding the marriage relationship."[3]

In *Eisenstadt v. Baird*[4] (1972), the U.S. Supreme Court extended the right of contraceptive use beyond the protection of marital privacy:

> *It is true that in Griswold the right of privacy ... inhered in the marital relationship. Yet the marital couple is not an independent entity with a mind and heart of its own, but an association of two individuals each with a separate intellectual and emotional makeup. If the right of privacy means anything, it is the right of the individual, married or single, to be free from unwarranted governmental intrusion into matters so fundamentally affecting a person as the decision whether to bear or beget a child.*[5]

Canada's Charter protection of "life, liberty and security of the person" provides more direct support for personal choices affecting one's own body than is reflected in the "penumbras" of the U.S. Constitution. Nevertheless, Canadian rulings often refer to American cases and concepts in the attempt to rule in uncharted territories. Exactly how far a "zone of privacy" or "security of the person" extends remains extremely unclear in situations involving reproductive partners, fetuses, and future children, not just one's own body. Further, Canadian rulings and policies at all levels are inconsistent regarding whether reproductive privacy applies only in marriage, extends equally to unmarried and/or same-sex couples, or is an individual expression of a right of self-determination.

ABORTION

Until 1988, the termination of pregnancy was the only medical or surgical procedure specifically governed by criminal law in Canada.[6] Under section 251 of the revised Criminal Code of Canada, abortions were permitted only if several provisions were met: (1) the abortion must be performed in an "accredited or approved" hospital; (2) the hospital must have a "therapeutic abortion committee" consisting of at least three doctors appointed by the hospital board; (3) the doctor performing the abortion must not be a member of the committee; and (4) the majority of the hospital committee must determine that continuing the pregnancy would endanger the life or health of the pregnant woman, and issue a certificate to this effect to her doctor. Access to abortion under such rules varied widely, as "therapeutic abortion committees" did not exist at some accredited health facilities, and accredited hospitals themselves may not have been accessible from remote areas. Also, among the abortion committees, the interpretation of "endangering the health" of a pregnant woman and the likelihood of approval for an abortion differed greatly.

Dr. Henry Morgentaler crusaded to ensure the availability of safe pregnancy termination procedures for Canadian women by provoking a series of court cases, several of which landed in the Supreme Court of Canada. In 1976, the Court ruled in *Morgentaler v. the Queen*[7] that the inability to be heard or be represented by counsel before the abortion committee was not a denial of due process. Since abortions were illegal procedures, exemptions granted by the committees turned unlawful conduct into a lawful act. Accordingly, any form of inaction or refusal by the committee could not affect one's lawful rights.

The Canadian Charter of Rights and Freedoms offered new grounds for judicial review of abortion legislation. The landmark case overturning the Criminal Code provision was *Morgentaler, Smoling and Scott v. The Queen,* indexed as *R. v. Morgentaler,*[8] in 1988. Writing for the 5–2 majority (Justices McIntyre and La Forest dissenting), Chief Justice Dickson emphasized the pregnant woman's right to security of her person at physical and emotional levels, with concern for the additional stress of losing decision-making power. "Forcing a woman, by threat of criminal sanction, to carry a fetus to term unless she meets certain criteria unrelated to her own priorities and aspirations, is a profound interference with a woman's body and thus a violation of security of the person."[9]

It is notable that in *Morgentaler* the Supreme Court specifically declined to address the question of fetal rights under the Canadian Charter. The matter at hand could be settled merely by evaluating whether section 251 achieved a fair balance between the government's interests in the protection of the fetus and the pregnant woman's right to security of the person. The Court reaffirmed a state interest in the well-being of fetuses and left open the possibility that a different piece of legislation to limit abortions might pass Charter muster; section 251 was simply flawed due to its arbitrariness and lack of proportionality. The protection of women's rights to privacy and security of the person are thus far from absolute under *Morgentaler,* and termination of pregnancy is not itself a right under the Canadian Charter.

Morgentaler differs importantly from the 1973 U.S. Supreme Court abortion ruling in *Roe v. Wade,*[10] in which the constitutional right of privacy identified in *Griswold* was extended to include abortion. Although section 7 of the Canadian Charter is more direct in its protection of security of the person, the Canadian Supreme Court's abortion ruling in terms of the woman's needs and aspirations is less sweeping than the constitutional right to an expansive "zone of privacy" as articulated in *Griswold* and *Roe.* Chief Justice Dickson noted in *Morgentaler* that it was "neither necessary nor wise ... to explore the broadest implications of s. 7 ... I prefer to rest my conclusions on a narrower analysis than that put forward by the appellants."[11] Further, although *Roe*'s restrictions during late pregnancy deny an *absolute* right to abortion, the U.S. Constitution does *not* contain a "notwithstanding" clause to abrogate the right of privacy.

A further important comparison between the Canadian and U.S. rulings concerns the treatment of pregnancy over time. *Morgentaler* identifies the need to balance fetal and maternal rights throughout the pregnancy. *Roe* established a trimester framework: abortions are considered a private matter between a woman and her doctor for the first third of pregnancy (12 weeks); the state may reasonably regulate abortion to ensure the health of the mother during the second trimester, when abortions become more risky; and greater state interest in the *viable* fetus may lead to more extensive regulation in the third trimester. The trimester framework is a classic example of judicial activism, and has remained deeply contentious in U.S. legal criticism. Advances in neonatal medicine also pose a practical challenge to the trimester framework: *Roe* designates viability at the start of the third trimester (24 weeks), but premature babies born after only 22 weeks of gestation now have a roughly 50 percent chance of survival.

The problem of abortion remains a greater political obsession in the United States than in Canada, as activist groups and episodes of violence accompany numerous U.S. Supreme Court challenges and political manoeuvring.[12] Three cases in 1983 reinforced *Roe*,[13] but access to abortion was severely undermined by Supreme Court approval of the Reagan administration policy of restricting federal funds to pay for abortion services[14] or even to discuss the option of abortion.[15] In 1989, the U.S. Supreme Court approved a state law that required viability tests from 20 weeks onward, thus extending the state's protection of fetuses into the second trimester, not just the third.[16] In *Planned Parenthood v. Casey* (1992), the Court reaffirmed the right to have an abortion, but revoked the definition of that right as "fundamental" and allowed restrictions on pre-viability abortions so long as they do not constitute an "undue burden" to the woman.[17] Overturning previous decisions, *Casey* also allowed (1) a mandatory 24-hour waiting period between signing the consent form and having the procedure, (2) state-mandated information about abortion and fetal development designed to persuade the woman not to have an abortion, and (3) a requirement for parental consent (or a judicial waiver) for minors seeking abortions. A requirement to notify the husband before an abortion could be performed was considered unduly burdensome and was struck down, confirming an earlier ruling[18] that denied the husband's right to consent to an abortion.

Although Canadian rulings have not been as extensive as their American counterparts, the 1988 *Morgentaler* ruling did not settle Canadian political difficulties surrounding abortion either. Dr. Morgentaler has since challenged several provincial attempts to prevent free-standing (nonhospital) abortion clinics, winning his case against Nova Scotia in the Supreme Court of Canada in 1993.[19] The Court ruled that such attempts to return abortion to a criminal framework were outside the jurisdiction of the province, as the Criminal Code is a federal matter.

Does the father of the fetus have any right to prevent a woman from having an abortion? The Supreme Court of Canada ruled in *Tremblay v. Daigle* that the relationship between the expectant father and mother is "a civil action between two private parties and there is no state action which is being impugned."[20] In this case, Mr. Tremblay had not identified any law that infringed on his or anyone else's rights, nor had he made a Charter appeal. Accordingly, the Court ruled that fathers cannot prevent women from having abortions. This case is discussed in more detail later in this chapter under the heading "Fetal Status."

DEVELOPING TRENDS: WRONGFUL BIRTH AND WRONGFUL LIFE

Many genetic and developmental abnormalities can be detected prior to birth, but sometimes such anomalies are missed or the pregnant woman is not warned about risks involved in her pregnancy. As a result, the woman may continue a pregnancy that she would have terminated if she had known the risks involved. Two types of tort cases are possible in these circumstances. In *wrongful birth* cases, parents sue clinicians for failing to advise them of fetal abnormalities that would have led them to terminate the pregnancy. Such cases usually involve claims for financial support to meet the special needs of a child with serious illness or disabilities, but may also involve punitive damages or compensation for distress to the parents and siblings. *Wrongful life* suits are filed by severely disabled children (or their representatives) against their parents and/or clinicians for allowing them to be born. No court in Canada has upheld a wrongful life claim, as this amounts to an assertion that some lives are not worth living.

The one wrongful birth case reviewed by the Supreme Court of Canada, *Arndt v. Smith*[21] focused on the definition and limits of informed consent. In 1986, a pregnant woman contracted chicken pox and gave birth to a child with varicella syndrome, which made necessary both continuous tube feeding and many operations. The plaintiff, Ms. Arndt, claimed that, had she known about the risks that her having chicken pox posed to her offspring, she would have terminated the pregnancy. In 1994 the trial court convicted Dr. Smith of medical negligence for failing to disclose all material risks to Ms. Arndt. However, the losses suffered by the plaintiff in caring for the child were judged by the Supreme Court in 1997 to be causally unrelated to this negligence, since "a reasonable and prudent expectant mother"[22] would not have had an abortion under the circumstances. In other words, while the doctor had a duty to disclose the risks, the trial court supposed that no reasonable person who knew those risks would terminate the pregnancy.

This case thus raises debate about patient consent. Note, for example, that the Court of Appeal had earlier (in 1995) approached the case with a different assumption about abortion choices: "What happens if some reasonable patients in the actual patient's position would have undergone the treatment, and others would not?"[23] The Court of Appeal reviewed the "reasonable person in the plaintiff's position" standard for informed consent established by the Supreme

Court in *Reibl v. Hughes*,[24] and found that the trial court had not applied the standard correctly. Accordingly, a new trial was ordered.

To understand the complexities of the consent issue, a glance at the landmark informed consent decision in *Reibl* is helpful. In 1970, a patient suffered a disabling stroke as a side effect of surgery to clear a blockage from an artery. While the patient had consented to the surgery, he claimed it was not an *informed* consent due to the doctor's failure to disclose this rare but devastating complication. The Supreme Court outlined three possible models for appropriate disclosure and truly informed consent for a medical procedure. The first, the "professional standard," reflects what most doctors would tell a patient. This model has a long history in practice, but fails to reflect the *patient's* perspective, which is crucial to giving consent. The second is the "reasonable person standard," an objective test that reflects what a typical, reasonable person would need to know to make an informed decision. The third model tailors the disclosure of information to a specific patient's needs, fears, beliefs, and so on. While most satisfying from the patient's perspective, it is impossible in practice to know exactly what another person would find relevant. The Supreme Court settled on a modified version of the "reasonable person standard," injecting a dose of subjectivity to create the "reasonable person in the plaintiff's position standard." That is, not all patients are in the same position in life, and the information relevant to their choices might vary according to such factors as their cultural or religious background, family needs, time to retirement, or other underlying health conditions. The question thus is not what a generic reasonable person would need to know, but what a reasonable person in *this* patient's position would need to know.

In *Arndt v. Smith*, the Supreme Court rejected the trial court's interpretation of informed consent and reaffirmed the standard of disclosure from *Reibl*. The Court also upheld the Court of Appeal's ruling for a new trial in order to reconsider the conviction for medical negligence in light of the proper informed consent framework. However, the majority agreed with the trial court's conclusion that Ms. Arndt would not have terminated the pregnancy had she known the risks, given her "desire for children and her suspicion of the mainstream medical profession."[25]

The ruling in *Arndt* remains controversial, as the Supreme Court (like the trial court) assumed that consensus exists about not terminating pregnancies in this situation. Further, the burden of getting information is delegated to the patient: "[w]hile [Arndt] did make a very general inquiry concerning the risks associated with maternal chickenpox, there was nothing to indicate to the doctor that she had a particular concern in this regard."[26] It appears from this ruling that patients must make an active effort to announce their concerns *prior* to being given information that a reason to be concerned might exist.

FETAL STATUS

While *Morgentaler* specifically avoided the question of the fetus's legal status, the Supreme Court articulated more precisely the status of fetuses under Canadian law in the *Tremblay v. Daigle* abortion ruling. The Court identified its task as "fundamentally normative" rather than descriptive, since recognition of legal standing results in the recognition of rights and duties. Accordingly, "[m]etaphysical arguments may be relevant but they are not the primary focus of inquiry. Nor are scientific arguments about the biological status of a fetus determinative in our inquiry." The *Tremblay* case presented "a matter which falls outside the concerns of scientific classification."[27]

The Court reviewed the specific provisions of the Civil Code of Lower Canada, Quebec's Charter of Rights and Freedoms, and prior case law in Quebec, concluding unanimously that a fetus could only claim the rights provided by the Quebec's Civil Code following live birth and independent existence. The Court also reviewed the status of the fetus in English common law, quoting the British Court of Queen's Bench: "[t]he foetus cannot, in English law ... have a right of its own at least until it is born and has a separate existence from its mother."[28] Similar rulings had been issued by the Ontario High Court: "[t]he law has selected birth as the point at which the fetus becomes a person with full and independent legal rights."[29] Accordingly, the Supreme Court ruled that the fetus has no standing in Canadian common law, either.

The question of whether fetuses are persons under the Charter was pointedly raised, but not directly addressed, by the Supreme Court in *Borowski v. Canada*.[30] Mr. Borowski challenged the Criminal Code provisions on abortion as a violation of the fetus's rights to life and equality under sections 7 and 15 of the Charter. The Court of Appeal (1987) noted the historic availability of abortion in Canada; that the fetus was not recognized under Canadian common law, civil law, or in other jurisdictions; and that the legislative history of the Charter showed no intent to change the legal status of fetuses. Accordingly, the Court of Appeal concluded that the fetus is not included in the terms of "everyone" or "every individual" under sections 7 and 15 of the Charter, and thus abortion could not be considered a violation of the fetal rights. The Supreme Court held on appeal in 1989 that the case had become moot the year before, when *Morgentaler* struck down the abortion provisions of the Criminal Code. The Court further noted that a ruling on fetal rights would be contrary to the public interest in the absence of a legislative context. By recounting the Court of Appeal summaries of fetal status under Canadian law, however, *Borowski* supports the Supreme Court's ruling in *Tremblay* that common law gives no right to a fetus to be born alive.

In *R. v. Sullivan*[31] in 1991, the Supreme Court reaffirmed its previous rulings on the status of fetuses, this time in the context of criminal law. Two midwives had been charged with criminal negligence when the infant they were attempting to deliver died during birth. The British Columbia Court of Appeal reduced the charge to criminal negligence causing bodily harm to the mother, rather than criminal negligence causing death to the fetus, who was not yet a distinct individual. The Supreme Court affirmed the Court of Appeal's finding that there was no indication that Parliament had intended the word "person" in the Criminal Code to differ from that of "human being," which was defined as a child who "has completely proceeded, in a living state, from the body of its mother."[32]

Accordingly, the fetus could not be a person within the meaning of the criminal negligence provisions of the Criminal Code.

PREGNANCY INTERVENTION

While the Court has ruled repeatedly that fetuses have no legal standing in Canada, there remains a state interest (noted in *Morgentaler*) in the well-being of fetuses insofar as they become children. That is, a *fetus qua fetus* has no legal standing in Canada, and thus may be aborted, but a *fetus qua future child* may have future interests that are appropriately protected by the state prior to the child's birth.[33] In *Winnipeg Child and Family Services v. D.F.G.*[34] the Supreme Court ruled that forced treatment or confinement of pregnant women is unjustified. During a hospital admission in May 1996 for complications arising from solvent abuse (nausea, confusion, lack of muscle control), D.G. was found to be 13 weeks pregnant. She agreed to drug treatment, but no beds were immediately available. By the time a treatment space became available, she was intoxicated and refused to go; Child and Family Services then petitioned for a court order to compel the drug treatment. The initial court found D.G. incompetent and issued the order, despite a psychiatric assessment that D.G. was competent, but this ruling was overturned by the Manitoba Court of Appeal. The case reached the Supreme Court in October 1996, but the Court withheld its ruling until October 1997.

The Royal Commission on New Reproductive Technologies had earlier concluded that state intervention in pregnancy is never justified, even when the health of the child is at risk.[35] The Supreme Court, in a 7–2 majority ruling, followed this reasoning and quoted the Commission's justifications regarding the inability of judicial intervention to prevent harm. Instead, judicial intervention is more likely to create crisis and conflict, deny the pregnant woman her right to self-determination, and damage her relationships with her partner and physician. Further, the chain of legal precedents discussed above establishes that fetuses are not persons under the law:

> The position is clear. Neither the common law nor the civil law of Quebec recognizes the unborn child as a legal person possessing rights. This principle applies generally, whether the case falls under the rubric of family law, succession law or tort. Any right or interest the fetus may have remains inchoate and incomplete until the birth of the child.
>
> It follows that under the law as it presently stands, the fetus on whose behalf the agency purported to act in seeking the order for the respondent's detention was not a legal person and possessed no legal rights. If it was not a legal person and possessed no legal rights at the time of the application, then there was no legal person in whose interests the agency could act or in whose interests a court order could be made.[36]

Under common law, governments reserve a power called the doctrine of *parens patriae*, which authorizes the state to act like a parent to protect persons who cannot protect themselves. Since fetuses are not persons under the law, *parens patriae* cannot be extended to them. The Court also recognized that extending tort law to allow the detention of a pregnant woman to protect the off-spring, and/or extending *parens patriae* to fetuses, would involve sweeping rather than incremental changes to the current law. Such changes are appropriately made only in the legislative arm of government, not the judiciary. The magnitude of allowing children to sue their mothers is summarized nicely in Justice McLachlin's majority opinion:

> To permit an unborn child to sue its pregnant mother-to-be would introduce a radically new conception into the law; the unborn child and its mother as separate juristic persons in a mutually separable and antagonistic relation. Such a legal conception, moreover, is belied by the reality of the physical situation; for practical purposes, the unborn child and its mother-to-be are bonded in a union separable only by birth. Such a dramatic departure from the traditional legal characterization of the relationship between the unborn child and its future mother is better left to the legislature than effected by the courts.[37]

The dissenting opinion raised new and potentially revolutionary arguments. Justice Major (with Justice Sopinka) argued that once a woman has decided not to terminate the pregnancy through a legal abortion, she has made a commitment to the pregnancy, and her moral and legal obligations to the fetus change. When maternal behaviour such as drug use constitutes a clear risk to the future child, she should be held responsible for (and *parens patriae* may be invoked to prevent) injury to that future child. It is important to notice the shift in perceptions of abortion in only ten years. Prior to 1988, abortion was a criminal activity in Canada. By 1997, two Supreme Court justices considered abortion so routine that opting not to have one would allow state intervention in a continued pregnancy. Sanda Rogers interprets the shift more ominously, noting that abortion had been defended as a right of liberty and security of the person, but was now being promoted as a last resort to avoid prosecution.[38]

Just before this volume went to press, the Supreme Court ruled that children cannot sue their mothers for injuries caused during pregnancy. In *Dobson (Litigation Guardian of) v. Dobson*,[39] a pregnant woman negligently caused an automobile accident that in turn resulted in the premature birth of a son with permanent mental and physical impairment. The child's grandfather sued on the child's behalf to force the mother's insurance company to pay for the child's medical needs. Justice Cory, writing for the 7–2 majority, affirmed that the relationship between a pregnant woman and the fetus is "truly unique" and cannot be meaningfully compared to a child's action for negligence against a third party.

> The actions of a pregnant woman, including driving, are inextricably linked to her familial role, her working life, and her rights of privacy, bodily integrity and autonomous decision-making.... The imposition of tort liability in this

context would have profound effects upon every pregnant woman and upon
Canadian society in general ... and may make life for women who are pregnant
or who are merely contemplating pregnancy intolerable. The best course, there-
fore, is to allow the duty of a mother to her foetus to remain a moral obligation
which, for the vast majority of women, is already freely recognized and
respected without compulsion by law.

Justice Major (with Justice Bastarache) argued in a dissenting opinion that the duty of care that Ms. Dobson had to her fetus is no greater than the duty of care she already owed to other users of the highway or passengers in her car. "To grant a pregnant woman immunity from the reasonable foreseeable consequences of her acts for her born alive child would create a legal distortion as no other plaintiff carries such a one-sided burden, nor any defendant such an advantage."

Despite the general trend to protect women's rights to liberty and security of the person in matters involving pregnancy, women's rights are ambiguously and incompletely defined. While *Dobson* acknowledges the "very demanding biological reality that only women can become pregnant and bear children," the Supreme Court has failed to address the implications of section 15 of the Charter regarding equal protection regardless of sex.[40] The fact that women carry pregnancies while men do not means that *any* restriction or intervention in pregnancy necessarily affects women and men differently. Since damage may occur to fetuses before pregnancies are even identified, restrictions have sometimes been imposed on all females between the ages of adolescence and menopause, thus affecting women as a class.[41] The Supreme Court of Canada will no doubt face a section 15 challenge in the near future.

STERILIZATION

While voluntary surgical sterilization is much like general contraceptive use, sterilization *without* consent of the person to be sterilized raises difficult new problems. A legacy of abuses committed in the name of eugenics prompts caution. In the U.S. Supreme Court, a much-criticized 1927 opinion sustained a state law that allowed sterilization of institutionalized "mental defectives" and summarily rejected due process claims by asserting that "three generations of imbeciles are enough."[42] In an apparent about-face in 1942, the U.S. Court invalidated a state law that provided for compulsory sterilization after a third conviction for a felony involving "moral turpitude," such as larceny, but excluding such felonies as embezzlement. In a widely quoted passage, the majority in *Skinner v. Oklahoma* framed the matter in terms of "one of the basic civil rights of man [sic]. Marriage and procreation are fundamental to the very existence and survival of the race."[43] However, the ruling did not establish a general right to procreate, nor did it provide protection for other inmates who might face sterilization. Instead, it merely prohibited discrimination between larcenists and embezzlers.[44]

Canada also has an unfortunate history of sterilizing individuals residing in government institutions. In Alberta, the Sexual Sterilization Act created a

Eugenics Board that authorized the sterilization of 2832 residents of province-run mental health institutions from 1928 to 1972. A 1996 provincial Court of Queen's Bench ruling in favour of the first plaintiff to file suit for wrongful sterilization[45] led to approximately 750 similar cases by 1998. The provincial government's attempt to limit compensation for sterilization victims by invoking the notwithstanding clause (s. 33 of the Charter) sparked widespread protest and was retracted the following day, and an out-of-court settlement for 504 victims was reached a few months later. Although no cases connected with these sterilizations have yet reached the Supreme Court of Canada, it is possible that one may yet appear.

The Supreme Court's rulings have been somewhat inconsistent in the sterilization cases that it has heard. In *E. (Mrs.) v. Eve*,[46] a mother (Mrs. E.) sought a court order to allow surgical sterilization of her mentally handicapped adult daughter on the grounds that pregnancy and labour would be traumatic for Eve, and that Eve would be unable to provide care for a child. The Court declined to authorize the sterilization, affirming that forced sterilization constitutes a "grave intrusion on a person's rights" and is an "irreversible and serious intrusion on the basic rights of the individual."[47] However, a 1995 decision by the Supreme Court declined to provide similarly strong language to protect individuals from sterilization. In *Chan v. Canada*,[48] a Chinese man sought refuge in Canada due to his fear of persecution and forced sterilization for violating China's one-child policy. The Immigration and Refugee Board found that the appellant was not a Convention refugee as defined by the Immigration Act,[49] and held that forced sterilization did not constitute a form of persecution. The Federal Court of Appeal upheld the Board's decision. The Supreme Court of Canada identified the key issues to be considered in the appeal as those related to the definition of political refugee status: (1) whether forced sterilization is a form of "persecution" within the meaning of s. 2(1)(a) of the Immigration Act; (2) whether persons facing forced sterilization are members of a "particular social group"; (3) whether those refusing forced sterilization are expressing a "political opinion"; and (4) whether the appellant has a well-founded fear of forced sterilization or of other persecution.[50]

A four-member majority[51] rejected the appeal, arguing that Mr. Chan had demonstrated neither a subjective fear of persecution nor objective evidence that sterilization was inflicted on men in his area. The majority offered little reflection about the nature of compulsory sterilization as a violation of human rights or of Canadian laws and policy. The dissenting opinion, in contrast, found Mr. Chan's fears consistent with what was known about China's one-child policy, and expressed a strong defence of a right to be protected from sterilization. "Forced sterilization constitutes a gross infringement of the security of the person and readily qualifies as the type of fundamental violation of basic human rights that constitutes persecution. Notwithstanding the technique, forced sterilization is in essence an inhuman, degrading and irreversible treatment."[52] When *Eve* and *Chan* are compared, it is thus unclear whether the Court would classify procreation as a human right. The majority in *Eve* stated that the notion of a right to procreate was gaining credence in some circles, despite the risks to Eve and her child, and the burdens for Mrs. E. in raising an unwanted child if Eve became pregnant. However, when given the opportunity in *Chan* to entrench a right to procreate, the majority declined to address the issue.

REPRODUCTIVE TECHNOLOGIES

While there is support for a negative right to have one's reproductive health left undamaged, is there a positive right to have children that would support access to reproductive technologies? The challenge has not been presented to the Supreme Court of Canada, although a very recent case may reach the Court on appeal. In *Cameron v. Nova Scotia*,[53] a couple sued the province for failing to provide health insurance coverage for *in vitro* fertilization (IVF) and a variation called ICSI (intracytoplasmic sperm injection, in which a single sperm is injected into the ovum). They argued that since medical help is offered for most physiological impairments, it should also be offered for reproductive impairments. The Nova Scotia Supreme Court dismissed the claim, arguing that the provincial health care plan rightly declines to cover some services since it is impossible to provide all possible services for all citizens. The Nova Scotia legislation enabling the province to determine covered services was, moreover, judged to be legitimate, and it was found that appropriate due process had been followed in establishing the funding priorities that excluded IVF and ICSI as not medically necessary. Ontario provides coverage of IVF (but not any of its variants) only in cases in which both fallopian tubes are blocked, while no other province covers IVF or its variants at all.

The Nova Scotia ruling also noted that no court in Canada has defined the scope of the words *medically necessary* beyond a specific application, and thus limited its analysis strictly to IVF/ICSI. While IVF may be medically indicated in cases of infertility, and ICSI is becoming the treatment of choice for male infertility, neither category is equivalent to medically necessary procedures that must be covered by the health plan. Even the medical community has not yet applied to have IVF/ICSI deemed medically necessary. The claim that ICSI in particular is medically necessary is implausible given the risks and low success rate of the procedure, the absence of medical risk in declining the procedure, and the options to respond to male infertility with adoption, artificial insemination using donor sperm, or acceptance.

Finally, the Nova Scotia Supreme Court addressed the claim that the failure to fund IVF/ICSI represents a form of discrimination against persons with a disability, contrary to the equal protection clause in section 15 of the Charter. While it was noted that these procedures are likely of interest only to infertile individuals, it was also pointed out that the health plan excludes certain services (such as electrolysis) that may be of interest to both fertile and infertile persons, and that some other infertility diagnosis and treatment procedures are covered. The decision not to fund IVF/ICSI therefore was not discriminatory since it was "based on the nature of the treatment being sought, rather than the personal characteristics of those persons seeking the funding, the infertile."[54]

While it may be possible to construct arguments defending a right of access to infertility treatment under the Canadian Charter, such interpretations are debatable at several turns. In 1985, the Ontario Law Reform Commission[55] concluded that even if infertility were recognized as a disability under section 15, access to reproductive technologies might still be limited due to marital status, the economic ability of the parents to support a child, or other considerations, such as a history of violence, that are contrary to the best interests of the child. Further, the report contended, a wholesale ban on reproductive interventions would cause all members of society to be treated equally, since in that case access would be denied to all, regardless of marital or fertility status. For example, fertile people who want to use new technologies to prevent the transmission of a genetic disease would also have their reproductive options substantially limited.

The "best interests of the child" argument returns us to the earlier-discussed questions of wrongful birth and wrongful life, and the claims that children might make against their parents or physicians. A new challenge may arise that injury to a child (either by medical mishap or parental abuse) would have been prevented if infertility treatment had been denied.

REPRODUCTIVE TISSUES

While little case law exists regarding new reproductive and genetic technologies, one case establishes an important distinction between products and services when donated reproductive tissues are involved. In *ter Neuzen v. Korn*,[56] a recipient of artificial insemination (AI) in January 1985 contracted HIV through contaminated donor sperm, and sued the administering physician for malpractice. Dr. Korn was found guilty in the B.C. Supreme Court and ordered to pay damages, but the B.C. Court of Appeal overturned the conviction on the grounds that no accurate test for HIV was in general use when the AI was performed. The Supreme Court of Canada unanimously upheld the appellate court's ruling that a new trial be held, limited to malpractice other than failure to detect HIV at the time of treatment. What is most interesting in this case is not the discussion of standards of professional care and malpractice regarding HIV testing, but the consideration of reproductive technologies in light of contract law and the province of British Columbia's Sale of Goods Act. Is artificial insemination with donor sperm a *sale* of sperm, or is it instead the provision of a medical service in which goods are incidentally passed to the patient? The Court held that "the contract to perform the AI procedure on the appellant was primarily a contract for medical services ... Although donor semen was a necessary component of this process, the contract was not primarily for a sale of semen."[57]

The precedent set in *ter Neuzen v. Korn* may be challenged in the near future as the outright sale of ova and embryos becomes more common. Advertisements have appeared in university student newspapers in recent years offering to purchase ova, with occasional compensation offers as high as US$20 000 to $50 000 for eggs from healthy, young, and talented women. It is not immediately clear why the prohibitions on the sale of blood, organs, and tissues embodied in most provincial human tissue gift acts are not applied to the transfer of reproductive tissues. Any attempt to enforce such provisions in infertility clinics may spark a court challenge. We may also see a case in which the ovum provider and/or the clinicians are sued for failing to provide a healthy reproductive product (ovum, embryo, or perhaps infant). Further challenges may arise in "surrogate" gestational contracts in which the birth mother has bonded with the baby and refuses to give custody to the contracting parties; might living babies also be classified as commodities or mere "incidental goods" related to the service of carrying a pregnancy? The social ramifications of treating reproductive tissues or services, and especially the children that result from them, as commodities or incidental goods under the law, will require extensive analysis beyond the scope of this review.

CONCLUSIONS

Although the Supreme Court of Canada has judged relatively few cases involving reproductive matters, several interesting lines of argument have been advanced in a rapidly evolving social and medical context. Frequently, the matters raised in reproductive cases have more to do with non-reproductive matters such as informed consent, due process, or equal protection than with procreation itself, thus offering important contributions to other medical and legal contexts. On reproductive matters of substance, the rights of women to control their own bodies during pregnancy have been reinforced over several decisions following the decriminalization of abortion in 1988. However, challenges to women's medical and personal autonomy during pregnancy are still common, and the Court has not firmly established the scope of reproductive autonomy relative to the legitimate social need to protect future children from harm.

Canadians tend to believe that they are more supportive of collective values and the common good than are Americans, whom they perceive as being more focused on individual liberty, but the trends of reproductive law in the two countries do not fully play to this stereotype. The notwithstanding clause provides Canadians with a mechanism to override individual rights and liberties for the common good, but the attempt by Alberta to invoke the notwithstanding clause in relation to compensation for surgical sterilization met with immediate and devastating criticism. While the socialized health care plan in Canada excludes coverage for IVF, private clinics and reproductive arrangements flourish in the absence of regulatory control.[58] The Supreme Court of Canada rulings on abortion and pregnancy intervention tend to support women's individual liberties over state and paternal interests in the offspring. In contrast, the current trend of abortion decisions in the U.S. Supreme Court increasingly restricts women's autonomy in order to promote social values related to the well-being of fetuses and future children. Perhaps the differences in reproductive policy reflected in Canadian and U.S. Supreme Court rulings do not so much indicate differing emphases on autonomy versus the common good, but rather different perceptions of *whose* autonomy and *which* common goods are to be promoted.

Reproductive law will undoubtedly be an exciting field in the next several decades. Procreating is both deeply personal and socially important, affects the liberty of adults and the well-being of offspring, and is rapidly changing with new technologies. It is therefore unlikely that either nation's Supreme Court will pronounce its final words on the topic for quite some time.

ENDNOTES

1. *Griswold v. Connecticut*, 381 U.S. 479 (1965).
2. Advice about contraception is protected under the First Amendment's protection of a right to free speech. The Third (prohibition against quartering soldiers in citizens' homes) and Fourth (search and seizure) Amendments protect individuals' homes—and thus their bedrooms—from state intrusion. The Fifth Amendment (protection from self-incrimination) is routinely extended to spouses, providing further privacy within the marital relationship. The Ninth Amendment protects as rights of the people matters extending beyond the specific enumeration of rights in the previous eight Amendments in the Bill of Rights. Finally, the Fourteenth Amendment guarantees due process and equal protection under the law.
3. *Griswold*, 485–86.
4. *Eisenstadt v. Baird*, 405 U.S. 438 (1972).
5. Ibid., 453.
6. "Abortion in Canada," *Canadian Health Facilities Law Guide* (Don Mills: CCH Canadian Limited, 1993), 4061.
7. *Morgentaler v. the Queen* [1976] 1 S.C.R. 616.
8. *R. v. Morgentaler* [1988] 1 S.C.R. 30. Unless otherwise indicated, all further *Morgentaler* references are to the 1988 case.
9. Ibid., 32–33, 56–57.
10. *Roe v. Wade*, 410 U.S. 113 (1973).
11. *R. v. Morgentaler*, 51.
12. Summaries and full case rulings on key U.S. abortion cases are available on-line from Planned Parenthood at http://www.plannedparenthood.org/about/narrhistory/court.html (last accessed 31 May 1999). Several key Republican Party leaders in recent years have also supported a "human life amendment" to the Constitution that would grant full legal status to embryos and fetuses, thus overturning *Roe* and possibly subjecting abortion to extreme limitations.
13. *City of Akron v. Akron Center for Reproductive Health*, 106 S.Ct. 1517 (1983); *Planned Parenthood Association of Kansas City v. Ashcroft*, 103 S.Ct. 1532 (1983); *Simopolous v. Virginia*, 462 U.S. 506 (1983).
14. *Harris v. McRae*, 448 U.S. 297 (1980); *Williams v. Zbaraz*, 448 U.S. 358 (1980).
15. *Rust v. Sullivan*, 500 U.S. 173 (1991).
16. *Webster v. Reproductive Health Services*, 492 U.S. 490 (1989).
17. *Planned Parenthood of Southeastern Pennsylvania v. Casey*, 505 U.S. 833 (1992).
18. *Planned Parenthood of Central Missouri v. Danforth*, 428 U.S. 52 (1976).
19. *R. v. Morgentaler* [1993] 3 S.C.R. 463.
20. *Tremblay v. Daigle* [1989] 2 S.C.R. 532–33.
21. *Arndt v. Smith* [1997] 2 S.C.R. 539.
22. Ibid., 542.

23. *Arndt v. Smith* [1995] 7 W.W.R. 390.

24. *Reibl v. Hughes* [1980] 2 S.C.R. 880.

25. *Arndt v. Smith* [1997] 541.

26. Ibid., 540–41.

27. *Tremblay v. Daigle*, 552–53.

28. *Paton v. British Advisory Services Trustees* [1979] Q.B. 279.

29. *Dehler v. Ottawa Civic Hospital*, (1979) 101 D.L.R. (3d) 699.

30. *Borowski v. Canada (Attorney General)* [1989] 1 S.C.R. 342.

31. *R. v. Sullivan* [1991] 1 S.C.R. 489. Note: this case should not be confused with the U.S. Supreme Court case *Rust v. Sullivan* (also 1991) at note 15, above.

32. Criminal Code R.S.C. 1970, c. 34, sec. 206. See Martha Jackman, "The Status of the Foetus Under Canadian Law," *Health Law in Canada* 15, no. 3 (1995): 83–86.

33. The distinction between a *fetus qua fetus* and *fetus qua future child* may be clarified by the following example: if someone were to set a time bomb to explode in two hundred years, no currently existing person would be hurt. We assume, though, that *someone* will exist in the future, and the future person(s) may sustain injury caused by actions taken today. Thus, non-existent future persons have no legal standing, but their interests are morally and legally important if current actions cause future harms to *somebody*. See Joel Feinberg, "The Rights of Animals and Unborn Generations," *Philosophy and Environmental Crisis*, ed. William T. Blackstone (Athens, GA: University of Georgia Press, 1974), 43–68.

34. *Winnipeg Child and Family Services (Northwest Area) v. D.F.G.* [1997] 3 S.C.R. 925. For commentary on this case, see articles in the *Alberta Law Review* 36, no. 3 (July 1998).

35. Royal Commission on New Reproductive Technologies (RCNRT), *Proceed with Care: Final Report* (Ottawa: Minister of Government Services, 1993), vol. 2, ch. 30, 949–66. Commissioner Suzanne Scorsone dissented on this conclusion, arguing that while judicial or state intervention should be exceedingly rare, it is unreasonable to rule out exceptions. RCNRT, vol. 2, 1063–1065 and 1123–1143.

36. *Winnipeg Child and Family Services (Northwest Area) v. D.F.G.* [1997] 3 S.C.R. 939. Reproduced with the permission of the Minister of Public Works and Government Services Canada, 1999.

37. Ibid., 945.

38. Sanda Rogers, "State Intervention in the Lives of Pregnant Women," in Jocelyn Downie and Timothy Caulfield, eds., *Canadian Health Law and Policy* (Toronto: Butterworths, 1999), 294.

39. *Dobson (Litigation Guardian of) v. Dobson*, heard December 8, 1998, file no. 26152. Supreme Court of Canada ruling issued July 9, 1999.

40. Rogers, 296.

41. An example of such a class restriction is the denial of employment to all potentially pregnant women in jobs that involve exposure to lead or other known causes of birth defects. This policy was struck down by the U.S. Supreme Court in *Automobile Workers v. Johnson Controls, Inc.*, 499 U.S. 187 (1991).

42. *Buck v. Bell*, 274 U.S. 200 (1927) 207.

43. *Skinner v. Oklahoma*, 316 U.S. 535 (1942) 541.

44. Gerald Gunther, *Constitutional Law*, 11th ed. (Mineola, NY: The Foundation Press 1985), 503.

45. *Muir v. The Queen in right of Alberta* (1996), 32 D.L.R. (4th) 69 (AB QB).

46. *E. (Mrs.) v. Eve* [1986] 2 S.C.R. 388.

47. Ibid., 431, 432.

48. *Chan v. Canada (Minister of Employment and Immigration)* [1995] 3 S.C.R. 593.

49.   The definition of a Convention refugee in the Immigration Act [R.S.C. 1985, c. I–2, ss. 2(1)] draws upon several international covenants and conventions, including *The Convention on the Elimination of All Forms of Discrimination against Women,* 1 March 1989, Can. T.S. 1982 No. 31, Art. 15(1)(e) and the *International Covenant on Civil and Political Rights,* 19 December 1966, Can. T.S. 1976 No. 47, Art. 12(2). Further guidance is drawn from the United Nations High Commissioner for Refugees (UNHCR) *Handbook on Procedures and Criteria for Determining Refugee Status* (Geneva: United Nations, 1979).

50.   Ibid., 594.

51.   Only seven members of the Court were present for this case. Justice Sopinka wrote the majority opinion, joined by Justices Cory, Iacobucci, and Major, and with Justices La Forest, L'Heureux-Dubé, and Gonthier dissenting.

52.   *Chan v. Canada,* 596–97.

53.   *Cameron v. Nova Scotia (Attorney General)* [1999] N.S.J. No. 33, DRS 99-01803, S.H. No. 137396.

54.   Ibid., para. 154. On September 14, 1999, the two-member majority of the Court of Appeal considered infertility to be a disability that may give rise to claim of discrimination, but unanimously reaffirmed Nova Scotia's right to limit the list of covered services in Medicare.

55.   Ontario Law Reform Commission, "The Prohibition of Artificial Contraception Technologies: Is There a Right to Procreate?" *Report on Human Artificial Reproduction and Related Matters,* vol. 1 (Toronto: Ministry of the Attorney General, 1985), 39–51.

56.   *ter Neuzen v. Korn* [1995] 3 S.C.R. 674.

57.   Ibid., 709.

58.   Health Canada is expected to introduce federal legislation to regulate reproductive and genetic technologies shortly after this volume goes to press.

LEGISLATIVE AUTHORITY, NOTWITHSTANDING, AND PARLIAMENTARY SOVEREIGNTY

PART 4

FORD v. QUEBEC:

THE LANGUAGE OF
PUBLIC SIGNS

Pierre Coulombe

State intervention that aims at modifying the status of languages in a polity is not uncommon. Since most societies are to some degree multilingual, and languages in contact most often are unequal in prestige, transforming the linguistic behaviour of citizens in order to elevate the position of a given language is a widespread public policy issue. Such intervention is no trivial matter, however, for state language planning is linked to questions of justice, citizenship, and rights. And the more far-reaching a language policy is, the more likely it is to spark disagreement among citizens over its legitimacy and efficiency. This is especially the case when a language law limits rather than expands linguistic diversity.

One component of language planning concerns public signs. In Colombia, for example, all public signs must be exclusively in Spanish, except for those specifically geared to tourists.[1] In Mexico's federal district, the required permit for putting up signs is not issued unless the signs are in Spanish.[2] The Swiss canton of Tessin, for its part, requires the predominance of Italian on all public signs.[3] In Quebec, too, legislative provisions regulate the use of languages on public signs. In its latest version (1993), the Charter of the French Language, a provincial law otherwise known as Bill 101, requires the marked predominance of French on public signs.

Quebec's language of signs policy is the product of twenty-five years of democratic deliberation. A Supreme Court of Canada ruling central to this deliberation is *Ford v. Quebec*. This chapter will examine the language of signs policy in light of the *Ford* decision. I will first describe historical events leading up to the enactment of the Charter of the French Language, and explain the justifications that can be given for having such a law. I will then focus on the nature of the dispute at hand and the decision of the Supreme Court. A discussion of the political fallout from the decision will follow. The question asked in the concluding section is whether *Ford* constitutes a morally sound judgment.

THE LANGUAGE OF SIGNS

The idea of legislating the public use of languages in Quebec took root in the late 1960s when, in the aftermath of the Quiet Revolution, the Québécois (i.e., French-speaking Quebeckers) saw themselves as a majority in the province rather than as a minority in Canada. The rationale for intervening then still applies today: in Quebec, language transfers of allophones (people who are neither francophone or anglophone) tend naturally to benefit the English-speaking community; put differently, if left free to choose, allophones who abandon their mother tongue adopt English more often than French. Even with language laws in place that limit this choice, recent data indicates that immigrants who settle in Montreal are as likely to learn English as they are to learn French.[4] The fact that more than 80 percent of Quebeckers (i.e., all people living in Quebec) are francophone seems to be an insufficient reason for immigrants to be drawn to the learning of the French language rather than the English language. For many immigrants, settling in Quebec means settling in North America, where the English language naturally constitutes the means of communication. Successive Quebec governments have sought ways of sending a clear message to the allophone community: Quebec is a French-speaking society.

Language policy in Quebec has traditionally attempted to promote the use of French in four sectors: in the legislature and courts, in schools, in the workplace, and on public signs. This last component, which was the object of dispute in the *Ford* ruling, is therefore part of a complex and far-reaching language planning effort. In 1969, with An Act to Promote the French Language in Quebec (Bill 63), the objective of making French the predominant language of public signs was invoked for the first time.[5] Five years later, the government of Robert Bourassa brought in the Official Language Act (Bill 22), the first law to impose the use of French on public signs, but without forbidding additional languages.[6] In 1977, shortly after René Lévesque's Parti Québécois took power, the Charter of the French Language (Bill 101) was enacted. It required the exclusive use of French on all public signs, except for signs with humanitarian, political, or religious purposes. Alongside other important measures, the promotion and eventually the imposition of French on public signs was a visual means of communicating the linguistic nature of Quebec society to the immigrant population. Quebec's language policy thus rejects freedom of choice as a principle to govern the language of use on public signs.

At the outset, we may ask what the justifications are for adopting coercive, rather than persuasive, measures. To invoke the fragility of French in contrast to the strength of English does not, in itself, constitute a justification for state intervention. After all, everyone knows languages cannot be of equal strength; so why not let the free market of languages decide which will dominate instead of compelling citizens to use one in particular? The two distinct answers to this question point to the dual nature of Quebec's language policy. The first can be labelled the "collective rights" argument. What is invoked here is the right of the French-speaking majority to its cultural survival. It is an argument founded on the notion of historical continuity, whereby a people's identity ought to be preserved through time. Hence the use of collective rights discourse as a moral tool for a people to state its claims. The Québécois, the argument goes, have the *right* to promote their language, even if such promotion limits some individual rights. The second answer hinges on liberal-democratic principles. In this case, what is invoked is the need for a common public language in order to foster social cohesion and equal participation. It is an argument founded in French and American republican thought, whereby no divisive identity-related features, such as language, ought to come between citizens. Since Quebec is an overwhelmingly French-speaking society, the argument goes, French ought to be the language by which citizens of all descents integrate, not unlike English in Newfoundland, Italian in Italy, or Spanish in Puerto Rico.[7]

The defence of Quebec's language policy has included both the "collective rights" argument and the "liberal-democratic" argument,[8] although the latter clearly dominates today in a liberal-minded public discourse. It is indeed striking to hear how recent justifications for language laws no longer invoke collective rights, and instead solely call on liberal-democratic principles. This evolution in the discourse is part of the broader evolution of Quebec nationalism. The Quebec nation is no longer described in terms of a French-Canadian majority whose right to cultural survival is rooted in history, but rather in terms of a pluralistic society whose members of diverse origins ought to use a common language in the public sphere.

In 1977, with the Charter of the French Language, the Quebec National Assembly "resolved therefore to make of French the language of Government and the Law, as well as the normal and everyday language of work, instruction, communication, commerce and business."[9] In the private realm, citizens may use the language of their choice; however, in communicating with other citizens in the public realm, they ought to use French. In short, French should become the public language of Quebec society. As part of this general objective, the law imposed for the first time the exclusive use of French on public signs. If the visual environment were to remain ambiguously bilingual, according to the National Assembly, it would dissuade nonfrancophones from learning French, given the powerful attraction of English.[10] The linguistic landscape must be resolutely French so that nonfrancophones, especially newcomers, are conditioned into seeing it as Quebec's public language. State intervention to pursue this goal is justified by the collective right of Québécois to continue to live, work, and play in their language, and by the need to foster social cohesion as a precondition for an equal citizenship.

Not everyone, however, believed that French-only signs were a legitimate means of pursuing this objective. Among those who disagreed were business owners in the Montreal area who, in 1984, jointly challenged the language of signs provisions of Bill 101 in Quebec's Superior Court. They had received a summons from the Commission de surveillance de la langue française (the office responsible for investigating presumed infractions to the Charter of the French Language) advising them that their bilingual commercial signs were illegal. For example, one of those charged, Valerie Ford, who operated a retail store specializing in the sale of wool, displayed an exterior sign that included both "laine" and "wool." The other businesses involved in the case were charged for similar offences. The case eventually landed before the Supreme Court of Canada, which, in *Ford v. Quebec,* rendered a unanimous decision on December 15, 1988.

THE *FORD* CASE

The significance of court decisions such as *Ford* lies in how they shape the law by enunciating some of society's fundamental values—values that should be considered during public deliberations and policy making. Governments usually formulate policies that reflect the preferences of their electorate or that serve the pursuit of a particular agenda, but in the process sometimes neglect—because of political expediency or sheer incompetence—to consider the costs of these policies in terms of human rights and freedoms. One of the judiciary's roles is, therefore, to articulate where the limits of state intervention ought to be fixed. Court decisions are authoritative, though by no means flawless, and constitute counterweights to legislative power. With the entrenchment of the Charter of Rights and Freedoms in the Constitution, Canadian courts have had to explore much more often the relationship between the state and citizens, and between laws and liberties. Not surprisingly, the question of whether Bill 101 unduly restricted rights and freedoms was soon put before them.

The provisions of the Charter of the French Language at issue were section 58, which declared that public signs and commercial advertising had to be solely in French, and section 69, which declared that only the French version of a firm's name could be used. As for the rights and freedoms presumably infringed on, they are guaranteed by the Quebec Charter of Human Rights and Freedoms (henceforth referred to as the Quebec Charter) and, to a lesser extent, by the Canadian Charter of Rights and Freedoms (henceforth referred to as the Canadian Charter). These are the right to freedom of expression found in section 3 of the Quebec Charter and section 2(b) of the Canadian Charter, as well as the right against discrimination based on language found in section 10 of the Quebec Charter, but absent from the Canadian Charter. The two charters also recognize that rights and freedoms are not absolute. Section 9.1 of the Quebec Charter states: "In exercising his fundamental freedoms and rights, a person shall maintain a proper regard for democratic values, public order and the general well-being of the citizens of Quebec. In this respect, the scope of the freedoms and rights, and limits to their exercise, may be fixed by law." Similarly, section 1 of the Canadian Charter states: "The Canadian Charter of Rights and Freedoms guarantees the rights and freedoms set out in it subject only to such reasonable limits prescribed by law as can be demonstrably justified in a free and democratic society."

The Supreme Court was first asked whether "the freedom of expression guaranteed by s. 2(b) of the Canadian Charter and by s. 3 of the Quebec Charter include the freedom to express oneself in the language of one's choice."[11] Both the Superior Court of Quebec and the Quebec Court of Appeal had answered in the affirmative, noting the intimate relationship between expression and language. The Attorney General of Quebec had argued that a distinction should be made between the message and the medium, that the challenged provisions of

Bill 101 did not regulate the content of expression, but the language used to express content. But, quoting a well-known sociolinguist, Joshua Fishman, the Supreme Court concurred with the lower courts in saying that language "is not merely a *carrier* of content ... Language itself *is* content."[12] Moreover, the Court pointed out that the Charter of the French Language itself recognizes the value of a language as being more than a simple means of expression when it states in its preamble that "the French language ... is the instrument by which that people has articulated its identity."[13] The significance of the language–identity link, manifestly, cannot apply only to the French Québécois.

Having determined that freedom of expression does include the freedom to express oneself in the language of one's choice, the Supreme Court had to consider whether freedom of expression extends to *commercial* expression, since the challenged provisions concerned businesses. Again, both the Superior Court and the Court of Appeal had argued that it does, that the value of commercial expression stems from its function of assisting consumers to make informed economic choices. The Attorney General of Quebec had submitted that commercial expression is not a fundamental freedom, that Charter guarantees of freedom of expression are meant to protect *political* expression as an essential component to democracy. To place commercial expression and political expression on the same footing, he had argued, would be to trivialize the latter. The Supreme Court, however, felt that the commercial purpose in using English on signs does not have the effect of removing it from the scope of protected freedoms, and thus that commercial expression is not undeserving of constitutional protection. For these reasons, the Court concluded that sections 58 and 69 of the Charter of the French Language infringe on freedom of expression guarantees found in both the Quebec and Canadian Charters.

But is the infringement justified under section 1 of the Canadian Charter and section 9.1 of the Quebec Charter? To answer this question, the Supreme Court first had to establish whether the objective underlying the Charter of the French Language is a legitimate one. The material submitted by the Attorney General of Quebec, in that regard, convinced the Court of the pressing need to address the vulnerable position of the French language in Quebec, a view that was shared by the respondents themselves. A number of reasons for taking seriously Quebec's language policy were given: the declining birth rate of Quebec francophones, the integration of immigrants into Quebec's anglophone community, and the subordinate place of French in the economy. In the days before language planning, wrote the Court, the linguistic landscape

> *strongly suggested to young and ambitious francophones that the language of success was almost exclusively English. It confirmed to anglophones that there was no great need to learn the majority language. And it suggested to immigrants that the prudent course lay in joining the anglophone community ....*
> *The threat to the French language demonstrated to the government that it should, in particular, take steps to assure that the "visage linguistique" of Quebec would reflect the predominance of the French language.*[14]

The Court thus saw "a rational connection between protecting the French language and assuring that the reality of Quebec society is communicated through the 'visage linguistique.'"[15] Simply put, a language of signs policy is a sensible prescription for offsetting the asymmetry between the French and English languages in Quebec.

While the Supreme Court agreed that the objective underlying Quebec's sign law is a legitimate one, and that a language of signs policy is a rational means of meeting this objective, it did not, however, see the necessity of prohibiting languages other than French. The Attorney General of Quebec had pointed out that the Charter of the French Language contains a number of exceptions that attenuate the infringement to commercial expression, but had not submitted an argument to justify the exclusive use of French. Thus, if lawmakers wished to reflect the reality of Quebec society, that is, the predominance of the French language, the Court felt they could do so by requiring the display of French on public signs. In fact, taking on a policy-making role, the Court argued that imposing the *marked predominance* of French "would be proportional to the goal of promoting and maintaining a French 'visage linguistique' in Quebec and therefore justified under s. 9.1 of the Quebec Charter and s. 1 of the Canadian Charter."[16] However, prohibiting other languages is not proportional to this goal. In the words of the Court, the predominant display of French

> would ensure that the "visage linguistique" reflected the demography of
> Quebec: the predominant language is French. This reality should be communi-
> cated to all citizens and non-citizens alike, irrespective of their mother tongue.
> But exclusivity for the French language has not survived the scrutiny of a pro-
> portionality test and does not reflect the reality of Quebec society.[17]

In other words, to require the exclusive use of French is out of proportion with the end in question, that is, ensuring that the predominance of the French language be reflected in public postings.

The final question put before the Supreme Court was whether sections 58 and 69 of the Charter of the French Language violate the right against discrimination based on language in section 10 of the Quebec Charter. As was mentioned above, only the Quebec Charter applied here, since its Canadian counterpart does not include language in the list of items against which discrimination is prohibited. Section 10 of the Quebec Charter states that discrimination occurs when a distinction, exclusion, or preference based on language has the effect of impairing the right of persons to the full and equal recognition and exercise of their human rights and freedoms. Unlike section 3 of the Quebec Charter, which guarantees freedom of expression, section 10 is not subject to section 9.1 limitations. The Superior Court and the Court of Appeal had ruled, in agreement with the Attorney General of Quebec, that since the challenged provisions applied to everyone, regardless of their language of use, they did not constitute discrimination. No doubt they imposed on nonfrancophones a heavier burden, but such indirect discrimination was not, in their opinion, ground for finding them unconstitutional. The Supreme Court, however, disagreed. Referring to an argument made in a prior decision, *Forget v. A.G. Quebec*, it claimed that the *effect* of French-only signs had to be taken into account, regardless of the fact that the law applied to everyone indiscriminately. That effect is differential, in the sense that the requirement of French-only signs impinges "differentially on different classes of persons according to their language of use."[18] For the Court, this distinction impairs the right of nonfrancophones to full and equal recognition and exercise of the freedom to express themselves in the language of their choice, construed as a fundamental freedom.

For all these reasons, section 58 of the Charter of the French Language, which stated that public signs and commercial advertising are required to be solely in French, and section 69, which stated that only the French version of a firm name can be used, were declared unconstitutional.

BILL 178 AND THE UNITED NATIONS

The *Ford* decision arrived in the midst of heated debates surrounding the Meech Lake Accord, which would have amended the Constitution to recognize the distinct character of Quebec society. With public opinion already on edge, the government of Robert Bourassa had to respond to the ruling, knowing full well that whatever decision it took would likely displease many Quebeckers and Canadians. The Quebec government could comply with the ruling and be denounced by those who objected to any form of bilingualism on signs. Or it could make use of the override clauses (also known as the notwithstanding clauses) in both Quebec and Canadian Charters in order to uphold the integrity of the law, and be denounced by those who objected to the prohibition of other languages. The compromise the government proposed is Bill 178, enacted on December 22, 1988, which amended the Charter of the French Language. According to the new law, the rule of unilingualism would continue to prevail for outside signs, but other languages would be allowed inside establishments as long as French was predominantly displayed. Given its partial compliance with *Ford*, Bill 178 therefore included a disposition so as to be shielded for a period of five years from any court challenge based on section 2(b) of the Canadian Charter and sections 3 and 10 of the Quebec Charter. In other words, the notwithstanding clauses of the Canadian and Quebec Charters were invoked. Bill 178 was not greeted as a pragmatic compromise that could preserve the outside visibility of the French landscape while respecting the right of consumers to make informed economic choices where these are usually made, that is, inside businesses. Instead, it was criticized as an awkward piece of legislation brought forth by a government caving in to either anglophone or nationalist interests.

One consequence of the government's decision to override the judgment rendered by the Supreme Court in *Ford* is the appeal launched by three Quebec anglophones (a painter, a designer, and an undertaker) to the Human Rights Committee of the United Nations. Bill 178, they maintained, prevented them from advertising their services on exterior commercial signs in English, the language spoken by most of their customers. They challenged the legitimacy of Bill 178 under the International Covenant on Civil and Political Rights, of which Canada is a signatory—and as a result, ironically, the inculpated party in the case—alleging that the law violated the Covenant's guarantees relating to freedom of expression and to the right against discrimination. Furthermore, they claimed that the Quebec government's use of the override procedure (the notwithstanding clause) effectively denied them any further domestic remedy. The Committee agreed to hear the claim and reported its decision on May 5, 1993. Such decisions are not legally binding, although they do carry some moral weight.[19]

The Committee's main conclusion was that section 58 of the Charter of the French Language, as amended by Bill 178, violates freedom of expression guarantees under article 19 of the Covenant. In the words of the Committee, "[a] State may choose one or more official languages, but it may not exclude, outside the spheres of public life, the freedom to express oneself in a language of one's choice."[20]

Some interesting elements of this case are worth noting. First, the federal government, as the state party in the case, unsuccessfully argued that the extraordinary use of the notwithstanding clause allows a duly elected assembly of representatives to limit the powers of the judiciary:

> A system in which the judiciary is given full and final say on all issues of rights adversely impacts on a key tenet of democracy—that is, participation of citizens in a forum of elected and publicly accountable legislatures on questions of social and political justice ... he 'notwithstanding' clause provides a limited legislative counterweight in a system which otherwise gives judges final say over rights issues.[21]

Second, the Committee observed that the alleged victims could not invoke the protection of section 27 of the Covenant, which affirms the right of minorities to use their own language in their communities with the other members of their group. The anglophone community's status, the Committee argued, is that of a majority within the Canadian *state.* Consequently, anglophones have no claim under section 27, even though they constitute a minority within the *province.*

Third, the Committee concluded there had been no violation of section 26 of the Covenant, which affirms the right to equality before the law. Against the Supreme Court's reasoning, it argued that Bill 178 prohibited both anglophones *and* francophones from using English on outdoor signs, and therefore that no discrimination was involved.

Finally, it is also worth noting the dissenting opinion of Birame Ndiaye. He argued that the Charter of the French Language, as amended by Bill 178, pursues the same goal as that aimed at by section 27 of the Covenant, that is, the survival of a minority as an entity, which applies to the French-speaking community of Canada, not to the anglophone community of Quebec. Limitations to freedom of expression, as guaranteed by section 19 of the Covenant, are justified, considering

that the goal of the Charter of the French Language is compatible with the substance of section 27. It is important to provide francophones with a sense of linguistic security, he argued, and hence it is reasonable that, in the process of
pursuing this objective, freedom of expression be subject to certain restrictions,
including those brought about by Bill 178. He deplored the fact that

> [f]or the Committee, there is no linguistic problem in Canada or, if it does
> exist, it is not so important as to merit the treatment which the authorities of
> that country have chosen to extend to it. I can only disassociate myself from its
> conclusions.[22]

Except for Ndiaye's dissenting opinion, we can say that the Human Rights
Committee agreed with the Supreme Court that the Charter of the French
Language, as amended by Bill 178, violates freedom of expression, but disagreed
that it constitutes discrimination against nonfrancophones.

Following the Human Rights Committee's observations, and given the expi-
ration of the five-year override provision included in Bill 178, the National
Assembly enacted Bill 86, which once again amended the Charter of the French
Language. Interestingly, the Quebec government could have renewed the use of the
notwithstanding clause for another five years, but decided not to. Even though the
Human Rights Committee's decision was not binding, it constituted the judgment
of an international body, a fact that the Quebec government was quick to point out
in its justifications for restoring bilingualism on signs. So with Bill 86, French as a
rule must appear on public signs and commercial advertising and must be used in
firm names. However, and in compliance with the Supreme Court's and the Human
Rights Committee's decisions, other languages can be used as well. The rule of the
marked predominance of French applies for public signs and commercial advertising, and the rule of equality, for firm names. Three exceptions to this general rule
should be mentioned. First, when the message conveyed is of a nonprofit religious,
ideological, or humanitarian nature, French is not required.[23] This exception was
included in the first version of the Charter of the French Language (1977) and has
been maintained ever since. Second, when commercial billboards are sixteen square
metres or more in size and are visible from a public road, the exclusive use of French
is mandatory.[24] Third, when a commercial advertisement is on or in any public
means of transportation, the exclusive use of French is required.[25]

Since then, no further amendment to the Charter of the French Language
has been made with regard to the language of signs. An interesting phenomenon is
the decision of large companies not to use other languages in addition to French,
even though they have the legal right to do so. When, in 1998, some of these companies faced the possibility of a boycott by English-rights groups for not posting
bilingual signs, French-rights groups subsequently also threatened them with a
counter-boycott should the companies cave in to the pressure from the English-
rights groups. This led some company officials to suggest that a return to the policy
of unilingualism would be desirable, since it would divert the protest away from
them and towards the National Assembly. What is certain is that the credibility of

the Charter of the French Language would suffer from any significant amendment. Consistency is necessary for newcomers to take seriously the resolve of the National Assembly to make French the public language, over and above partisan considerations. In that regard, the Parti Québécois, which devised the policy of unilingualism, and the Liberal Party, which invoked the notwithstanding clause following *Ford*, both accept the reasonableness of the present policy.

BEHIND A VEIL OF IGNORANCE

In *A Theory of Justice*, American philosopher John Rawls proposes a theoretical procedure for determining the principles of justice that ought to govern society. If the procedure is fair, then the principles agreed on will be just. But for such a procedure to be fair, he argues, we first need to exclude contingencies that would taint the deliberations. Put differently, as delegates who deliberate on the principles of justice, we should not be able to exploit our personal circumstances to our advantage. The device he proposed is called the "veil of ignorance." The idea is to place ourselves behind a veil where we have no knowledge of particular facts about ourselves, such as our natural attributes, personal interests, or social position, nor any knowledge of particular facts about society, such as its history, political culture, or institutional structure. Rawls argues that behind the veil of ignorance, we would agree on a most basic principle of justice: equal liberty for all. This is, however, only the first step in a four-stage sequence at each stage of which the veil is partially lifted, revealing more information about society. At each subsequent stage we also inherit the constraints agreed upon in the previous stages. The second stage is the constitutional convention. At this point, we know the general facts about our society (but remain ignorant of our particular situation), so that we are able to incorporate in the constitution the concrete forms the principle of equal liberty will take. The next step is the legislative stage, at which laws and policies are made from the perspective of a lawmaker who still has no knowledge about his particular place in society. Finally, the last stage corresponds to the application of rules, namely by judges, with the restrictions of the veil of ignorance lifted completely.[26] The general idea of this device is to control the information available to individuals in order to establish an impartial point of view from which they can consider the terms of justice.

We could ask ourselves how Quebec's original policy of French-only signs would have fared in such a scheme. Assuming that the principle of equal liberty would have been chosen at the first stage, we can safely say—as does Rawls—that the rights to freedom of expression and to protection against discrimination would have been entrenched at the constitutional stage. These rights are, indeed, included in both the Quebec and Canadian Charters. Derived from these rights are the freedom to use the language of one's choice and the guarantee to not be discriminated against on the basis of one's language. They are not particular species of rights, but rather concrete forms of the basic respect for the autonomy and dignity of the individual.[27]

It is unlikely that collective language rights would have been considered at this stage, regardless of the importance they may hold for human well-being. In the abstract, delegates behind the veil of ignorance might recognize the good of cultural and linguistic identity to individuals. But they would lack the information required to give any shape to this recognition, since collective rights concern individuals as members of particular communities claiming particular goods. Moreover, even in the abstract, delegates would hesitate to recognize groups as right-holders, fearing that group claims would have parity with individual rights. Collective rights would ill serve as constitutional principles for adjudicating conflicting values and interests. In that respect, suggestions to entrench Bill 101 in the constitution of a sovereign Quebec, or even in its present Charter of Human Rights and Freedoms, and thus elevate it to the rank of fundamental right, have had little support. However important the law is for the recognition of language rights, few wish to see it placed on an equal footing with traditional civil rights.

It is at the legislative stage that language policy might be conceived and drafted. The veil of ignorance partially lifted, the lawmaker would discover a multilingual society. Inheriting the principles of a constitutional democracy from the previous stage, he or she might see the need for social cohesion in order to maximize the participation of every citizen in Quebec's institutions. If so, he or she would probably also see the need for a common public language to serve as an integrating tool. Given the presence of a large majority of francophones, but also the asymmetrical power of attraction between the French and English languages, legislating the compulsory use of the majority language on public signs would seem reasonable. But, however important this objective is for democracy itself, the lawmaker might nevertheless hesitate to prohibit other languages. The value of expression and that of public participation and integration are on the same footing, and the reasonable course would be to maximize the promotion of both. A law that imposes the use of French on all signs, but without prohibiting other languages, would seem a fair reconciliation of these equally worthy values.

The lawmaker would also hear groups make conflicting claims for the preservation of their linguistic identity. The francophone community, whose members largely share the same origins, would ground in history its collective claims to cultural continuity. But so would the anglophone minority. It, too, could invoke its historical presence in Quebec—rather than its status as part of English Canada's numerical majority—and insist that its language not be relegated to the private sphere. Aware of such general facts about these groups' conflicting claims, but not knowing to which he or she belongs, the lawmaker might propose a language of signs policy that provides some security to the francophone community as a regional majority, but a minority in Canada, and that also provides comfort to the anglophone community as a majority in Canada, but a regional minority in Quebec. This policy might resemble that of marked predominance for the threatened language, combined with allowances for ensuring the public visibility of the regional minority's language.

Delegates subject to the constraints of the veil of ignorance would likely reach a conclusion similar to the one Justices of the Supreme Court reached in

Ford v. Quebec: Imposing the use of French on public signs is legitimate, but prohibiting other languages is not. This theoretical exercise is interesting because it brings out a twofold rationale for today's language of signs policy that was implicit in the Supreme Court's decision, namely, the importance of liberal-democratic principles and collective rights.

A consensus on the justifications for the present-day policy arises from the deliberations of Canadian courts, the Human Rights Committee, and delegates behind the veil of ignorance. A first set of justifications speaks of the need for the promotion of French in the name of equal citizenship: every Quebec resident should have equal access to public institutions and deliberations. A necessary condition for such equality is inclusion, of which a common public language is an important ingredient in a multilingual society such as Quebec. A second set of justifications speaks of the need for the promotion of French in the name of the francophone community. The language rights of the French Canadians of Quebec are rooted in history, and thus acquire moral weight when various claims to language protection conflict. But both kinds of justifications cannot avoid consideration of respect for other languages, namely, English. Consideration cannot be avoided because nonfrancophones have the freedom to express themselves in their own language, a principle that is central to equal liberty, and because English-speaking Quebeckers are members of a settled community with equally valid historical claims to the preservation of their identity.

Today, the Charter of the French Language, in accordance with the Supreme Court's conclusions in *Ford*, meets these requirements of justice.

ENDNOTES

I would like to thank Noële Racine, Diane Roussel, and the editors of this volume for their comments.

1. Jacques Leclerc, *La guerre des langues dans l'affichage* (Montréal: VLB Éditeur, 1989), 164–66. Also see Jacques Leclerc and Jacques Maurais, *Recueil des législations linguistiques dans le monde*, vol. 6 (Québec: Centre international de recherche en aménagement linguistique, 1994).

2. Leclerc, *La guerre des langues dans l'affichage*, 257. Also see Leclerc and Maurais, *Recueil des législations linguistiques dans le monde*, vol. 6.

3. Leclerc and Maurais, *Recueil des législations linguistiques dans le monde*, vol. 3.

4. The 1996 census seems to confirm this phenomenon. In the city of Montreal, the language transfers of allophones are towards English and French equally; in the Communauté urbaine de Montréal, two-thirds transfer to English. See Jean Chartier, "Le français n'est parlé que dans 44,8% des foyers de la CUM, hormis Montréal," *Le Devoir* (Montreal), 30 March 1999, A3.

5. Section 4 of Bill 63 stated that the Office de la langue française is to "advise the government on any legislative or administrative measures which might be passed in regard to public posting to ensure the priority of the French language therein."

6. Section 35 of Bill 22 stated that "[p]ublic signs must be drawn up in French or in both French and another language...."

7. Jean Dansereau, legal adviser for the Office de la langue française, writes: "En donnant le nom de charte à sa loi linguistique, et en qualifiant de fondamentaux les droits

linguistiques qu'elle prévoit (sans pour autant lui accorder la préséance sur la *Charte québécoise des droits et libertés*), il paraît non seulement avoir voulu faire passer la langue française du statut de langue dominée à celui de 'langue prédominante' (selon l'expression utilisée par la Cour suprême dans l'arrêt Ford), mais la proposer comme valeur d'intégration à toute la société québécoise, selon un processus qui affecte l'ensemble des rapports sociaux et qui implique une transformation qualitative de son statut." Jean Dansereau, "Droits linguistiques individuels et droits linguistiques collectifs," paper presented at the symposium *Droits linguistiques et droits culturels*, 23–25 April 1992, Girona (Catalonia), 34.

8. For example, in a 1978 article, Camille Laurin, the architect of Bill 101, justified Quebec's new language policy as the concrete expression of the right of the Quebec people, understood here as the French-speaking Québécois, to preserve its French identity. However, he also wrote that "Québec also needs a common language to ensure the cohesion of its community and the normal, smooth, and efficient functioning of its institutions." See "French Language Charter," *Canadian Review of Sociology and Anthropology* 15, no. 2, (1978): 122.

9. Charter of the French Language, Preamble.

10. José Woehrling, "La conformité de certaines modifications projetées au régime linguistique de l'affichage public et de la publicité commerciale découlant de la *Charte de la langue française* avec les chartes des droits et libertés," *Avis sur d'éventuelles modifications à la Charte de la langue française* (Conseil de la langue française, 1993), 11–12.

11. *Ford v. Quebec (A.G.)* [1988] 2 S.C.R., 733.

12. Joshua Fishman, *The Sociology of Language*, 1972, 4, quoted in *Ford v. Quebec*, 750.

13. Charter of the French Language, preamble, quoted in *Ford v. Quebec*, 750.

14. *Ford v. Quebec*, 778.

15. Ibid., 779.

16. Ibid., 717.

17. Ibid., 780.

18. Ibid., 787.

19. I thank José Woehrling for clarifying this point.

20. Human Rights Committee, Forty-seventh session, 5 May 1993, 16.

21. Quoted in Human Rights Committee, 10.

22. Birame Ndiaye, in Human Rights Committee, 20.

23. Charte de la langue française, 1993, section 59. Also see Règlements, section 22.

24. Charte de la langue française, Règlements, 1993, section 15.

25. Ibid., section 16.

26. John Rawls, *A Theory of Justice* (Cambridge: The Belknap Press of Harvard University Press, 1971), 195–201.

27. I develop this distinction further in *Language Rights in French Canada* (New York: Lang Publishing, 1995), 89–92.

ACCEPTABLE LAW, QUESTIONABLE POLITICS:

THE CANADA ASSISTANCE PLAN REFERENCE

Paul Barker

Federal–provincial fiscal arrangements represent an important element in Canadian politics. They involve the transfer of financial assistance from the federal government to provincial authorities for the purpose of helping to fund programs in such areas as health, welfare, and postsecondary education.[1] In the 1990s, these arrangements experienced a great deal of turbulence, largely because of budgetary problems at the national level. In the early part of the decade, the federal government placed limits on increases in payments to provinces in an effort to deal with large budget deficits and the resulting cost of servicing the growing public debt. In 1995 it took more drastic action: it reduced the level of funding and changed the structure of the most important fiscal arrangements. At the end of the 1990s, the emergence of budget surpluses allowed for a partial restoration of payments.

One of the earliest events in this roller-coaster ride in federal–provincial financing concerned the Canada Assistance Plan (CAP), a major fiscal arrangement affecting provincial welfare services. In early 1990, the federal government announced that the growth in CAP transfers in each of the next two fiscal years would be limited to 5 percent for the well-off provinces of Ontario, Alberta, and British Columbia. Shortly thereafter, the government of British Columbia challenged the constitutionality of the limit in the courts. Using a newly developing legal doctrine, the province argued it had a "legitimate expectation" that any immediate changes in CAP required the consent of the provinces, and that the relevant law seemed to support such a challenge. The *Canada Assistance Plan* [*Act*], the legislative authority for CAP, stated that each province could enter into an agreement with Ottawa to provide for the federal sharing of welfare costs *and* that the amendment or termination of this agreement necessitated either the consent of both parties or one year's notice by either the federal government or the province in question. The individual agreements themselves included the same provisions. But Ottawa had neither sought the consent of British Columbia nor given the appropriate notice. It had simply said that in less than two months limits would be placed on CAP payments to the well-off provinces. The government of British Columbia succeeded at first with its argument. The B.C. Court of Appeal agreed that the province did indeed have a legitimate expectation that its consent was required before any changes could be made to CAP. But the province lost its case on appeal to the Supreme Court of Canada. The highest court in the land ruled that the principle of parliamentary sovereignty gave the federal government all the authority necessary to make unilateral changes to federal–provincial fiscal arrangements.

By itself, judicial review is usually unable to shape the course of federal–provincial relations dramatically. But, in this instance, the courts could have caused relations to take a more desirable direction. If the Supreme Court of Canada had decided in favour of British Columbia, the federal government would have been forced to make adjustments to the fiscal arrangements in partnership with the provinces. This is not to say that the Court made a poor decision, for a judgment based on the supremacy of Parliament is on solid ground. Nevertheless, a different decision most likely would have better protected health and social programs at the provincial level, given that the limits and reductions in federal financing hurt the operation of hospitals, universities, and social welfare plans. More importantly, a decision that found against unilateral actions might have provided for more cordial relations between the two levels of government. In a country beset by unity problems and fractious relations between national and provincial authorities, this would not have been an insignificant benefit.

LIMITS ON CAP

On February 20, 1990, the federal government, in its annual budget statement, outlined a new strategy for controlling program spending at the federal level. Since its election in 1984, the Progressive Conservative government of Brian Mulroney had been committed to dealing with large budget deficits and the high cost of financing the growing public debt. The new strategy, called the Expenditure Control Plan, was the latest move in the fight to "restore health to the nation's finances."[2] One of the areas affected by the control plan was transfers to the provinces. Over the years, Ottawa and the provinces together had agreed to a set of fiscal arrangements whereby the federal government transferred cash and taxing authority to the provinces to help pay for health, education, welfare, and other services. The inability of the provinces to finance such services under their jurisdiction had helped precipitate the arrangements, and so had the desire of

Ottawa to establish comparable social programs in the provinces. By the end of the 1980s, federal cash transfers to the provinces for the largest arrangements equalled nearly $25 billion, representing about one-quarter of total federal program spending. A further $10 billion had been transferred in the form of increased taxing authority.

Clearly, there was, in a fiscal sense, good cause to include the transfers in a deficit-reduction program. The transfers were simply too large to be ignored. The rapid increases in these transfers suggested the same; the average annual rate of growth of transfers in recent years was twice that of overall federal spending. But, in a political sense, the focus on federal transfers to the provinces meant trouble. Federal–provincial fiscal relations had always been a difficult area. The federal government typically sought in the relations control over the level and use of transferred monies. The provinces strove for the opposite, to ensure a steady flow of federal funding while at the same time minimizing the conditions attached to the funds. The result was frequent conflict, and conflict that threatened the very viability of the federation. Nevertheless, Ottawa determined that fiscal transfers to the provinces would not be spared.

Under the Expenditure Control Plan, increases in per capita payments for the largest federal–provincial fiscal arrangement, Established Programs Financing, were frozen for the next two years. This action was a continuation of a series of attempts made in the 1980s to limit federal spending for this arrangement, which covered health care and postsecondary education. But there was something new in the control plan dealing with fiscal arrangements. For the first time, CAP would be affected. The plan dictated that increases in CAP payments for fiscal years 1990–91 and 1991–92 would be limited to 5 percent for the relatively rich or "have" provinces of Ontario, Alberta, and British Columbia.[3] Under CAP, the federal government agreed to pay up to 50 percent of the costs of provincial (and territorial) expenditures on social assistance payments and welfare services; in return, the provinces were obliged to observe a few conditions concerning the operation of their welfare programs. Until now, CAP had been an open-ended arrangement: Ottawa would finance half of eligible or shareable provincial expenditures on welfare. But the Expenditure Control Plan changed that for three of the provinces. For these provinces, the federal government would, in the next two fiscal years, share costs *up to a point*, namely, to where provincial expenditures increased by 5 percent. Beyond this point, Ontario, Alberta, and British Columbia were on their own, and the belief of all concerned parties was that spending on welfare would increase by more than 5 percent.

Ottawa defended its proposal for introducing limits into the CAP arrangement. The proposal involved only those provinces best able fiscally to handle reductions in transfers. Of the three affected provinces, the federal Finance Minister said, "[W]e have asked them to accept a slightly greater responsibility."[4] The action also sent a message to some of the provinces—Ontario in particular— that their expenditures on social assistance were rising too rapidly. The provinces, especially those directly affected, were unpersuaded. The limits represented an attempt, they said, to shift the federal deficit to the provinces. A federal problem would now become a provincial one. More directly, Ottawa would be withholding much-needed funding, and the need would become even greater with the expected downturn in the economy. To stop the federal government from moving forward with the "cap on CAP," the provinces had some "weapons" at their disposal.[5] One such weapon was to object to the constitutionality of the federal limits. The provinces, however, had not issued a constitutional challenge when the federal government had placed restraints on transfers in the 1980s. The provinces had not done so in part because there seemed to be little ground for such a challenge. The Constitution and supporting case law recognized the authority of the federal government to disburse money in areas of provincial jurisdiction and to attach any conditions to the spending of these monies. In making changes to the fiscal arrangements, Ottawa was merely exercising its power to spend.

The seeming lack of constitutional grounds notwithstanding, a week after the announcement of the Expenditure Control Plan, the government of British Columbia indicated its intention to challenge the constitutionality of the 5 percent limit on CAP payments to itself, Alberta, and Ontario. The immediate question was, on what basis could the provincial government make its case? The answer has to do with the federal statute supporting CAP, the *Canada Assistance Plan* [*Act*], which required that the federal government and each of the provinces enter into an agreement specifying the details of the transfer of federal funds. More significantly, the law stated that "an agreement may ... be amended or terminated at any time by *mutual consent* of the Minister and the province," and the same provision was repeated in the individual agreements with the provinces.[6] The agreement could also be terminated unilaterally by either party, so long as they provided one year's notice. The other major fiscal arrangements lacked the same kinds of detailed agreements, so this quality made a constitutional challenge based on CAP an inviting proposition. And, of course, the limit on CAP increases meant that detailed agreements for Ontario, Alberta, and British Columbia had been amended, yet none of the affected provinces had given consent (nor received one-year notices of termination). Also relevant was that, in the past, any proposed and actual changes affecting CAP had involved discussions and agreement between Ottawa and the provinces. But the federal government in this instance had acted unilaterally. In light of all this, the government of British Columbia turned to the legal doctrine of "legitimate expectations." This doctrine essentially voided government actions if it was felt that such actions took insufficient notice of procedural requirements and expected behaviour. And this is what the government of British Columbia said had happened. "We have a legitimate expectation that when an agreement is made," said the province's Attorney General, "the aspects of that agreement will not be nullified by the unilateral acts by the minister of finance."[7] Ottawa needed the consent of British Columbia, but it had acted alone.[8]

The challenge was, strictly speaking, only in relation to CAP. But a successful challenge could have implications for *all* the federal–provincial fiscal arrangements. If the courts accepted the doctrine of legitimate expectations, then it might be applied across the board. Though the other major arrangements were without the detailed agreements and provisions requiring the consent of the provinces, they certainly involved expectations and beliefs by the provinces that the federal government would consult with them on any changes. At a minimum, a victory would give the provinces more leverage in their dealings with the federal government. Other aspects of the challenge also revealed that the case had implications that went beyond CAP and the doctrine of legitimate expectations. The Canadian judicial system permits parties other than those directly involved in a case to make representations before the courts (these are called "interveners"). In this case, the governments of Ontario, Manitoba, and Alberta all intervened and made arguments intended to supplement British Columbia's basic contention *and* to erect more legal obstacles to unilateral federal changes to federal–provincial fiscal arrangements.[9]

To expedite the case, the government of British Columbia relied on a little-known element of the judicial system. This element, called the reference procedure, allows governments (and no others) to ask the courts for an opinion on a government action. The opinion is only advisory—it has no legal force—but it typically has the effect of a binding decision. The attractiveness of the procedure for governments lies in part with its capacity to move matters forward quickly, and the B.C. government wanted swift action—it did not wish to lose funding under the new limit. Ideally, any government directing a reference to a court would prefer to send it to the highest and most powerful court in Canada, the Supreme Court of Canada. But only the federal government may do this. The provinces, however, are authorized to ask for an opinion from their provincial courts of appeal, and there is an automatic right of appeal of reference decisions to the Supreme Court of Canada. The first stop in the challenge of the new arrangement for CAP would thus be the B.C. Court of Appeal, with the expectation that any decision of this court would be appealed to the Supreme Court of Canada.

GETTING TO THE SUPREME COURT

The government of British Columbia referred two questions to the B.C. Court of Appeal:

> 1. Has the Government of Canada any statutory, prerogative or contractual authority to limit its obligations under the *Canada Assistance Plan Act*, R.S.C. 1970, c. C-1 and its Agreement with the Government of British Columbia dated March 23, 1967, to contribute 50 per cent of the cost to British Columbia of assistance and welfare services?
>
> 2. Do the terms of the Agreement dated March 23, 1967 between the Governments of Canada and British Columbia, the subsequent conduct of the Government of Canada pursuant to the Agreement and the provisions of the *Canada Assistance Plan Act*, R.S.C. 1970, c. C-1, give rise to a legitimate expectation that the Government of Canada would introduce no bill into Parliament to limits it obligation under the Agreement or the *Act* without the consent of British Columbia?[10]

On June 15, 1990, the B.C. Court of Appeal responded to the reference with three separate judgments.[11] On the first question, all three justices agreed. They interpreted the question as asking whether the federal cabinet has the authority to change its obligations under CAP without accompanying legislative enactments. This was an easy question to answer. No government can act in the absence of the appropriate legislative authority, and the limit of payments to 5 percent to designated provinces would be inconsistent with provisions in the *Canada Assistance Plan*. But this was not fatal to the purposes of the federal government. Suitable legislative authority in the form of the *Government Expenditures Restraint Act* had been introduced and would soon become law. On the second question, the Court of Appeal issued three distinct opinions. Two of the justices answered in the affirmative, that a legitimate expectation did indeed exist, but the two gave different reasons. Justice Lambert premised his opinion on the belief that a legitimate expectation existed if it could be shown that "there is an obligation, binding on Canada, to pay to British Columbia 50% of the cost of providing assistance to those in need...."[12] To determine the existence of an obligation, the Court had to interpret the meaning of the provision in the agreement that committed Canada to contributing to the financing of assistance and welfare services in British Columbia. Did it mean Canada must pay the proportion authorized when the agreement was made (which was 50 percent), or did it require the federal government to pay the amount that might be specified in any subsequent amendments? Justice Lambert said that the former interpretation, a "static" interpretation, was the right one, and so Ottawa was obligated to cover one-half the cost of welfare services in British Columbia.[13]

In the other opinion finding in the affirmative, Justice Toy (supported by two other justices) centred his decision on the legal doctrine of legitimate expectations. Justice Lambert had eschewed this approach, preferring to address the question in a way that focused on the ordinary or commonsense interpretation of the term "legitimate expectations." Justice Toy observed that the doctrine and supporting case law required public authorities to comply with any procedural requirements outlined in the law. A failure to do so amounted to a "procedural impropriety."[14] For Justice Toy, this reading of the doctrine of legitimate expectations made it simple to find that British Columbia did indeed have an legitimate expectation that no unilateral changes would be made to the cost-sharing arrangement. In coming to this decision, Justice Toy wanted to make it clear that he acknowledged the power of the federal Parliament to amend the *Canada Assistance Plan* on its own. His decision was not to be seen as a challenge to the principle of parliamentary sovereignty and the legal right of all legislative bodies in parliamentary democracies to make laws. Rather, he was saying that the federal government, the executive branch at the national level, was required under the doctrine of legitimate expectation to receive the consent of British Columbia before proposing changes to the House of Commons.

The third opinion of the Court of Appeal, one in the minority, ruled that no legitimate expectation existed. In her brief judgment, Justice Southin argued that there was nothing in the Canadian Constitution that provided for the kind of limit on the executive proposed in the second question of the reference. The government of British Columbia, the judge said, was asking the Court "to engraft onto the executive power in the *Constitution Acts, 1867 to 1982* a doctrine of 'legitimate expectation.'" But this was, she wrote, "simply wrong." The doctrine was "no more than 30 years old" and had evolved out of a series of English cases unrelated to "our made-at-home Constitution."[15]

Opinions in reference cases have no legally binding effect, but in practice they are followed. Accordingly, in view of its loss in the B.C. Court of Appeal, the federal government desisted from implementing the 5 percent limit on CAP payments. The matter, though, was far from over. Ottawa was determined to overturn the reference decision through an appeal to the Supreme Court of Canada, and it began this process in its written comments or "factum" to the Supreme Court. In its factum, the federal government contended that the questions involved in the reference were inappropriate for judicial review, i.e., were not justiciable. The B.C. government was using the courts in a political dispute with the federal government, a dispute bereft of any legal content. It also claimed that British Columbia and the Court of Appeal failed to respect the principle of parliamentary sovereignty. In the Canadian context, this principle recognizes the ability of Parliament and provincial legislative bodies to make any law, unencumbered by any impediment other than the Charter of Rights and Freedoms and the federal division of powers.[16] The federal government argued that the application of the doctrine of legitimate expectations to the executive had the effect of making it impossible for Parliament to enact new laws and amend existing ones. The majority in the Court of Appeal decision, along with the government of British Columbia, had "misconceived" the workings of parliamentary government in thinking that the executive and the legislature were separate.[17] In reality, the two combined to exercise the legislative function. The forming and introducing of legislation, done by the executive, was just as important to the legislative process as the enactment of legislation in Parliament.

In its written comments to the Court, the government of British Columbia said that the questions dealt with legal issues and hence were clearly justiciable. As to the question of the existence of legitimate expectations, British Columbia had an answer for this as well: the relevant legislation, the agreement, and the past behaviour of the two parties in relation to CAP had created the expectation that no unilateral changes would be made. The factum said that this position did not amount to an attack on the principle of parliamentary sovereignty. Contrary to the claims of the federal government, it was possible to make a distinction between the executive and legislative branches and to apply the doctrine of legitimate expectations to the former. Parliament could legislate, but the executive was obliged to secure the consent of British Columbia before introducing changes to the CAP arrangement.[18]

The appeal attracted the interest of the other affected provinces, as well as the governments of Manitoba and Saskatchewan.[19] All participated as interveners. The government of Ontario, in its comments to the Court, argued that a constitutional convention prohibited the kind of unilateral adjustment to CAP proposed by the federal government. Constitutional conventions are unwritten rules and traditions that serve to shape the operation of a constitution, and in the Canadian Constitution they play an important role.[20] Courts are unable to enforce conventions, but they may recognize them, and this recognition can influence the actions of government. For Ontario, a constitutional convention stipulated that any changes to cost-sharing agreements, including CAP, must either receive the approval of both Ottawa and the provinces or be carried out in accordance with the terms of any agreements (which for CAP meant consent of both parties or a one-year notice of termination). The province acknowledged the principle of parliamentary sovereignty, but contended that this principle had to be seen in light of the convention.[21] In its factum, Alberta dissented on the widespread belief that the doctrine of legitimate expectations had applicability only for the executive functions; it could be applied, said Alberta, to legislative acts as well. Similarly, it had been understood that the doctrine related to procedural matters, but again Alberta differed, saying that legitimate expectations also pertained to substantive issues.[22] For its part, the province of Manitoba argued that the CAP agreement between Canada and British Columbia should be "adjudicated upon in the same way as in the case of contracts between private parties."[23] Manitoba also said that the limit of CAP payments had implications for the federal spending power. The most direct implication was that the use of the power to restrict payments was equivalent to the "regulation or control of a matter outside federal authority...."[24] It was well understood in law that the regulation of a provincial matter represented an unconstitutional employment of the spending power.

DECISION OF THE SUPREME COURT

On August 15, 1991, the Supreme Court of Canada released its decision in the Canada Assistance Plan Reference.[25] In a single, unanimous judgment, the Court answered that the government of Canada had the authority to limit its contributions to the financing of assistance and welfare services in British Columbia. It also answered in the negative to the question of whether there existed a legitimate expectation that the government of Canada would propose no changes to Parliament without the consent of the government of British Columbia. With its opinion, the Court overturned the majority decision of the B.C. Court of Appeal. The federal government could proceed with its limits on fiscal transfers under CAP.

The decision of the Court was written by one of its then newest members, John Sopinka, a former trial lawyer with no previous experience as a judge. Justice Sopinka saw three issues inherent in the two questions before the Court. These were the justiciability of the case, the interpretations of federal–provincial agreements, and the doctrine of legitimate expectations and its impact on the executive part of government or cabinet. On the issue of justiciability, the Court dismissed the federal government's claim that the questions under review were political matters that should be resolved in the political arena. The test for determining justiciability, said Justice Sopinka, was whether the questions had a "sufficient legal component to warrant the intervention of the judicial branch."[26] This did not mean that a question or issue had to be totally devoid of a political component, but only that it contain a legal or constitutional component. In the judge's mind, the questions in the Canada Assistance Plan Reference did entail such a component. The first question involved the interpretation of a piece of legislation and an agreement; the second dealt with the legal doctrine of legitimate expectations.

The next issue in the appeal concerned the first question in the reference: Did the government of Canada have the authority to limit its initial obligation to pay 50 percent of the cost of assistance and welfare services in British Columbia? The Court of Appeal interpreted this as asking whether the cabinet or executive could make adjustments to the CAP arrangements without legislative enactment. But the Supreme Court read it to be whether the agreement under CAP required the federal government to pay the percentage stipulated at the time of the agreement or that amount that is specified "from time to time."[27] This had been central to the opinion of Justice Lambert, but in relation to the second question.

Justice Sopinka had little difficulty in determining that the federal government was committed only to paying that amount authorized in the law at any moment in time.[28] Thus, the answer to the first question was yes. In his reasoning, Justice Sopinka observed that all parties were aware of the authority of Parliament to amend the provisions of the Canada Assistance Plan. To believe otherwise would be to deny the principle of parliamentary sovereignty and to overlook federal legislation that stipulated the power of Parliament to amend any act of the federal legislature. Also, the parties knew that an amendment of CAP would have to be initiated by the government or executive as outlined in the Constitution Act, 1867. In view of this, Justice Sopinka wrote, the governments of British Columbia and Canada surely would have noted in the agreement their intention to freeze the contribution rate at 50 percent and "arrest" the introduction of the legislative changes.[29] Yet, this was not done. In fact, the agreement did not even contain the contribution formula. Only the legislation, the Canada Assistance Plan, included the formula, and it could be amended. As a result, the commitment contained in the agreement to make payments to British Columbia could only mean that the "obligation is to pay what is authorized from time to time."[30] The federal government, therefore, could change its obligation to pay 50 percent of the costs.

To buttress his opinion, Justice Sopinka outlined why Justice Lambert was wrong to believe that the contribution rate was fixed at 50 percent. The Court of Appeal had listed a variety of reasons for a static interpretation of the agreement, and the Supreme Court found all of them to be wanting. Justice Lambert had contended that British Columbia would have refrained from entering into an agreement that permitted only Ottawa to change it unilaterally. But, said Justice Sopinka, British Columbia did have the right to terminate the agreement on its own; it could simply exercise its legislative power to amend provincial welfare legislation supporting the agreement (and which the CAP legislation recognized). Justice Lambert also argued that normal rules of legal interpretation favoured a static interpretation, but Justice Sopinka said cited case law was inapplicable to this particular case. Justice Lambert also recognized that the absence of the contribution formula in the agreement might weaken his argument; so he maintained

that the formula had been included in the legislation to support the "fragile constitutionality of the federal spending power," which authorized CAP arrangements.[31] But this reasoning only allowed Sopinka to return to his original
argument. By placing the formula in legislation, the participating governments
knew that the formula was subject to amendment *without* some attempt to place
a "fetter on the amending power."[32] But no such attempt was made. The Court
went on to examine other arguments made by Justice Lambert (and the B.C. government), and determined each to be unconvincing.

   Justice Sopinka made one last comment on the first question. He acknowledged that the agreement lacked a binding effect. The federal government could
change the agreement at will through the principle of parliamentary sovereignty.
This quality made the agreement, the justice conceded, different from a normal
contract. But, said Justice Sopinka, this was not a contract in the ordinary sense of
the term. It was a political arrangement, an "agreement between governments," in
which the binding role was performed by the "perceived political price to be paid
for non-performance."[33] The Court here was trying to remind all concerned that
this was a case in constitutional law, and not contract law.

   As for the second question, the Court saw it as an invitation to examine the
legal doctrine of legitimate expectations and its ability to impede the actions of
government. In this, the Court followed the lead of Justices Toy and Southin and
rejected Justice Lambert's commonsense interpretation of the term. Justice
Sopinka examined the relevant case law and found himself swayed by a precedent
that concluded that the doctrine of legitimate expectations was "simply an extension of the rules of natural justice and procedural fairness."[34] What the doctrine
did was to provide for procedural rights. But British Columbia's claim argued for
a "substantive right to veto proposed federal legislation."[35] This was the effect of
saying that the province had to give its consent before the government of Canada
could amend the act. As a result, British Columbia's argument could not be
accepted:

> There is no support in Canadian or English cases for the position that the doc-
> trine of legitimate expectations can create substantive rights. It is a part of the
> rules of procedural fairness which can govern administrative bodies. Where it is
> applicable, it can create a right to make representations, or to be consulted. It
> does not fetter the decision following the representations or consultation.[36]

   A further problem was that the doctrine could only be applied to the
administrative actions of government. The legislative function was beyond its
reach. Yet, the attempt to apply the doctrine in this case constituted an attempt to
affect the ability of the federal government to legislate. The government of British
Columbia and Justice Toy had tried to get around this problem by arguing that the
executive was separate from the legislative process. But Justice Sopinka denied this
proposition, saying it "ignores the essential role of the executive in the legislative
process of which it is an integral part."[37] The practical effect of applying the doctrine, said the justice, would be to inhibit the operation of parliamentary govern-

ment. "The business of government would be stalled while the application of the doctrine and its effect was argued out in the courts," he wrote.[38] The doctrine would also deny the constitutional principle that a government cannot be constrained or "bound" by a preceding government, and, of course, it would be "a fetter on the sovereignty of Parliament itself."[39]

The Court ended with some observations on arguments made by the interveners. The Court quickly rejected the argument for a constitutional convention effecting changes to federal–provincial fiscal arrangements. The question of conventions, it said, could be considered only in relation to the doctrine of legitimate expectations. And since the latter was not applicable to the case, the issue of the existence of a convention was "irrelevant."[40] As for the claim that normal contract law applied to the case, the Court said that the principle of parliamentary sovereignty overrode any private rights of contract. On the matter of the federal spending power, the interveners fared no better. "The simple withholding of federal money which had previously been granted to fund a matter within provincial jurisdiction," wrote Justice Sopinka, "does not amount to the regulation of that matter."[41]

SIGNIFICANCE OF THE DECISION

The significance of a judicial decision that addresses relations between federal and provincial governments is usually couched in terms of its legal and political effects. The legal impact of a decision refers to the effect on the constitutional powers of the two orders of government. What is of interest here is whether the decision has enhanced the "constitutional capacity" of a government.[42] A decision might give the federal government more authority to make policy in a hitherto disputed area of jurisdiction, or it could provide the provinces with a greater ability to impede federal initiatives. It can, of course, affirm present understandings of the Constitution; but this, too, may be seen as a change in constitutional capacity, for the decision consolidates the authority of a government. Political effects include the immediate impact of the decision on the policy area in question and its beneficiaries. A decision will allow a policy to proceed, or cause it to be withdrawn or be substantially reshaped to mesh constitutionally with the decision of the Court. A more long-term effect at the political level is how the decision combines with other political resources to make an order of government more willing to undertake actions in the arena of federal–provincial relations. One order might have public opinion on its side and be possessed of an able set of negotiators, but feel it lacks the legal grounds for taking aggressive actions. A court, with a favourable decision, can remedy this situation. As Russell says, judicial decisions "should be studied in terms of how they combine with the other resources of federal and provincial politicians within a particular political or policy context."[43]

One of the legal effects of the CAP decision was to confirm the primacy of parliamentary supremacy and the power of Parliament to act unencumbered by the doctrine of legitimate expectations. "*CAP Reference* indicates that parliamentary sovereignty reigns and that Parliament or a legislature," writes Swinton, "has the ability to change its agreements without warning or in an unfair manner...."[44] In the Court's opinion, the doctrine of legitimate expectations deserved very little attention; it related to procedural matters and applied only to administrative actions and not legislative ones. If the provinces wanted to enforce financial agreements between themselves and the federal government, they would have to find a means other than the doctrine of legitimate expectations. Interestingly, this is exactly what they attempted to do. The Charlottetown Accord of 1992, which outlined a set of constitutional amendments, included a mechanism for protecting intergovernmental agreements against unilateral change. That this was directed right at CAP was evident: the accord said that it was "the intention of governments to apply this mechanism to future agreements related to the Canada Assistance Plan."[45] The accord, however, was rejected in a nationwide referendum, and with it went the constitutional protection against unilateral adjustments.

Another legal effect of the decision involved the federal spending power. In the past, the courts had offered opinions on this power, but these opinions were either ambiguous or uttered by judicial bodies lacking the standing of the Supreme Court of Canada.[46] The absence of a clear articulation of the federal spending power also stemmed from a lack of opportunity for the Court to adjudicate on the matter. Governments over time had been reluctant to press for such an articulation for fear of a harmful opinion; instead, they preferred to seek a resolution of differences in relation to the application of the power through other avenues.[47] But arguments in the Canada Assistance Plan Reference permitted the Supreme Court to speak to this matter, and in so doing the Court gave strength to the spending power. Justice Sopinka made it clear that the power enabled the federal government to spend in areas of provincial jurisdiction. He also said that adjustments in the terms of any federal–provincial arrangement—such as the limits on CAP—did not represent an unconstitutional use of the spending power. Manitoba had argued that the limits amounted to a *regulation* of a provincial matter, which if true meant that the setting of the limits was beyond the authority of the federal government. But the Court ruled that limiting payments under CAP and other such amendments in federal–provincial arrangements fell short of a regulatory action. The Court conceded that such action affected a provincial matter, but this was "clearly not enough to find that a statute encroaches upon the jurisdiction of the other level of government."[48] Although the Court's ruling on the spending power was not central to the case, it was significant enough to be cited in a later Supreme Court decision, suggesting that the Canada Assistance Plan Reference would now serve as the guiding precedent on the power.[49]

One last legal effect to be discussed related to the treatment of constitutional conventions. Ontario had made a plausible case for a constitutional convention that compelled the federal government to seek the agreement of the provinces before making changes to federal–provincial fiscal agreements. The test for the existence of a convention stipulates that precedents or past behaviour must suggest such a convention; also, those individuals involved in the precedents have to believe themselves constrained by the rule inherent in the convention, and there must be good reasons for the convention. The Ontario government recounted numerous instances in which provincial consent or the absence of such consent influenced the behaviour of the federal government in developing federal–provincial fiscal arrangements. The province also showed that the utterances of federal officials revealed the "binding nature of the convention," and it argued rather convincingly that there were good reasons for a convention prohibiting unilateral actions.[50] Yet, the Supreme Court of Canada rejected all this in a few sentences. In some respects, this was unfortunate. A decade earlier, the Supreme Court had ruled that a convention prohibited the federal government moving forward with constitutional reforms without some degree of provincial support. Surely, the major federal–provincial fiscal agreements approach constitutional amendments in significance. These agreements arrange for the provision of services essential to the well-being of Canadians, and do so in a way that respects and sustains the federal structure of the country and its Constitution. But the Supreme Court appeared to believe otherwise. The written rules of the Constitution would shape judicial determination of federal–provincial fiscal relations.[51]

The decision in the Canada Assistance Plan Reference also had some important political effects, some of which were quite immediate. Upon release of the decision of the Supreme Court, the federal government implemented the 5 percent limit on CAP expenditures for the three affected provinces. Moreover, even before the decision, Ottawa indicated that the limit would be extended for a further three years, to 1994–95. Eventually, the restrictions on CAP would cost the three provinces $8.5 billion over the five years, with Ontario losing the most, $6.8 billion.[52] The limits meant that the federal government came nowhere near sharing one-half of welfare costs in Ontario and British Columbia (Alberta was little affected because of its own limits on welfare spending). In Ontario, for example, the federal share fell to a little less than 30 percent of total costs, and this at a time when the province was experiencing its "worst recession since the 1930s."[53] Clearly, a national program had become less national. Another effect connected to the decision related to the introduction in British Columbia in 1995 of a rule whereby individuals could become eligible for welfare only if they had resided in the province for at least three months. The provinces received CAP payments partly on the condition of no residency requirements, but British Columbia now argued that the limits on CAP meant that the arrangement no longer applied. The federal government disagreed, withheld CAP payments, and British Columbia initiated a lawsuit against Ottawa to recover the payments. A year and a half later, the two parties came to an agreement: British Columbia dropped the lawsuit and eliminated the residency requirement, while the federal government partially restored the withheld payments and provided additional funding for related matters. Both players applauded the agreement, but the Canada Assistance Plan Reference had almost generated another full-blown legal and political conflict over CAP.

More significant than these immediate effects was the more general impact on the federal government. As Russell says, judicial decisions can be used as political resources to pursue desired aims, and with the decision in the CAP case the federal government was free to turn its attention to serious change in the fiscal arrangements.[54] In 1993, the Liberal government of Jean Chrétien assumed power at the federal level, and like the preceding government it emphasized the importance of getting rid of budget deficits and the need for reform in the fiscal arrangements. Two years later, in 1995, the federal government announced—without consulting the provinces—that CAP and the Established Programs Financing program would be combined to create a new arrangement, the Canada Health and Social Transfer (CHST). More important, federal funding in the first year of the new arrangement, 1996–97, would be $2.5 billion less than the $29.4 billion projected for CAP and Established Programs Financing. Also, an additional cut of $4.5 billion would be made the following fiscal year, leaving CHST at $25.1 billion. There was, to be sure, something in the new arrangement for the provinces. Conditions under CAP would be reduced, giving the provinces more flexibility in the design of their welfare plans. But the *cuts* in transfers (and not limits on increases) clearly took prominence; they affected, negatively, both public policy and relations between the two orders of government.

This exercise in "unilateral federalism" galvanized the provinces into making an attempt to put an end to the federal government acting on its own when it came to federal–provincial fiscal relations.[55] Thus, a further political effect of the Court decision, operating through the CHST, was the endeavour on the part of the provinces to effect a new kind of federalism in the area of social programs. During the last half of the 1990s, the provinces worked at creating "a rulebook for how the two levels of government—national and provincial—should interact on social policy."[56] The federal government resisted the initiative, but eventually agreed, in early 1999, to a framework for a new "social union."[57] The agreement (which Quebec refused to sign) stipulated a number of matters that affected federal–provincial fiscal arrangements; but one section related directly to the CAP limits:

> The Government of Canada will consult with provincial and territorial governments at least one year prior to renewal or significant funding changes in existing social transfers to provinces/territories, unless otherwise agreed, and will build due notice provisions into any new social transfers to provincial/territorial governments.[58]

The limits on CAP had angered the most powerful provinces in the federation. With the social-union agreement, these provinces were now trying to do what the Supreme Court had refused to do, which was to prevent any further unilateral initiatives by the federal government.

The social-union agreement suggested a movement towards a different brand of federalism. But the trappings of the unilateral approach were still evident. The agreement itself revealed this. The federal government would merely "consult" with the provinces; limits like those placed on CAP could still be introduced. The refusal of Quebec to sign the social-union framework was relevant on this point as well. Also, by now Ottawa had a budget surplus, due in part to the cuts in transfers to the provinces. At the same time as the social-union agreement was signed, the federal government used this surplus to effect an increase of $11.5 billion in funding for CHST over the next five years. More directly related to the CAP limits, it indicated that differences in funding among the provinces caused by the limits would be eliminated by fiscal year 2001–02. All of this, fiscally speaking, was good news for the provinces. But the provinces had to accept new conditions associated with health care—a provincial area of responsibility—in order to receive the increase in funding. More telling, the funding decision affecting CAP was, again, a federal decision. Ottawa had taken the money away and now it was giving it back.

CONCLUSION

The Supreme Court's decision in the Canada Assistance Plan Reference is difficult to contest from a strictly legal point of view. Parliamentary sovereignty is a cornerstone of government in Canada, and legislative authorities must have the authority to exercise their powers. "Legally, the decision is a victory for constitutional common sense," wrote the editors of *The Globe and Mail* at the time of the decision, and one would be hard-pressed to dispute such a sentiment (even in light of the argument for a constitutional convention prohibiting unilateral changes in fiscal arrangements).[59] But the larger political effects of the decision can be questioned. The limits on CAP and other unilateral changes to financial arrangements played havoc with provincial programs. Social policy, in short, was not a beneficiary of the Court's wisdom. The decision also encouraged Ottawa to act without much consultation with the provinces, and this, too, seemed an unwanted outcome because of the resulting bitterness in federal–provincial relations.

Of course, it is possible to interpret the decision differently. The federal government gained control of its spending, and the shock of reduced payments prompted the provinces to make some advisable changes to their social programs. Also, the decision of the Supreme Court prodded the provinces to seek a *political* solution (the social-union agreement) to differences between themselves and the federal government, which in a democracy is preferable to relying on appointed judicial officials to sort out the difficulties. It is also possible that the decision had no real effect, especially on the important area of federal–provincial relations. It may be that the desperate financial situations of public authorities in the early 1990s meant that conflict between the two orders of government was inevitable.

All of this is feasible. Of particular interest is the last contention concerning the inevitability of tension between federal and provincial governments. Perhaps no amount of discussion between the two parties would have led to a satisfactory handling of the federal deficit problem. But it seems more likely that at least an attempt to consult the affected provinces on the CAP limits would have lessened the degree of animosity. It was, after all, the blatant violation of the CAP agreement that so angered the three provinces (and some others too). Accordingly, a Court decision that forced a meeting of the two orders of government would have increased the chances of a less stormy kind of federalism. But, instead, the

Supreme Court issued a decision that helped usher in a period of intense and hostile relations between Ottawa and the provinces, hardly a desirable development in a country whose unity is in constant question.

ENDNOTES

1. The territories are also recipients of financial assistance under many of these arrangements.
2. Canada, Department of Finance, *The Budget*, 20 February 1990, 12.
3. Formally speaking, the limits applied to provinces ineligible for payments under the federal Equalization program. The Equalization program transfers funds from the national government to provinces with weak tax bases, which usually means all provinces except for Ontario, Alberta, and British Columbia.
4. Mark Hume, Justine Hunter, and Peter O'Neil, "B.C. Reels from Budget, Couvelier Seeks Summit," *Vancouver Sun*, 21 February 1990, A1.
5. Peter H. Russell, "The *Anti-Inflation* Case: the Anatomy of a Constitutional Decision," *Canadian Public Administration* 10, no. 4 (Winter 1977): 663.
6. R.S.C. 1970, c. C-1 (emphasis added).
7. Keith Baldrey, "Ottawa Suit Mulled by B.C. over CAP Cuts," *Vancouver Sun*, 27 February 1990, A7.
8. Another factor precipitating the legal challenge was the anger of the three affected provinces. The limits on the Established Programs Financing arrangement touched all the provinces, but not the limits affecting CAP. For Ontario, Alberta, and British Columbia, the "cap on CAP" was thus unfair. It was also considered inappropriate because CAP was not supposed to favour some provinces over others. Payments directed towards bettering the conditions of the less well-off provinces were to be made under the federal Equalization program.
9. The government of Saskatchewan also intervened in the appeal to the Supreme Court of Canada, but the brief nature of its comments to the Court suggests that its role was only to give support to British Columbia and the other interveners. See *Factum of the Attorney General of Saskatchewan* (Court File No. 22017).
10. The reader will note that the two questions incorrectly refer to the legislation supporting CAP as the *Canada Assistance Plan Act*. The correct title of the legislation is the *Canada Assistance Plan*.
11. *Re Canada Assistance Plan* (1990) 71 D.L.R. (4th) 99.
12. Ibid., 112.
13. Ibid., 119.
14. Ibid., 132.
15. Ibid., 138–39.
16. Peter H. Hogg, *Constitutional Law of Canada*, 3rd ed. (Toronto: Carswell, 1992), ch. 12.
17. *Factum of the Appellant, Attorney General of Canada* (Court File No. 22017), 20.
18. *Factum of the Respondent, Attorney General of British Columbia* (Court File No. 22017), 28.
19. The involvement of two provinces unaffected by the CAP limits may seem odd. But, as noted, the case had implications for arrangements affecting all the provinces. It should be noted as well that the list of interveners also included the Native Council of Canada and United Native Nations of British Columbia.

20. Hogg, 17–26.
21. *Factum of the Intervenor, Attorney General of Ontario* (Court File No. 22017), 13.
22. *Factum of the Intervenor, Attorney General of Alberta* (Court File No. 22017), 6–9.
23. *Factum of the Intervenor, Attorney General of Manitoba* (Court File No. 22017), 4–5.
24. Ibid., 5.
25. *Re Canada Assistance Plan* [1991] 2 S.C.R. 525.
26. Ibid., 545.
27. Ibid., 548.
28. Ibid.
29. Ibid., 549.
30. Ibid.
31. *Re Canada Assistance Plan* (1990) 71 D.L.R. (4th), 117.
32. *Re Canada Assistance Plan* [1991] 2 S.C.R., 550.
33. Ibid., 553–54.
34. Ibid., 557.
35. Ibid.
36. Ibid., 557–58.
37. Ibid., 559.
38. Ibid.
39. Ibid., 559–60.
40. Ibid., 561.
41. Ibid., 567.
42. Peter H. Russell, "The Supreme Court and Federal–Provincial Relations: the Political Uses of Legal Resources," in R.O. Olling and M.W. Westmacott, eds., *Perspectives on Canadian Federalism* (Scarborough: Prentice Hall, 1988), 91.
43. Ibid., 97.
44. Katherine Swinton, "Federalism under Fire: The Role of the Supreme Court of Canada," *Law and Contemporary Problems* 55, no.1 (Winter 1992): 143.
45. Kenneth McRoberts and Patrick J. Monahan, eds., *The Charlottetown Accord, the Referendum, and the Future of Canada* (Toronto: University of Toronto Press, 1993), 296; and Peter W. Hogg, "Division of Powers in the Charlottetown Accord," in ibid., 88–90.
46. Hogg, *Constitutional Law of Canada*, 153.
47. J. Stefan Dupre, "Section 106A and Federal–Provincial Fiscal Relations," in Katherine Swinton and Carol J. Rogerson, eds., *Competing Constitutional Visions: the Meech Lake Accord* (Toronto: Carswell, 1988), 209.
48. *Re Canada Assistance Plan* [1991] 2 S.C.R., 567.
49. *Eldridge v. B.C. (A.G.)* [1997] 3 S.C.R 624.
50. *Factum of the Intervenor, Attorney General of Ontario* (Court File No. 22017), 25.
51. At this point, it might of interest to note that in 1993 the Supreme Court decided another matter dealing with CAP. In the Canada Assistance Plan Reference, the issue was the amendment of obligations; in the 1993 case, the issue was the enforcement of obligations under CAP. Also, interestingly, the latter case stemmed not from a tussle between governments, but rather from the challenge of a private citizen. See *Finlay v. Canada (Minister of Finance)* [1993] 1 S.C.R 1080.
52. Thomas J. Courchene, "Canada's Social Policy Deficit: Implications for Fiscal Federalism," in Keith G. Banting, Douglas M. Brown, and Thomas J. Courchene, *The Future of Fiscal Federalism* (Kingston: School of Policy Studies, 1994), 98.
53. George E. Carter, "Federal Restraints on the Growth of Transfer Payments to the Provinces Since 1986–87: An Assessment," *Canadian Tax Journal* 42, no. 6 (1994): 1525.

54.   Russell, "The Supreme Court and Federal–Provincial Relations."

55.   The term "unilateral federalism" is borrowed from Margaret Briggs, *Building Blocks for Canada's New Social Union* (Ottawa: Canadian Policy Research Networks, 1996), 40. See also Gerard Boismenu and Jane Jenson, "A Social Union or a Federal State?: Competing Visions of Intergovernmental Relations in the New Liberal Era," in Leslie A. Pal, ed., *How Ottawa Spends 1998–99: Balancing Act: the Post-Deficit Mandate* (Toronto: Oxford University Press, 1998), 64.

56.   Edward Greenspon, "Social-Union Talks a Balancing Act," *The Globe and Mail*, 8 August 1998, A4.

57.   *A Framework to Improve the Social Union for Canadians*, 4 February 1999.

58.   Ibid., 5–6.

59.   "The Right of Ottawa to Alter Its Transfer Payments," *The Globe and Mail*, 16 August 1991, A10. There are some who are less supportive of the decision. See David Dyzenhaus, "Developments in Administrative Law: the 1991–92 Term," (1993), 4 *S.C.L.R.* (2d), 189–95.

COMMUNITIES, INTEREST GROUPS, AND THE COURT

PART 5

THE SUPREME COURT AND COLLECTIVE RIGHTS:

TAKING COMMUNITY SERIOUSLY?

Andrew M. Robinson

Both individual and collective rights are embedded in the Canadian constitutional fabric. While the meaning of the individual rights is by no means settled, even less is certain about rights that extend special recognition to communities. We can distinguish two important interpretations of collective rights that have currency in contemporary political thinking. One describes collective rights as rights that individuals exercise by virtue of being members of particular communities. According to this view, once it is determined that a person belongs to the community in question, no other facts about his or her life are of any importance. We might call this the "individualistic conception" of collective rights. A second interpretation places less emphasis on the individual and more on the collectivity or community. This "communitarian conception" focuses on subnational groupings such as religious, ethnic, and familial communities that may be said to share a conception of a common good. In this view, the role of collective rights is to protect collectivities as "communities of shared goods" (i.e., a shared set of values or way of life) and to help ensure their survival.[1]

These interpretations have very different implications for the kind of powers that collective rights might entail. Will Kymlicka provides some useful terms to describe these powers. Individualistic collective rights are intended to provide members of groups with what Kymlicka calls "external protections," which "protect the group from the impact of *external decisions* (e.g. the economic or political decisions of the larger society)."[2] Thus, for example, linguistic education rights protect the ability of all members of the francophone community to have their children educated in French, no matter what the (nonfrancophone) majority or other francophones might have to say. In addition to external protections, communitarian collective rights may also empower communities to impose "internal restrictions" that "protect the group from the destabilizing impact of *internal dissent* (e.g. the decisions of individual members not to follow traditional practices or customs)."[3] Thus, for example, a religious community might be allowed to expel members whose beliefs or actions threaten its ability to carry out the common practices (i.e., shared goods) that define it as a community.

The distinction between individualistic and communitarian conceptions of collective rights helps us to understand two sources of tension that will always exist when communities receive special recognition. The first source of tension arises from the fact that, when special powers are extended to a community, some person or group is usually authorized to speak for the community, to define its membership, and to enforce its rules. This creates a temptation for some within a community to benefit themselves by marginalizing or excluding others who have legitimate claims to membership. A story that was recently in the news about an Indian band in northern Alberta may provide an example of such behaviour. It has been alleged that a dominant family used the band council's powers over the membership code, the budget, the allotment of housing, and the right to vote in council elections to exclude people who had legitimate claims to membership. The alleged motivation was the desire to gain control of the band's assets, which have an estimated value of $85 million. It has been reported that only 27 band members live on the reserve out of approximately 220 people who claim membership.[4] The appeal of the individualistic interpretation of collective rights is that it is not consistent with communities exercising such power over their members.

Tension may also arise when the right to full participation in a community is granted to people whose behaviour is thought by others to undermine the community's way of life or the values it embodies. Consider, for example, the Pueblo communities of the southwestern United States. For many Pueblos, what they value in their communities is inseparable from the traditional characteristics of those communities. These characteristics include "quasi-theocratic" forms of government in which there is little separation of church and state, societies that embody a mixture of Catholic and Native spirituality, and the general expectation that all members of the community will participate in communal religious ceremonies.[5] Given the nature of these communities, it is not surprising that when some Pueblos converted to Protestantism and refused to participate in communal ceremonies and practices, some Pueblo leaders reacted by trying to exclude the deviants from further participation in their communities.[6] From the perspective of many community members, the deviants ceased to be Pueblos when they became Protestants. Cases like this are often used to support the communitarian interpretation of collective rights and the internal restrictions it defends.

No formulation of collective rights can ever completely eliminate these tensions. If communities are given the power to control their membership, for instance, they may use it to marginalize or exclude legitimate members. If they are denied this power, they will always be vulnerable to threats posed by those who continue to belong but do not share their values or concerns. Thus, it seems, there will always be a role for the courts to determine whether rights have been properly exercised. Three cases are presented here to illustrate these tensions. In each, the Supreme Court's decision has, by and large, been consistent with the individualistic conception of collective rights to the detriment of the communitarian conception. The Court has generally opted to protect the individual while showing respect for governmental authority and looking only cautiously at empowering the collective group.

SKOKE-GRAHAM v. THE QUEEN

The appellants in this case were practising Roman Catholics who were "charged, pursuant to s. 172(3) of the Criminal Code, with wilfully disturbing the order or solemnity of an assemblage of persons who met for religious worship."[7] There had been a long-running dispute with the parish and diocesan church authorities over a change in the liturgy that required parishioners to stand rather than kneel when receiving Communion. The appellants were philosophically at odds with modern Catholic practices and beliefs. Charges were laid after the appellants protested by insisting on kneeling to receive Communion during a regular service. They were convicted.

This case requires us to consider how much power, if any, should be placed at the disposal of community leaders to enforce internal restrictions. On the one hand, the Catholic Church and its many local parishes are communities whose customs and traditions give purpose and meaning to the lives of many. The survival of such customs and traditions requires a certain degree of conformity among adherents. Were church leaders unable to exercise a certain amount of discipline over their members, these customs and traditions could wither away. On the other hand, no community or tradition is the property of its leaders. There must also be room for sincere dissent. *Skoke-Graham v. The Queen* required the Supreme Court to decide whether the means available to communal leaders to discipline dissenters should include the sanction of criminal law. This broader issue concerning conformity and internal discipline has clear implications for others, such as homosexuals in Christian communities, or Sikhs who reject the traditional practice of eating the *langar* meal on the floor.[8]

Specifically, the Court had to decide whether s. 172(3) of the Criminal Code was best applied as an external protection, intended to protect all members of religious communities from hostile *outsiders*, or as an internal restriction, designed to protect the community from its own *dissenters*. The lower court decisions had treated the case as one in which the collective group could appropriately have recourse to this form of sanction. Justice Hart, in the unanimous decision of the Nova Scotia Supreme Court, wrote:

> *If several persons disagree with the form of the religious service they may have the right to withdraw but not to insist upon their procedures against the will of*

the hierarchy of the church. The actions of the appellants although relatively
passive ... [constituted] the very type of conduct intended to be prohibited by
the provisions of the Criminal Code.[9]

Even the appellants, in making their appeal to the Nova Scotia Supreme Court, included an argument that was consistent with s. 172(3) being an internal restriction. They suggested that the bishop of the parish did not have the authority to change the liturgy, and thus the appellants had not defied a legitimate authority. The implication was that the criminal law should be available to church authorities to control dissenting members, but only when their authority is legitimate. Had the Court chosen to uphold any of these positions, it would have greatly extended the range of instruments through which religious authorities might maintain decorum and discipline members.

While the Supreme Court was unanimous in deciding that the convictions should be overturned, it was divided (5–2) on the reasons. Justice Dickson, writing for the majority, settled the matter without directly addressing the question of religious authority and the criminal law. First, his interpretation of the purpose of s. 172(3) was more consistent with its being an external protection than an internal restriction. He said it protects "people ... who have gathered to pursue any kind of socially beneficial activity, from being purposefully disturbed or interrupted."[10] More decisively, he restricted the meaning of "disturb" such that the law did not apply in this case. The meaning of the law, he wrote, was such that for an action to be criminal it must not only disturb the solemnity of the worship in the broadest sense of the word "disturb," but there must also be some activity in the nature of a disorder that occurs as a result of this conduct before a trial judge would be entitled to find the order or solemnity of a meeting had been disturbed.[11]

Justice Wilson refused to accept this restricted interpretation of the law and chose instead to directly address the issue of communal authority and the criminal law. She argued, *contra* Dickson, that the trial judge had "found on proper evidence that the appellants' conduct disturbed the order and solemnity of the service."[12] The problem with the earlier court rulings, she held, was that "kneeling to receive communion as a result of firmly-held convictions is [not] within the spirit of s. 172(3) of the *Code* even if it is within its literal wording."[13] She offered two arguments in support of this position. The first concerned the "legislative context and history of s. 172(3)." She said that Parliament did not intend "the provision to cover peaceful acts of defiance of religious authority."[14] The second argument was that there were "strong policy grounds" for restricting the application of the section:

when the legislature employs language as broad as it has here, I think it is open
to the Court to refine it in light of what it perceives to be the degree of public
condemnation any impugned conduct would be likely to attract. I believe also
that an interpretation ... which would make the criminal law available as a
tool for the enforcement of liturgical practice or the settlement of liturgical

> *disputes may represent an extension of the law into areas which a substantial*
> *segment of the public ... would find unacceptable.*[15]

There was thus an unwillingness to allow criminal law sanctions to be used to impose internal restrictions within religious communities. This decision is consistent with an understanding of s. 172(3) as sustaining an individualistic collective right to the protection of a private space within which religious debate can occur.

NATIVE WOMEN'S ASSN. OF CANADA v. CANADA

Native Women's Association of Canada v. Canada arose in the context of discussions leading up to the Charlottetown Accord in 1992. These federal–provincial discussions appeared likely to result in the definition and constitutionalization of a significant Aboriginal right—the right to self-government. Especially contentious was the question of whether the Canadian Charter of Rights and Freedoms would apply to self-governing institutions. Given the importance of these discussions, the government of Canada decided in the fall of 1991 to invite four Aboriginal groups to participate in a parallel process of consultation. These were the Assembly of First Nations (AFN), comprised of all Indian band chiefs in Canada; the Native Council of Canada (NCC), an organization that represents Métis, nonstatus Indians, and off-reserve registered Indians; the Métis National Council (MNC), a federation of provincial and territorial organizations representing the Métis people; and the Inuit Tapirisat of Canada (ITC), which represents the Inuit of the Northwest Territories, northern Quebec, and Labrador. The government provided $10 million to fund the participation of these groups, a portion of which was earmarked for women's issues. On March 12, 1992, these same groups were invited to participate in a multilateral process of constitutional discussions that was intended to prepare constitutional amendments. On March 18, the Native Women's Association of Canada (NWAC)—an interest group that believed that the equality of Native women would be threatened if the Charter did not apply to self-government—went to court to request an "order of prohibition" that would prevent the government from disbursing any more money to the four other Aboriginal groups until NWAC received equal funding and the right to participate in the process on the same terms.

While the specific question before the Court concerned the extension of funding by the federal government, it could not be answered without addressing the more general question of who could legitimately speak for the Aboriginal community. The two interpretations of collective rights would suggest very different answers. If communities have shared goods, as suggested by the communitarian conception, then these goods may be adequately represented by legitimate community organizations such as the AFN and the ITC so long as these groups are organized to allow an overall collective view to be formulated and maintained. The individualistic conception, conversely, assumes that the interests of some individuals can be, and often are, sacrificed in the pursuit of collective agendas.

Accordingly, it suggests that individuals must be permitted to defend their own interests, either personally or through representatives whom they have explicitly chosen.

In recognizing and affirming the "existing aboriginal and treaty rights of the aboriginal *peoples* of Canada,"[16] the Canadian Constitution Act, 1982, appears to be consistent with the communitarian conception of collective rights. Since the Charter, including its many individual rights, applies to Aboriginal peoples, however, the Court must give at least prima facie consideration to the kinds of claims we have associated with the individualistic conception. Among these individual rights are s. 2(b) guarantees of freedom of thought and expression. The resulting tension is illustrated in the second of four questions the Court felt it needed to address in deciding *Native Women's Assn. of Canada v. Canada*:

> Did the Government of Canada violate the freedom of expression of the individual respondents or of Aboriginal women represented by the respondent NWAC, as guaranteed by s. 2(b) read together with s. 28 of the Canadian Charter of Rights and Freedoms, by funding the four aboriginal organizations and permitting their participation in the constitutional discussions while not providing an equal right of participation and funding to NWAC?[17]

In claiming that the federal government had violated its members' freedom of expression by not explicitly seeking their input in the constitutional discussions, NWAC seemed to be saying that while its members might not have a right to represent *themselves* personally in the discussions, they did have the right to have their *views* represented, even if these views had been rejected by their communal organizations. If accepted, this position would have seriously undercut the ability of communal organizations to represent the broader interests of their members.

NWAC's position relied on the Court's earlier decision in *Haig v. Canada* ([1993] 2 S.C.R.) in which L'Heureux-Dubé, writing for the majority, had stated:

> While s. 2(b) of the Charter does not include the right to any particular means of expression, where a government chooses to provide one, it must do so in a fashion that is consistent with the Constitution.... Thus, while the government may extend such a benefit to a limited number of persons, it may not do so in a discriminatory fashion, and particularly not on a ground prohibited under s. 15 of the Charter.[18]

NWAC suggested that, by extending funding and the right to participate in discussions to the other Aboriginal organizations, the federal government had provided a means for expression in a fashion that discriminated against Native women.

The Court was unanimous in denying NWAC's request. The majority decision was written by Justice Sopinka. Before considering the factual basis of NWAC's position, Sopinka made it clear that he believed that the *Haig* decision did not limit the government's discretion in selecting its advisers such that every time the government consulted one organization it had to consult groups representing opposing views. Rather, *Haig* only required the government to consult a particular group when a prior decision to consult some other group or groups had "the effect of suppressing another's freedom of speech,"[19] a situation he judged to be uncommon. This set a very high standard for the evidentiary foundation of NWAC's position.

> *The s. 2(b) argument advanced is dependent upon a finding that the funding of and participation by NWAC were essential to provide an equal voice for the rights of women. A corollary to this submission is that the funded groups are not representative of Native women because they advocate a male-dominated aboriginal self-government.*[20]

Assessment of NWAC's claim required a consideration of the representativeness of all five Native organizations. Sopinka found that there was no evidence to support either the contention that the AFN, NCC, MNC, and ITC were less representative than NWAC of the viewpoint of Aboriginal women on the Constitution, or that NWAC received any higher level of support from Aboriginal women than did the four funded groups.[21] Thus, he concluded that "there was no evidence in the case to suggest that the funding or consultation of the four Aboriginal groups infringed the respondents' equal right of freedom of expression."[22]

While the Court ruled against NWAC, Sopinka's decision should not be understood as an endorsement of the communitarian conception of collective rights. While he accepted that the four Aboriginal organizations did act as legitimate representatives of their communities in this case, Sopinka clearly worked within a framework of sensitivity to the individualistic conception: NWAC's case was adjudicated largely in light of concerns over freedom of expression and equality rather than the collective representational needs of the larger Aboriginal community. Further, the Court's rejection of NWAC's claims was driven more by traditional respect for the authority of the Parliamentary executive than by communitarian concerns. Nevertheless, the outcome of this decision was promising to the extent that it appeared to strike a balance between the individualistic and communitarian conceptions. Rather than rejecting the right of communal organizations to represent their members, the Court insisted on ensuring that the interests of individual members not be ignored or marginalized.

CORBIERE v. CANADA (MINISTER OF INDIAN AND NORTHERN AFFAIRS)

Corbiere v. Canada concerned the legitimacy of limitations on the voting rights of members of Indian bands. The Batchewana Band chose its chiefs and council according to s. 77(1) of the Indian Act, which required that, to be eligible to vote in band elections, a band member be 18 years old and "ordinarily resident on the reserve." The case began when John Corbiere, a resident of one of the Batchewana reserves, and three other members who lived off-reserve, challenged the requirement that members be "ordinarily resident on the reserve" on the grounds that it violated the equality provisions of s. 15(1) of the Charter of Rights and Freedoms.[23]

Can the exclusion of some band members from full participation in the community ever be justified? According to the communitarian conception, internal restrictions, such as the denial of full participation, may be justified when the behaviour of some community members is irreconcilable with, or threatens the existence of, the community's way of life. Does choosing to live away from the reserve constitute such a challenge? According to the individualistic conception, conversely, anyone who qualifies as a member of a community has an equal right to participate in it and to enjoy the benefit of its protection. Should individuals who choose to live away from the reserve retain full privileges of membership?

While divided (5–4) on its reasons, the Court exhibited broad agreement on the points that are of interest to us.[24] The majority decision written by Justices McLachlin and Bastarache illustrates these key points. They evaluated the issues in light of the equality protections in s. 15 of the Charter. Denying voting rights to off-reserve members was deemed to constitute a distinction conferring unequal benefits or burdens, and to have been made on analogous grounds to those prohibited by s. 15. Such distinctions involve personal characteristics understood as immutable, such as race, or alterable only at great personal cost or sacrifice to personal identity, such as religion. "Aboriginal-residency" was to be regarded as analogous, and therefore distinctions made on that basis warranted judicial examination.[25] The question then became whether this distinction constituted discrimination. Justices McLachlin and Bastarache offered two reasons for thinking that it did. First, they said that the denial of the right to vote "perpetuates the historic disadvantage experienced by off-reserve band members." Second, they said the distinction denies the important interests that off-reserve members have in band governance. For instance, band councils exercise jurisdiction over "the surrender of band lands, the allocation of land to band members, [and] the raising of funds and making of expenditures for all band members"; the representation of the community in negotiations with the government; and, of central importance to Aboriginal identity, the preservation of the "ancestral place," rituals, ceremonies, and traditions.[26]

McLachlin and Bastarache's position was consistent with a very strong interpretation of the individualistic conception of collective rights. An individual's claim to participate in a community is based on her interest in the community and should not be affected by any other decisions she has made about how to lead her life.

> Even if all band members living off-reserve had voluntarily chosen this way of life and were not subject to discrimination in the broader Canadian society, they would still have the same cause of action. They would still suffer a detriment by being denied full participation in the affairs of the band to which they would continue to belong while the band councils are able to affect their interests....[27]

Section 77(1) is discriminatory on this account because, by forcing band members

> *to choose between living on the reserve and exercising their political rights, or*
> *living off-reserve and renouncing the exercise of their political rights ..., it*
> *implies that off-reserve band members are lesser members of their bands or*
> *persons who have chosen to be assimilated by the mainstream society.*[28]

Consistent with the individualistic conception, this decision suggested that the standards to which people can be held in order to exercise collective rights must not be open to communal manipulation. Thus, rather than allowing communities to set minimal standards based on their way of life, the Court insisted that the right to participate fully in the community could depend only on ascriptive characteristics (race) and self-identification (cultural identity)[29]—neither of which is within the community's control. If individuals meet these standards, there can be no legitimate grounds for excluding them.

The consistency of this decision with the individualist conception was enhanced when McLachlin and Bastarache considered whether s. 77(1) could be justified under s. 1 of the Charter as being "demonstrably justified in free and democratic society." This required determining whether the legislation's objective was "pressing and substantial" and whether the means employed were proportional to that objective. It is revealing that, in attributing an objective to the legislation, the communitarian conception was not considered. From the communitarian perspective, the legislation serves to protect the reserve community from the corrosive influence of those who have been assimilated into the dominant culture. Arguments of this nature had gained prominence in the debate over Bill C-31. Until 1985, the Indian Act had required Aboriginal women who married non-Aboriginal men to relinquish their legal status as Indians. Non-Aboriginal women who married Aboriginal men, however, became status Indians. Bill C-31 addressed this injustice by extending Indian status to many Aboriginal women and children who had been affected by this provision. Some within the Aboriginal community argued that these "Bill C-31 Indians" should not automatically be allowed to return to live on their reserves. For instance, one Native witness argued before a Commons committee that this would "accelerate the loss of the Cree language and culture because .... many of the reinstatees and their children no longer speak Cree, and many have little appreciation of Cree culture."[30] The Court, however, did not consider such arguments. Instead, it assumed that the legislation's aim was to give "a voice in the affairs of the reserve only to the persons most directly affected by the decisions of the band council." Given this objective, the Court would accept only one ground for differentiating the right to participate in band governance: Those who do not live on the reserve should not have a say in purely local reserve matters. It is not at all surprising that, having excluded the communitarian perspective in determining the legislation's intent, the Court found that the means employed in s. 77(1) were not proportionate to its objective, since they failed to minimally impair off-reserve members' s. 15 rights. Thus, the offending phrase was struck out of s. 77(1).

In deciding *Corbiere v. Canada*, the Court left little room for the communitarian conception of collective rights to be applied in defining the rights of community members. By protecting the right of everyone who has a claim to membership to participate fully in the community, the court severely restricted the ability of Aboriginal communities to protect themselves from members who might threaten their survival. The only exception to this general conclusion was that the Court left the door open a crack for the communitarian conception by accepting that "if another band could establish an Aboriginal right to restrict voting,... that right would simply have precedence over the terms of the *Indian Act*."[31]

CONCLUSION

The Supreme Court appears headed towards denying many exotic and valuable communities the strong communitarian, perhaps even internally restrictive, powers they may need to survive. The Court did not endorse the communitarian conception in any of the decisions considered here. (In the case of *Skoke-Graham* the minority explicitly rejected it.) A bias in favour of the individualistic conception and individual rights in general may be understandable given the central place of such rights in the Charter. This is especially so given the fact that there will always be factions within communities that will be tempted to marginalize and silence those who do not share their vision of the community. Nevertheless, when such emphasis is placed on the individualistic conception, we must question why collective rights should have been extended at all. If such special rights and privileges are extended because they express certain values or embody ways of life that their members cannot experience outside of the community, then it seems reasonable to suggest that communities should be empowered to protect these core values and ways of life. This may require providing communal leaders with the authority to speak for their communities, to define their membership, and to discipline those whose actions threaten core values. From this perspective, the problem with the decisions we have examined is not that they recognized the importance of the individualistic perspective, but that they did not balance it against the equally important interests reflected in the communitarian perspective. The Court would do well to focus less on protecting community members from their leaders and more on ensuring that these leaders only exercise their authority in legitimate attempts to protect what is valuable in their communities.[32]

ENDNOTES

1. The terms *individualistic conception* and *communitarian conception*, as used here, are mine. For further study of the issues surrounding such competing conceptions of community, see Will Kymlicka, *Multicultural Citizenship* (Oxford: Clarendon Press, 1995), esp. 91–92; and Michael Sandel, *Liberalism and the Limits of Justice* (Cambridge: Cambridge University Press, 1982).

2. Kymlicka, 35.

3. Ibid.

4. Erin Anderssen, "How the Sawridge Millions Tore Apart a Native Community," *The Globe and Mail*, 31 October 1998, A1, 8–9.

5. See Edward P. Dozier, *The Pueblo Indians of North America* (New York: Holt, Rinehart, and Winston, Inc., 1970).

6. See Florence Hawley, "The Keresan Holy Rollers: An Adaptation to American Individualism," *Social Forces* 26 (1–4): 272–80.

7. *Skoke-Graham v. The Queen*, [1985] 1 S.C.R. 106.

8. Robert Matas, "Religious Ruling Comes as a Blow to Liberal Sikhs," *The Globe and Mail*, 28 April 1998, A2.

9. Quoted in *Skoke-Graham v. The Queen*, [1985] 1 S.C.R. 113–14.

10. *Skoke-Graham v. The Queen*, [1985] 1 S.C.R. 114.

11. Ibid., 118.

12. Ibid., 108.

13. Ibid., 134.

14. Ibid., 130.

15. Ibid., 134.

16. S. 35(1). My emphasis.

17. *Native Women's Assn. of Canada v. Canada*, [1994] 3 S.C.R. 645.

18. Quoted in ibid., 655.

19. Ibid., 657.

20. Ibid.

21. Ibid.

22. Ibid., 664.

23. *Corbiere v. Canada (Minister of Indian and Northern Affairs)*, at paras. 25–27. Since this decision has not yet been published in Supreme Court Reports, the reader is directed to the appropriate paragraph(s) in the decision. The judgment, delivered on May 20, 1999, is available at the following Web site: http://www.droit.umontreal.ca/doc/csc-scc/en/rec/html/batchewa.en.html.

24. The key difference concerned how the Court should treat enumerated and analogous grounds associated with s. 15(1) of the Charter. The majority said they are "constant markers of suspect decision making or potential discrimination," while the minority insisted that "contextual factors" must be considered. *Corbiere v. Canada (Minister of Indian Affairs)*.

25. Ibid., at paras. 13–14.

26. Ibid., at paras. 17, 19.

27. Ibid., at para. 19.

28. Ibid.

29. Ibid.

30. House of Commons, "Minutes of the Proceedings and Evidence of the Standing Committee on Aboriginal Affairs and Northern Development" (Ottawa: Canadian Government Publishing Centre, Issue No. 39, April 27, 1988), 56.

31. *Corbiere v. Canada (Minister of Indian Affairs)*, at para. 22.

32. While *Native Women's Assn. of Canada v. Canada* came closest to reflecting this approach, its motivation was not respect for the interests of communities as communities, but rather, respect for executive discretion.

LOBBYING THE SUPREME COURT

Ian Brodie

It is hard to study the Supreme Court of Canada these days without studying the role of interest groups. Groups representing feminists, civil libertarians, language minorities, unions, business interests, and others regularly appear before the Court to argue legal issues of interest to their members. Journalists rely on comments by interest group leaders in their reporting on the Court's work. Interest groups even lobby behind the scenes over who will be appointed to the Court.[1] Today, the Supreme Court is just as much a forum for interest-group activity as cabinet, the bureaucracy, the House of Commons, or the Senate.

Interest groups pay attention to the Supreme Court because interest groups pay attention to any institution that wields political power, and the Supreme Court certainly wields political power. Some groups pay attention to the Court because they want to achieve short-term goals. They want the Court to change a specific government policy—by interpreting a piece of legislation in a particular way, by striking down a policy as unconstitutional, or by expanding a policy to include the group's members. For these groups, court action might be a last-ditch effort to change a government's mind when other avenues of lobbying have failed. Other groups have long-term goals. They want to influence the Court's decisions on a particular issue over time. These groups might pressure many political institutions, including the Court, or they might see court action as their preferred strategy for advancing their goals. Either way, groups with long-term goals plot their court actions carefully, and plan to be active in trying to influence the Supreme Court for years or decades. Being a regular participant in the Court's work makes a group a policy "player" and gets it into the government's networks of decision makers. The Supreme Court also benefits from the attention of interest groups. It gets access to information that interest groups have about issues before the Court, and, by listening to interest groups, the Court also adds to its legitimacy as a political institution.

There is nothing new about political and community interests using the courts to try to influence public policy.[2] A century ago, Manitoba francophones and Roman Catholics sued the provincial government to protect their language and schooling rights.[3] In the 1920s, Canadian feminists sued the federal government to be recognized as "persons" and be eligible to be appointed to the Senate.[4] In the 1950s, Jehovah's Witnesses in Quebec appealed to the Supreme Court many times when the Duplessis government tried to suppress their religious activities.[5] For many decades, business interests have used court action to roll back economic regulation by governments.[6] Still, most of these early efforts were short-term attempts to influence government actions. Since the 1970s, the Supreme Court and other Canadian courts have seen a new kind of interest group activity—not sporadic efforts by loosely organized communities or ad hoc coalitions, but systematic, planned litigation campaigns by groups organized to wage long-term battles in the courts.

A NEW ROLE FOR THE SUPREME COURT, A NEW ROLE FOR INTEREST GROUPS

Until the 1970s, the Supreme Court had a low political profile among Canadian political institutions. It did not become Canada's final court of appeal until 1949. Until then, Canadians could appeal court decisions to the Judicial Committee of the Privy Council (JCPC), a British institution. The Canadian Supreme Court worked in the JCPC's shadows. Even after 1949, the Supreme Court rarely became involved in policy issues. There were two important reasons for this.

First, the Court's judges saw their role as declaring, not making, the law. They thought of the law as already existing. Their job was to find the law in the statutes passed by legislatures, decisions in prior court cases (especially the British courts), and the principles implicit in prior decisions. They then used the law to resolve specific disputes between two or more parties. For more than two decades after the abolition of appeals to the JCPC, Canadian Supreme Court judges did not think of their role as "creative." They did not make new law. They thus avoided having to decide whether government policies were advisable, since they could accept the law as it was established by legislatures or other courts.[7]

The Supreme Court also kept a low profile in the two decades after 1949 because it could not control its own workload. Until 1975, a case could be appealed to the Supreme Court automatically if more than $10 000 was at stake. Even in the 1950s and 1960s, many court cases involved more than $10 000, and in every one of them, the party that lost before the next lower court could force an appeal to the Supreme Court. This rule meant the Court spent much of its time deciding routine commercial lawsuits. Few of these cases raised new legal issues, but they took up the time and energy of the Supreme Court's judges all the same.

Until the late 1960s, then, the Supreme Court's focus on declaring the law and resolving routine commercial disputes meant interest groups had little reason to pay attention to the Supreme Court and the Supreme Court had little reason to pay attention to interest groups. Canadian judges rarely tried to influence policy decisions, and the Supreme Court beavered away at the flood of commercial cases it was required to hear. By the late 1960s, political forces were coming together that would change the Supreme Court's role in Canadian politics.

THE TRUDEAU REFORMS AND THE SUPREME COURT

When Pierre Trudeau entered federal politics in the mid-1960s, he intended to give the Canadian courts—including the Supreme Court—a bigger role as policy makers. He wanted judges to think of themselves as important lawmakers, working with Parliament and other institutions in developing the law. He hoped they would see cases as opportunities to contribute to public policy matters, rather than as opportunities to "declare" the law. Trudeau was interested in changing the role of the courts for two reasons. First, he wanted to promote the prospects for law reform in Canada (as Minister of Justice, he proposed legislation that loosened Canada's laws on abortion and homosexuality), and he hoped that getting the Supreme Court more involved in policy making would advance the cause of law reform. Second, Trudeau thought that amending the Constitution to include a bill of rights and a guarantee of French-language schooling outside Quebec and bilingualism in both the federal and provincial governments would strengthen national unity.[8] He hoped that the courts, including the Supreme Court, would take a leading role in forcing the provinces to go along with his language policies.[9]

Trudeau implemented three reforms to shift the Supreme Court's role away from adjudication and make it more of a policy maker. First, he changed the kind of judges appointed to the Court. Previous governments had appointed judges who saw their job as "declaring" the law rather than making public policy. Trudeau appointed judges who were more amenable to taking on a policy-making role. The judges he appointed had experience in law reform and the academic world. Bora Laskin, who had been Dean of Law at the University of Toronto and a well-known critic of the Supreme Court's reluctance to get involved in policy making, went to the Court in 1970 and became Chief Justice in 1973. Two more former law deans (Beetz and LeDain) and a former member of the Law Reform Commission of Canada (Lamer) followed him to the Court during Trudeau's years as prime minister. As Trudeau had hoped, these new judges were not content just to "declare" the law and did want the Court to take an active role in making policy. Brian Mulroney appointed some judges who were primarily known as practising lawyers (L'Heureux-Dubé, Sopinka, Cory, Gonthier, Major), but he also appointed a number of former law professors (La Forest, McLachlin, Stevenson, Iacobucci) and a former Law Reform Commission member (La Forest) to the Court and made Lamer Chief Justice. Jean Chrétien has appointed one judge who was best known as a practising lawyer (Binnie) and one who was a prominent language rights activist and law school dean (Bastarache). By the mid-1980s, the Court was dominated by reform-minded judges eager to get involved in complex policy issues.

Second, Trudeau gave the Court more control over the cases it heard. By the early 1970s, many lawyers and politicians thought the Court should have more leeway to select which cases it would hear. In 1974, Parliament agreed to abolish the right of appeal in cases involving more than $10 000 and gave the Court's judges more control over which cases they would decide. Only certain kinds of criminal cases and references cases would still be eligible for appeal. Freed from hearing routine commercial cases, the Court could devote its time to cases with broader policy implications. The effect of the change was striking. In 1970–71, the Court heard 151 cases, but it had chosen to hear only 15 percent of them. Ten years later, in 1980–81, the Court heard 115 cases, and the Court chose 74 percent of them. The remainder were criminal or reference cases appealed by right.

Finally, between 1980 and 1982, Trudeau patriated the Canadian Constitution with a Charter of Rights that "guaranteed" a number of fundamental freedoms, criminal rights, equality rights, and minority language educational rights. All the Charter's provisions were enforceable by lawsuit. The Charter therefore invited the courts to become more deeply involved in making public policy decisions across Canada.

These reforms gave the Court a new mandate to become an active policy maker. This new mandate meant a new role for interest groups at the Court. As the Court delved into complex policy issues, some interest groups started to take an interest in its work. At the same time as the Court became more involved in making policy decisions, it also found it needed the help of interest groups. It needed information from them to help make decisions, and it needed their guidance on what legal and political issues were important to them.

LEGAL MOBILIZATION

While the Trudeau government was reforming the Supreme Court's role in Canadian politics, Canadian society was changing as well. New civil liberties and civil rights movements were emerging across the democratic world. In Canada, these movements produced new kinds of interest groups with an interest in the law, law reform, and rights issues. Governments were also beginning to fund legal work and law reform efforts. The legal profession itself was beginning to change. All these factors created what Epp calls a "support structure for legal mobilization"—the social infrastructure that lets interest groups pursue their political objectives in the courts.[10]

In the years after World War II, the Western world saw a new interest in human rights issues.[11] The United Nations drafted and ratified the Universal Declaration of Human Rights in 1948. In Canada, some politicians began to press for better protection of civil liberties and basic freedoms. A few of them doubted that parliamentary government could protect rights effectively, and they agitated for a constitutional bill of rights. When the black civil rights movement began to win court challenges to racial segregation in the United States, some Canadians began to think about the potential for public interest litigation in Canada too.

Between 1960 and 1985, a number of groups were established to promote civil liberties or the rights of various groups across Canada.[12] The British Columbia Civil Liberties Association was formed in 1962, and the Canadian Civil Liberties Association was formed in 1964. In the 1970s, the Canadian feminist movement produced several groups interested in women's rights, such as the National Action Committee on the Status of Women and the National Association of Women and the Law. In 1985, Canadian feminist lawyers created the Women's Legal Education and Action Fund (LEAF) to pursue feminist objectives in the courts. In the 1980s, the Advocacy Resource Centre for the Handicapped, the Canadian Disability Rights Council, and Equality for Gays and Lesbians Everywhere were formed to advance the interests of other groups through the courts. In 1960, Canada had few groups interested in law reform or rights issues. By 1985, the country had a network of them.

At the same time, governments started to fund law reform and rights advocacy work.[13] All the provinces created legal aid programs between 1966 and 1975. They made legal help available to a wider clientele, and this encouraged lawyers to devote more attention to the rights of criminal defendants. The federal government began funding litigation by Indian groups and language groups. This funding similarly encouraged lawyers to think more about Indian rights and language rights issues. The federal government and several of the provinces established law reform commissions. All provincial governments and the federal government set up human rights commissions. These new commissions drew on new schools of legal research that were investigating the law, equality, and human rights to create a base of ideas about law reform and rights across the country. They also trained new cohorts of reform-minded activist lawyers.

Canada's legal profession also changed.[14] New law schools were established, and law school enrolments grew quickly. Full-time professors, rather than practising lawyers, were hired by the law schools, which also became more independent from the rest of the legal profession. In their teaching, the schools put new emphases on theoretical, constitutional, and law reform issues rather than on commercial and private law. Law professors became involved in law reform efforts themselves, acting as consultants to law reform commissions or activists for community and public interest groups. The legal profession became more diverse both demographically and in political outlook.

New interest groups, new ideas about the law, and a new kind of legal profession, combined with the changes at the Supreme Court, made it possible for interest groups to make frequent use of litigation to influence the law and public policy in a way that would have been impossible in the 1960s. LEAF is the best example of the new kind of interest group that uses the courts. It has successfully put feminist ideas about equality before the Supreme Court on issues such as sexual assault, pornography, abortion, and social welfare benefits.[15] It has done so by combining the expertise of law professors and sympathetic officials at human rights and law reform commissions with the activism of practising lawyers, using donations from lawyers and a regular stream of government grants.

HOW TO GET INTO COURT

Once a group decides to advance its interests through the courts, how does it get its views into a courtroom? Whether a group wants to launch a one-time lawsuit over a specific government policy or a strategic campaign that will influence the courts over several years, it can get its views before a judge in two ways. It can either launch a lawsuit or intervene in someone else's lawsuit.

LAUNCHING A LAWSUIT

When most people want to get an issue before the courts, they sue someone and launch a lawsuit. To launch a lawsuit, they must meet the "rules of standing." Canada's rules of standing made it very difficult for interest groups to launch lawsuits over public policy until the late 1970s. For example, no one could sue a government just because they thought the government was acting unconstitutionally. Only individuals, corporations, or governments who had live, concrete legal disputes with other individuals, corporations, or governments could sue. Therefore, interest groups did not have much room to challenge legislation or government action on their own. A group had to find someone who did have standing and then offer to pay their legal costs. So, as part of its move away from the adjudicative model of judging, the Supreme Court rewrote the rules of standing for the Canadian court system, starting in 1975. By 1981, it had made it easier for interest groups to sue.[16] Today, a group can launch a lawsuit over a piece of public policy if there is no other way for its constitutionality to be challenged in court.

Launching a lawsuit or sponsoring a test case can be useful for an interest group that wants to change public policy. When a group launches a lawsuit, it decides which legal issues to raise and naturally picks whichever issues are most favourable to its cause. It sets the timing of the case. It might coordinate a court case with other lobbying and public relations campaigns. Launching a lawsuit also has some important drawbacks. For one thing, fighting a lawsuit is dauntingly expensive. Even a lawsuit that asks for a simple policy change will be heard by a trial court and probably one appeals court. If a lawsuit involves an important policy, it could head to the Supreme Court and cost hundreds of thousands of dollars. A lawsuit is also time consuming. It might occupy a group's leaders and resources for well over five years. So a group that wants to launch its own lawsuits must have a lot of money and be able to wait years for a final resolution.

A good example of the pros and cons of interest group lawsuits arose in 1983, when the Trudeau government decided to allow the American government to test its cruise missile in Canadian airspace. Operation Dismantle, a disarmament group, announced it would try to force the government to change its mind using demonstrations, petitions, lobby efforts, and a lawsuit. Operation Dismantle's lawsuit argued that testing the cruise missile increased the risk of a nuclear war and violated Canadians' right to life under section 7 of the Charter of Rights. In a preliminary motion, the federal government challenged the group's right to launch the case. Even though one of Operation Dismantle's supporters called the group's legal case "weak,"[17] a Federal Court judge denied the federal motion and upheld the group's right to sue. The federal government appealed, and the preliminary motion eventually ended up at the Supreme Court.

In 1985, the Court ruled that Operation Dismantle could not proceed with its case. To say the government's decision to allow the missile tests increased the chance of nuclear war involved assumptions and hypotheses about the field of international relations. The Court's majority decided that saying how other countries would react to Canada's decision was pure speculation. No one could prove in court how other countries would react to the missile testing, and so Operation Dismantle could not prove that the tests would increase the threat of nuclear war.[18] Operation Dismantle had to drop the court case. In the meantime, although the case did get Operation Dismantle some publicity in the media, the group had put so much money and effort into the lawsuit that its other tactics for pressuring the government fizzled out. Soon after the Supreme Court handed down its decision, the group was left with nothing.

INTERVENING IN A CASE

An interest group does not have to launch a lawsuit to gets its views before a court. It can also ask for permission to intervene in someone else's case. Intervention allows a group (or a government, corporation, or person) to provide a court with a written brief of about twenty pages, setting out the intervener's views about the legal issues at stake in a particular case. The intervener might make its own arguments about how the Constitution, a piece of legislation, or precedents apply to a case. Usually, the court expects an intervener to take a broader perspective than the parties to a case, and to draw on a wider range of arguments and sources in its submissions. An intervener may also ask permission to argue its point of view orally when the court hears the case.

Until the 1970s, the Supreme Court was reluctant to hear from interveners. When the Court thought its primary duty was to resolve disputes, it did not usually need help from interveners. As the Court moved towards a policy-making role in the 1970s, it experimented with hearing from interest group interveners.[19] The Court heard from interveners only sporadically during the mid-1980s, prompting an outcry from groups that wanted to appear before the Court but could not. Eventually, the Court relented, and since the late 1980s, it has been hearing almost all the interest groups that want to intervene in its cases. Intervention is now the most common way for interest groups to appear before the Supreme Court.

The pros and cons of intervention mirror those of launching a lawsuit or sponsoring a test case. Intervention is a relatively inexpensive way for a group to get in front of the Supreme Court. An intervener does not pay the expense of getting the case to the Court. It only pays its own legal fees and expenses, which might be a few tens of thousands of dollars. Yet, it is hard to coordinate an intervention with other lobbying efforts, since the intervener does not control the timing of a case. Nor can an intervener decide which issues will be raised in a case. An intervener is usually limited to arguing about the issues already raised by the parties, and these might not be the best issues for the group's cause.

202 PART 5 COMMUNITIES, INTEREST GROUPS, AND THE COURT

Some groups have found that if they plan carefully they can minimize the drawbacks to intervention. Early in its life, LEAF, the feminist law reform group, realized that sooner or later someone charged with selling obscene materials would challenge the Criminal Code's obscenity provisions using the Charter's freedom of expression provision. LEAF activists knew that, once that case reached the Supreme Court, they would want to intervene and make their own arguments about how the Charter ought to apply to obscenity law in Canada. They began planning their legal arguments years before any obscenity cases reached the Court. In the meantime, LEAF intervened in other Supreme Court cases involving freedom of expression and persuaded the Court to read the Charter's right to freedom of expression in tandem with its rights to equality. Its intervention in *Butler* was the culmination of its efforts to shape the Court's decisions on freedom of expression. LEAF convinced the Court in this case that the need for free expression had to be balanced with the equal treatment of women and that obscenity law could ban pornography that degrades women.[20]

CONCLUSION

Interest groups are now often involved in the work of the Supreme Court of Canada. Some groups appear as interveners in Supreme Court cases. Others appear as parties to cases. Some appear before the Court only once or twice without thinking of long-term litigation. Others plan carefully for litigation campaigns that last for years. This new role of interest groups is partly a result of Trudeau's efforts to reform the Court, and partly a fallout from broader social changes. This new role is an integral part of the new role the Supreme Court has taken in Canada's political system over the past thirty years.

Canadian scholars are only beginning to ask whether interest group involvement in the Supreme Court's work makes a difference. Some observers say that reform-minded judges and special interest groups have become allies, pursuing unpopular social engineering experiments in areas such as gay rights that more democratically accountable institutions of government could not implement. Others argue that, since judges are usually wealthy and well-educated professionals, they are likely to favour business interests over unions and social movements such as feminism and gay rights. Judges, these people say, will usually tilt towards preserving social and political status quo.[21] This line of research is expanding rapidly. Regardless of who is correct, the new role of interest groups at the Supreme Court is gaining significance as the Court becomes a more and more important political institution.

ENDNOTES

The author thanks Ryan Schmidt for her research assistance with this chapter.

1.   See F.L. Morton, "To Bring Judicial Appointments Out of the Closet," *The Globe and Mail*, 22 September 1997, A15.

2. Kent Roach, "The Role of Litigation and the Charter in Interest Advocacy," in Leslie Seidle, ed., *Equity and Community: the Charter, Interest Advocacy and Representation* (Montreal: Institute for Research on Public Policy, 1993).

3. See Michael Mandel, *The Charter of Rights and the Legalization of Politics in Canada* (Toronto: Thompson Educational, 1994), 99; Roach, "The Role of Litigation," 161–63.

4. *Edwards v. Attorney General of Canada*, [1930] A.C. 124.

5. *Roncarelli v. Duplessis*, [1959] S.C.R. 121; *Boucher v. The Queen*, [1951] S.C.R. 265; *Switzman v. Elbing*, [1957] S.C.R. 285.

6. J.R. Mallory, *Social Credit and the Federal Power in Canada* (Toronto: University of Toronto Press, 1954).

7. The Court interpreted and enforced the federal–provincial division of powers under the 1867 constitution, a job that did involve the Court in controversial disputes between the two levels of government. As well, the federal government had the power to refer hypothetical questions to the Supreme Court. This gave the Court a nonadjudicative role from time to time. But, overall, the Court tried to stick as much as possible to resolving legal disputes between private parties or between private parties and governments.

8. See, for example, his 1965 essay "Quebec and the Constitutional Problem," in Pierre Elliott Trudeau, *Federalism and the French Canadians* (Toronto: Macmillan, 1968).

9. Peter Russell, "The Political Purposes of the Canadian Charter of Rights and Freedoms," *Canadian Bar Review* 61 (1983): 30–54; Rainer Knopff and F.L. Morton, "Nation-Building and the Canadian Charter of Rights and Freedoms," in Alan Cairns and Cynthia Williams, eds., *Constitutionalism, Citizenship and Society in Canada* (Toronto: University of Toronto Press, 1985); and Mandel, *Charter of Rights*, ch. 3.

10. Charles R. Epp, "Do Bills of Rights Matter? The Canadian Charter of Rights and Freedoms," *American Political Science Review* 90 (1996): 765–79.

11. Cynthia Williams, "The Changing Nature of Citizen Rights," in Cairns and Williams, eds., *Constitutionalism, Citizenship and Society in Canada*.

12. Epp, "Do Bills of Rights Matter?"

13. Ibid.

14. Ibid.

15. Sherene Razack, *Canadian Feminism and the Law: the Women's Legal and Education Fund and the Pursuit of Equality* (Toronto: Second Story Press, 1991).

16. *Thorson v. Attorney General of Canada*, [1975] 1 S.C.R. 138; *Nova Scotia Board of Censors v. McNeil*, [1976] 2 S.C.R. 265; and *Canada v. Borowski*, [1981] 2 S.C.R. 575.

17. Mandel, *Charter of Rights*, 75.

18. *The Queen v. Operation Dismantle*, [1983] 1 F.C. 745 (F.C.T.D.); *Operation Dismantle v. The Queen*, [1985] 1 S.C.R. 441.

19. *Attorney General of Canada v. Lavell*, [1974] S.C.R. 1349; *R. v. Morgentaler*, [1976] 1 S.C.R. 616.

20. *R. v. Butler*, [1992] 1 S.C.R. 452.

21. See F.L. Morton and Rainer Knopff, *The Charter Revolution and the Court Party* (Peterborough: Broadview, forthcoming); and Mandel, *Charter of Rights*.

To the owner of this book

We hope that you have enjoyed *Political Dispute and Judicial Review*
(ISBN 0-17-616744-7), and we would like to know as much about your experiences with this text as you would care to offer. Only through your comments and those of others can we learn how to make this a better text for future readers.

School _____ Your instructor's name _____

Course _____ Was the text required? _____ Recommended? _____

1. What did you like the most about *Political Dispute and Judicial Review?*

_____

_____

_____

2. How useful was this text for your course?

_____

_____

_____

3. Do you have any recommendations for ways to improve the next edition of
this text?

_____

_____

_____

4. In the space below or in a separate letter, please write any other comments
you have about the book. (For example, please feel free to comment on
reading level, writing style, terminology, design features, and learning aids.)

_____

_____

_____

_____

Optional

Your name _____ Date _____

May Nelson, Thomson Learning quote you, either in promotion for *Political
Dispute and Judicial Review* or in future publishing ventures?

Yes _____ No _____

Thanks!

You can also send your comments to us via e-mail at
college@nelson.com

MAIL ➤ POSTE
Canada Post Corporation
Société canadienne des postes

Postage paid	Port payé
if mailed in Canada	si posté au Canada
Business Reply	Réponse d'affaires

0066102399   01

0066102399-M1K5G4-BR01

NELSON, THOMSON LEARNING
HIGHER EDUCATION
PO BOX 60225 STN BRM B
TORONTO ON M7Y 2H1